SPARES DIVISION

SPARE PARTS CATALOGUE

for

JAGUAR 'E' TYPE
SERIES 2

GRAND TOURING MODELS

Open, Fixed Head Coupé, 2 + 2 Models

PUBLICATION IPL 5/2   PUBLISHED JUNE 1975

JAGUAR CARS LIMITED, COVENTRY, ENGLAND

This Interim Parts List was the only parts publication issued by Jaguar dealing with 'E' Type Series 2 vehicles. It contained no illustrations. Jaguar recommended that if users wished to identify components they should refer to two earlier 'E' Type Parts Catalogues - J37 which covered the 4.2 Series One open sportscars and coupés and J38 which covered the Series One 4.2 2+2 models.

To assist current owners we have included all illustrations from these publications in two supplements which can be found at the back of this book.

CONTENTS

SECTION A – ENGINE AND TRANSMISSION

CONTENTS – Continued

SECTION A – ENGINE AND TRANSMISSION (Continued)

CONTENTS - Continued

SECTION B - Body

CONTENTS - Continued

SECTION B - Body (Continued)

CONTENTS - Continued

SECTION C - Electrical Equipment

Supplement 1

Supplement 2

NOTES

<u>SERIES 2 'E' TYPE</u>.

<u>COMMENCING CHASSIS NUMBERS</u>.

<u>OPEN MODELS</u>.

1R.1001 FOR R.H.DRIVE.
1R.7001 FOR L.H.DRIVE.

<u>FIXED HEAD COUPE</u>.

1R.20001 FOR R.H.DRIVE.
1R.25001 FOR L.H.DRIVE.

<u>2+2 MODELS</u>.

1R.35001 FOR R.H.DRIVE.
1R.40001 FOR L.H.DRIVE.

PLEASE NOTE :- Prefix 'P' to a Chassis Number denotes that Power
Steering is Fitted.

Suffix 'BW' to a 2+2 Chassis Number denotes that
Automatic Transmission is fitted.

<u>COMMENCING ENGINE NUMBERS</u>.

7R.1001 FOR OPEN AND FIXED HEAD COUPE MODELS.

7R.35001 FOR 2+2 MODELS.

The Parts in this List are common to all models unless otherwise stated
and should be used in conjunction with Catalogues J.37 and J.38.

Items suggested for Distributor Stocking are marked ....*

Items suggested for Distributor/Dealer Stocking are marked.....................**

Items which have not previously appeared in a Jaguar Catalogue
are marked..+

PART NO.	Description.	NO. PER UNIT.	REMARKS

CYLINDER BLOCK.

PART NO.	Description.	NO. PER UNIT.	REMARKS
C.29524	Cylinder Block Assembly	1))	
C.21690	Cylinder Liner	6)	
C.15867	Oil Filter Flange Plug	1)	
C.16862/2	Core Plug	1)	
C.16862/8	Core Plug	6)	
C.29042	Blanking Plate	1)	
C.27877	Blanking Plate Gasket	1)	
UFS.125/4R	Setscrew, for Plate	6)	
FG.104/X	Spring Washer, on Setscrew	6)	
UFS.925/4H	Recessed Head Setscrew, for Plate	1)	
C.5022	Plug, for Bray Heater Hole	1)	
C.13478	Dowel, for Clutch Housing	2)	Fitted up to Eng.
C.13479	Dowel, for Timing Cover	2)	Nos.7R1914. Open
C.13479	Dowel Small, for Bearing Caps	7)	and F.H.C.
C.19340	Dowel Large, for Bearing Caps	7)	7R35388. 2+2
C.2157	Rear Oil Gallery Plug	1)	
C.2296/2	Copper Washer, on Plug	1)	**
C.2352	Side Oil Gallery Plug	6)	
C.2296/3	Copper Washer, on Plug	6)	**
C.2305	Front Oil Gallery Brass Plug	1)	
C.17522	Dipstick Adaptor Tube	1)	
C.29039	Cylinder Block Assembly	1)	
C.16862/2	Core Plug	1)	Fitted from
C.16862/5	Core Plug	4)	Eng.No.7R1915
C.16862/8	Core Plug	9)	'E'Type Open and
C.29038	Plug, for Bray Heater Hole	1)	F.H.Coupe
C.2296/16	Copper Washer, on Plug	1)	Eng.No.7R35389. 2+2
	All other items as for Cylinder Block C.29524		
C.23609	Cylinder Head Stud	3)	Fitted up to Eng Nos.
C.2269	Cylinder Head Stud	10)	7R1914.Open and F.H.C.
C.23610	Cylinder Head Stud (Dowel)	1)	7R35388. 2+2
C.29032	Cylinder Head Stud (Dowel)	1)	Fitted from
C.29033	Cylinder Head Stud	6)	Eng.No. 7R1915
C.29034	Cylinder Head Stud	3)	Open and F.H.C.
C.29035	Cylinder Head Stud	4)	Eng.No.7R35389.2+2
C.5846	Banjo Bolt, on Oil Feed Pipe	1	*
C.4146	Copper Washer, on Bolt	2	**
UFS.119/2R	Plug, for Oil Hole in Distributor Boss	1	
AW.102/E	Copper Washer, on Plug	1	
C.19687	Rear Cover Assembly	1	*
C.2470	Cap Screw, securing Cover	2	
C.2394	Dowel, in Cover	2	
C.19654	Oil Seal, in Cover	2	
C.2373	Ring Dowel, securing cover to block	2	
C.19686	Cap Screw, securing Cover to Block	1	
C.19685	Cap Screw, securing Cover to Block	2	
C.2262	Main Bearing Cap Bolt	14	
C.28082	Washer, on Bolt	11	**
C.2430	Sealing Ring, for Distributor	1	**

PART NO.	Description.	NO. PER UNIT.	REMARKS

Cylinder Block (Continued).

PART NO.	Description.	NO. PER UNIT.	REMARKS
UFS.125/4R	Setscrew, for Distributor	1	
FW.104/T	Plain Washer, under Setscrew	1	
C.724	Shakeproof Washer, on Plain Washer	1	
C.30380	Heating Element, in Cylinder Block(110V)	1	CANADA ONLY
C.29037	Adaptor, for Heating Element in Cylinder Block	1)))	Required from Eng.Nos.7R1915 and 7R35389
C.2354	Drain Tap, at L.H.S. of Cylinder Block	1	
C.2296/3	Copper Washer, on Tap	1	**
C.316	Fibre Washer, on Tap	As req'd	
C.23521/1	Crankshaft	1	
C.23761	Screwed Plug, in Camshaft	6	
C.757	Woodruff Key	4	
C.2226	Bush, in Crankshaft for Primary Shaft	1	*
11622	Main Bearing Kit	1	*
C.2316	Thrust Washer, at Centre Bearing Cap	2	*
C.2316/1	Thrust Washer, at Centre Bearing Cap	2	*
C.29370	Crankshaft Damper	1	*
C.23131	Crankshaft Pulley	1	
UFB.131/10R	Bolt, securing Damper to Pulley	4	
C.725	Shakeproof Washer, on Bolt	2	
C.2314	Oil Pump Drive Gear, on Crankshaft	1	*
C.2170	Timing Sprocket, on Crankshaft	1	*
C.23701	Oil Thrower	1	
C.2173	Distance Piece	1	
C.2466	Damper Cone	1	
C.5896	Crankshaft Bolt	1	
C.2468	Crankshaft Washer	1	
C.23158	Crankshaft Tab Washer	1	*
C.7917/2	Drilled Connecting Rod	6	
C.17164	Small End Bearing	6	
C.22236	Bolt, in Connecting Rod	12	
C.28535	Nut, on Bolt	12	
C.30003	Big End Bearing (Prs)	6	**
C.18517	Flywheel	1	
C.2313	Dowel, in Centre of Flywheel	2	
C.8631	Dowel, in Outer Face of Flywheel	3	
C.4855	Setscrew, Flywheel to Crankshaft	10	
C.4810	Lockplate, securing Setscrews	1	
C.28084	Piston Assembly 8:1 CR	6	**
C.28086	Piston Assembly 9:1 CR	6	
C.26629	Gudgeon Pin	6	
C.3964	Circlip, for Gudgeon Pin	6	
C.26634	Top Pressure Ring	6	
C.26635	Bottom Pressure Ring	6	
C.26636	Scraper Ring	6	

PART NO.	Description.	NO. PER UNIT.	REMARKS

Cylinder Block (Continued).

PART NO.	Description.	NO. PER UNIT.	REMARKS
C.24457	Oil Sump	1	
C.16315	Rear Oil Sump	1	
C.24611/2	Front Oil Seal	1	**
C.19590	Gasket Sump to Cylinder Block (Prs)	1	**
C.23435	Drain Plug	1	*
C.2296/1	Copper Washer, on Drain Plug	1	**
UFS.131/6R	Setscrew, securing Sump to Block	25	
C.14170	Setscrew, securing Sump to Block	1	
C.725	Shakeproof Washer, on Setscrews	26	
C.16741	Baffle, inside Oil Sump	1	
UCS.131/5R	Setscrew, securing Baffle	6	
C.725	Shakeproof Washer, on Setscrew	6	
C.16752	Filter Basket inside Oil Sump	1	
UFN.125/L	Nut, securing Filter Basket to Baffle	6	
C.724	Shakeproof Washer, under Nut	6	
C.16753	Oil Return Pipe, on Sump	1	
C.16756	Gasket, between Pipe and Sump	1	
C.16757	Stud, securing Pipe to Sump	3	
UFN.125/L	Nut, on Studs	3	
FG.104/X	Spring Washer, under Nut	3	
C.15949	Hose, Oil Cleaner to Oil Return Pipe	1	
C.2905/14	Clip, securing Hose	2	
C.30112	Dipstick Assembly, for Oil Pump	1	
C.15849	L.H.Front Engine Mounting Bracket	1	
C.15850	R.H.Front Engine Mounting Bracket	1	
UFS.143/6R	Setscrew, securing Brackets to Block	6	
C.727	Shakeproof Washer, on Setscrews	6	
C.18556	Front Engine Mounting Rubber	2	**
UFS.150/7R	Setscrew, securing Rubber Mountings to Engine Brackets	2	
FG.108/X	Spring Washer, on Setscrews	2	
FW.108/T	Plain Washer, under Spring Washer	2	
C.18242	Packing Piece, under Rubber Mountings	As req'd	
UFS.131/6R	Setscrew, securing Rubber Mountings to Front Frame	4	
C.8667/2	Nut, self-locking, on Setscrews	4	
C.12890	Stabilising Link, at Rear of Cylinder Block	1	*
C.10940	Bush, in Eye of Link	1	**
UFB.143/14R	Bolt, securing Link to Bearing Brackets	1	
C.8737/4	Nut, self-locking, on Bolt	1	
C.11607	Stepped Washer, on Link above Rubber Mounting	1	
C.11688	Stepped Bush, on Link below Rubber Mounting	1	
C.8667/3	Nut, self-locking at Top of Link	1	

PART NO.	Description.	NO. PER UNIT.	REMARKS	

Cylinder Block (Continued).

Part No.	Description	No. Per Unit	Remarks	
C.20217	Rubber Mounting, at Top of Link	1		
UFS.131/6R	Setscrew, securing Mounting to Body	1		
UFS.131/9R	Setscrew, securing Mounting to Body	1		
C.21201	Tapped Plate, receiving Setscrews	1		
C.14922	Bracket L.H. on Clutch Housing, securing Stabilising Link	1		
C.14923	Bracket R.H. on Clutch Housing, securing Stabilising Link	1		
UCS.131/6R	Setscrew, securing Brackets to Housing	4		
C.725	Shakeproof Washer, on Setscrews	4		
C.21333	Support Bracket, for Rear Engine Mounting	1	Open and F.H. Coupe	
C.25470	Support Bracket, for Rear Engine Mounting	1	2+2 Model only	
C.12335	Spring Seat Rubber, in Bracket	1		**
C.12265	Centre Bush Rubber	1		**
UFS.131/6R	Setscrew, securing Support Bracket to Body	5		
FW.105/T	Plain Washer, on Setscrew	5		
FG.105/X	Spring Washer, on Setscrew	5		
C.12299	Coil Spring, for Rear Engine Mounting	1		**
C.12335	Rubber Seat, at Top of Coil Spring	1		**
C.21932	Retainer, at Top of Coil Spring	1		
C.21336	Pin Assembly, securing Retainer to Gearbox and locating Support Bracket	1		
12245	Gasket Set, for Lower Part of Engine	1		**

PLEASE NOTE :- For complete Engine Gaskets use Gasket
Set 12245 and Decarbonising Gasket
Set 12244

Part No.	Description	No. Per Unit	Remarks	
10527	Seals Set, for Engine Overhaul	1		**

PART NO.	Description.	NO. PER UNIT.	REMARKS

WATER PUMP.

PART NO.	Description.	NO. PER UNIT.	REMARKS
C.31144	Water Pump Complete	1)	
C.28129	Body only	1)	
C.8167	Spindle and Bearing Assembly	1)	*
C.6773	Seal, on Spindle	1)	**
C.8256	Thrower, on Spindle	1)	Fitted up to Eng. **
C.23128	Screw, Locking Bearing in Body	1)	Nos.7R1914.Open and
UFN.225/L	Nut, locking Screw	1)	F.H.C.
C.22798	Impellor	1)	7R35388 2+2
C.25082	Carrier, for Pump Pulley	1)	
C.26852	By-Pass Adaptor	1)	
C.2296/2	Copper Washer, on Adaptor	1))	
C.2303	Gasket, between Pump and Cyl. Block	1)	**
C.30811	Water Pump Complete	1)	
C.28414	Body only	1)	
C.8167	Spindle and Bearing Assembly	1)	'
C.28089	Seal on Spindle	1)	**
C.28628	Thrower, on Spindle	1)	**
C.23128	Screw, locking Bearing in Body	1)	Fitted from
UFN.225/L	Nut, locking Screw	1)	Eng.No.7R1915.Open
C.28804	Impellor (Rotor)	1)	and F.H.C.
C.25082	Carrier, for Pump Pulley	1)	Eng.No.7R35389 2+2
C.26852	By-Pass Adaptor	1)	
C.2296/2	Copper Washer, on Adaptor	1))	
C.28656	Gasket, between Pump and Cyl. Block	1)	**
C.28609	Pulley, for Water Pump	1	
C.30630	Pulley, on Pump Driving Alternator	1	
UFS.125/8R	Setscrew, securing Pulleys to Carrier	4	
FG.104/X	Spring Washer, on Setscrews	4	
C.28955	Belt, Driving Water Pump	1	MANUAL STEERING **
C.31686	Belt, Driving Water Pump and Power Steering Pump	1	POWER STEERING **
C.29849	Belt, Driving Alternator	1	**
C.26853	By-Pass Hose	1	**
C.2905/8	Clip, securing Hose	2	

PART NO.	Description.	NO. PER UNIT.	REMARKS

OIL PUMP.

PART NO.	Description.	NO. PER UNIT.	REMARKS
C.21765	Oil Pump Complete	1	*
C.17656	Body only	1	
C.17664	Rotor Assembly	1	
C.21759	Cover, bottom of Oil Pump	1	
UFS.131/8R	Setscrew, securing Cover	2	
UCS.131/14R	Setscrew, securing Cover	2	
FG.105/X	Spring Washer, on Setscrews	4	
C.8649	'O'Ring, in Oil Pump Body for Delivery Pipe	1	**
C.21848	'O' Ring, in Oil Pump Cover for Suction Pipe	1	**
C.8646	Drive Shaft, Distributor to Coupling	1	
C.8647	Bush, for Drive Shaft	1	*
C.2393	Washer, on Shaft at Bottom of Bush	1	
C.2152	Helical Gear. Driving Pump and Distributor	1	*
C.753	Key, Gear to Drive Shaft	1	*
UFN.256/L	Nut, at Bottom of Drive Shaft	1	
C.2151	Special Washer, locking Nut	1	
C.8648	Coupling, between Pump and Drive Shaft	1	
C.9294	Dowel Bolt, securing Pump to Bearing Cap	2	
UFB.131/18R	Bolt, securing Pump to Bearing Cap	1	
C.7263	Tab Washer, locking Bolt	1	**
C.22595	Oil Delivery Pipe Assembly	1	
C.22598	Gasket, Pipe to Cylinder Block	1	**
UFS.131/8R	Setscrew, securing Pipe to Block	3	
C.22952	Tab Washer, locking Setscrews	2	**
C.28369	Strut, supporting Oil Delivery Pipe	1	
C.6824	Clip, securing Delivery Pipe to Strut	1	
UFS.125/5R	Setscrew, through Clip	1	
C.3968/1	Nut, (self-locking) on Setscrew	1	
FW.104/T	Plain Washer, under Nut	1	
C.21760	Oil Suction Pipe Assembly	1	
C.21794	Clip, securing Suction Pipe to Strut on Pump	1	
C.21793	Strut, on Pump supporting Suction Pipe	1	
UFS.125/5R	Setscrew, securing Clip to Strut	1	
C.3968/1	Nut, self locking, on Setscrew	1	
FW.104/T	Plain Washer, under Nut	1	
C.21850	Clip, rear, securing Suction Pipe to Strut	1	
C.21849	Strut, rear for Suction Pipe	1	
UFB.125/15R	Bolt, securing Clip to Strut	1	
C.22031	Distance Piece, on Bolt	1	
C.3968/1	Nut, self locking on Bolt	1	
FW.104/T	Plain Washer, under Nut	1	
C.21745	Plate, sealing bottom of Suction Pipe	1	
C.21744	Spring, behind Sealing Plate	1	
C.1221/4	Split Pin, retaining Spring and Plate on Pipe	1	

PART NO.	Description.	NO. PER UNIT.	REMARKS

OIL CLEANER.

PART NO.	Description.	NO. PER UNIT.	REMARKS
C.21911	Oil Cleaner Complete	1	Up to Eng.Nos. 7R2297 & 7R35582 *
7984	Canister Assembly	1	
6159	Spring, at Bottom of Canister	1	
6160	Plain Washer, Top of Spring	1	
6161	Felt Washer, under Pressure Plate	1	
6886	Pressure Plate	1	
7987	Bolt, through Canister	1	
6158	Rubber Washer, under Head of Bolt	1	
6163	Spring Clip, on Bolt	1	
11028	Element	1	**
9348	Anchor Insert	1	
9667	Clamping Plate, on Filter Head	1	
6883	Sealing Ring, Canister to Filter Head	1	**
10443	Filter Head	1	
9664	Balance Valve, in Filter Head	1	
9665	Seal, under Head of Valve	1	
2714	Relief Valve	1	**
8105	Spring, for Relief Valve	1	**
8106	Spider and Pin Assembly, under Spring	1	**
9663	Adaptor, for Hose	1	
9662	Washer, on Adaptor	1	
10444	Drain Plug, at Bottom of Filter Head	1	
8752	Washer, on Drain Plug	1	
C.21912	Gasket, Oil Cleaner to Cylinder Block	1	**
UFB.131/20R	Bolt, Oil Cleaner to Cylinder Block	4	
FW.105/E	Copper Washer, on Bolt	4	
C.15949	Hose, Oil Cleaner to Oil Sump	1	**
C.2905/14	Clip, securing Hose	2	
C.29554	Oil Cleaner, complete	1	Fitted from *
12249	Canister Assembly	1	Engine Nos
6159	Spring, at Bottom of Canister	1	7R2298 & 7R35583
11664	Washer, plain, Top of Spring	1	
11665	Washer, felt, under Pressure Plate	1	
11666	Pressure Plate	1	
12250	Bolt, through Canister	1	
11668	Rubber Washer, on Bolt	1	
6033	Spring Clip, on Bolt	1	
11028	Element	1	**
6883	Sealing Ring, Filter Head to Canister	1	**
11671	Filter Head Assembly	1	
11672	Relief Valve Assembly	1	*
9662	Sealing Washer, for Relief Valve, Plug and Adaptor	3	*
11673	Plug, in Filter Head	1	
11674	Adaptor, for Hose	1	
C.29105	Gasket, Oil Cleaner to Cylinder Block	1	**

PART NO.	Description.	NO. PER UNIT.	REMARKS

Oil Cleaner (Continued).

PART NO.	Description.	NO. PER UNIT.	REMARKS
UFB.131/21R	Bolt, Oil Cleaner to Cylinder Block	4	
FW.105/E	Copper Washer, on Bolt	4	
C.31171	Hose, Oil Cleaner to Pipe on Sump	1	**
C.2905/14	Clip, securing Hose	2	

CYLINDER HEAD.

PART NO.	Description.	NO. PER UNIT.	REMARKS
11346	Cylinder Head Assembly Complete (Comprising :- Cylinder Head, Valves Guides, Springs, Tappets, Camshafts, Camshaft Covers etc., but NOT Breather).	1))))	Fitted up to Eng. No.7R1914. Open and F.H.C. Eng.No.7R35388.2+2
12395	Cylinder Head Assembly Complete (Comprising:- Cylinder Head, Valves Guides, Springs, Tappets, Camshafts Camshaft Covers etc., but NOT Breather).	1))))	Fitted from Eng. No. 7R1915. Open and F.H.C. Eng.No.7R35389. 2+2
C.26202	Cylinder Head	1)	
C.2326	Stud, securing Cam Shaft Bearing Cap and Camshaft Covers	16))	
C.2373	Ring Dowel, on Studs	16)	
FW.105/T	Plain Washer, on Studs	16)	
UFN.131/L	Nut, securing Bearing Caps	16)	Fitted up to
FG.105/X	Spring Washer, under Nuts	16)	Eng.No.7R1914 Open
C.317	Core Plug, in Exhaust Face	2)	and F.H.C.
C.2157	Core Plug, (Headed) Top of Cylinder Head	3))	Eng. No.7R35388.2+2
C.2296/2	Copper Washer, on Headed Plug	3)	
C.27477	Guide, for Inlet Valve	6)	
C.26195	Guide, for Exhaust Valve	6)	
C.26199	Circlip, retaining Valve Guides	12)	
C.29122	Insert, for Inlet Valve	6)	
C.29124	Insert, for Exhaust Valve	6)	
C.7262	Guide for Tappets	12)	
C.27479	Seal, at top of Inlet Valve Guides	6)	
C.27081	Gasket, between Head and Block	1)	**
C.28391	Cylinder Head Details as for Cylinder Head C.26202	1)))	Fitted from Eng. No. 7R1915 Open and F.H.C. Eng. No. 7R35389. 2+2
C.28974	Gasket, between Head and Block	1)	**
C.2189	Stud (short) Head to Block	2	
UFN.131/L	Nut, on Studs	2	
FG.105/X	Spring Washer, under Nuts	2	
C.2189	Stud, Head to Timing Cover	2	
UFN.131/L	Nut, on Studs	2	
FW.105/E	Copper Washer, under Nuts	2	
C.11761	Stud, fixing Inlet and Exhaust Manifolds	29	
UFN.131/L	Nut, on Studs for Inlet Manifold	18	
UFN.131/Q	Nut, on Studs for Exhaust Manifold	16	
FG.105/X	Spring Washer, under Nuts	34	

PART NO.	Description.	NO. PER UNIT.	REMARKS

Cylinder Head (Continued).

C.7624	Stud, securing Exhaust Manifold Breather Pipe and Dipstick Location Clip	5	
C.6727/2	Stud, Front End of Head for Fixing Camshaft Covers	6)	4 only off each fitted
		)	from 7R2083 & 7R35463
C.2327	Dome Nut, on Studs	6)	on cars for U.S.A. and
FW.104/E	Copper Washer, under Dome Nut	6)	Canada.
C.6727	Stud, Front of Head for Breather Housing	4	
C.2327	Dome Nut, on Studs	4	
FG.104/X	Spring Washer, under Dome Nut	4	
C.23607	Engine Lifting Bracket	2	
C.2328	Dome Nut, securing Head to Block	14	
C.10301	Special Washer, under Dome Nuts	8	
FW.207/T	Bevelled Washer, under Dome Nuts	6	
12244	Decarbonising Gasket Set	1)	Fitted up to Eng. No. **
		)	7R1914.Eng. No.
		)	7R35388
10525	Seals Set, for use when Decarbonising Engine	1	
C.12444	Inlet Valve	6	**
C.21942	Exhaust Valve	6	**
C.7136/7	Valve Springs (Inner and Outer) Prs	12	**
C.27481	Seat, for Valve Springs	12	**
C.27480	Collar, at Top of Valve Springs	12	**
C.27482	Cotter, retaining Collar to Valve Prs.	12	**
C.7213	Tappet	12	**
C.2243/A to Z	Adjusting Pad, for Tappets	12	SELECTIVE SIZES **

PLEASE NOTE :- These Pads range from .085" thick to
.110" thick and each individual size
must be ordered separately (e.g. C.2243/A
= .085" thick: C.2243/B = .086" etc)

C.14985	Inlet Camshaft	1	*
C.13081	Exhaust Camshaft	1	*
C.2288	Bearing for Camshafts Prs	8	**
C.2324	Oil Thrower, Rear of Exhaust Camshaft	1	
UFS.137/4R	Setscrew, securing Thrower to Camshaft	1	
FW.106/E	Copper Washer, on Setscrew	1	
C.19043	Flanged Sealing Plug, L.H.Rear of Head	1	
C.19044	'O' Ring on Sealing Plug	1	**
UCS.125/5R	Setscrew, securing Sealing Plug	2	
FW.104/E	Copper Washer, on Setscrew	2	
C.14991	Seal, between Rear Bearing Cap and Inlet Camshaft Cover	1	**

PART NO.	Description.	NO. PER UNIT.	REMARKS

Cylinder Head (Continued).

PART NO.	Description.	NO. PER UNIT.	REMARKS	
C.26773	Flanged Sealing Plug R.H.Rear of Head	1		**
C.14990	'O' Ring, on Sealing Ring	1		
UCS.125/5R	Setscrew, securing Sealing Plug	2		
FW.104/E	Copper Washer, on Setscrew	2		
UFS.137/4R	Setscrew, Rear End of Inlet Camshaft	1		
FW.106/E	Copper Washer, on Setscrew	1		
C.27497	Cover, for Inlet Camshaft	1	Not U.S.A. or CANADA	
C.28890	Cover, for Inlet Camshaft	1	) U.S.A. and CANADA up to) Eng.Nos.7R2082 and) 7R35462	
C.30820	Cover for Inlet Camshaft	1)	) U.S.A. and CANADA from	
UCS.025/6H	Setscrew, Countersunk, at Front of Cover	1)	) Eng. Nos. 7R2083 and) 7R35463	
C.14988/1	Gasket for Cover	1		**
C.27277	Cover, for Exhaust Camshaft	1	Not U.S.A. or CANADA	
C.28889	Cover, for Exhaust Camshaft	1	) U.S.A. and CANADA up to) Eng. Nos. 7R2082 and) 7R35462	
C.30825	Cover, for Exhaust Camshaft	1	) U.S.A. and CANADA from	
UCS.025/6H	Setscrew, Countersunk, at Front of Cover	1	) Eng. Nos. 7R2083 and) 7R35463	
C.6735/1	Gasket for Cover	1		**
C.2327	Dome Nut, securing Covers to Head	16		
FW.104/E	Copper Washer, under Dome Nut	16		
C.27278	Oil Filler Cap	1		
C.25480	'O' Ring on Oil Filler Cap	1		*
C.25619	Oil Pipe Cyl.Block to Rear of Head	1		*
C.5846	Banjo Bolt, securing Oil Pipe	3		
C.4146	Copper Washer, on Banjo Bolt	6		*
C.25261	Front Cover, and Breather Housing Assy	1		*
C.18604/1	Gauze Filter, under Front Cover	1		*
C.2227	Gasket, Front and Rear of Filter	2		*
C.28247	Breather Pipe, long	1)	NOT U.S.A. or	
C.25268	Flanged Breather Pipe, on Air Box Base	1)	CANADA	
C.28710	Breather Pipe.Long	1)	FOR U.S.A. and	
C.28808	Flanged Breather Pipe on Air Box Base	1)	CANADA	
C.25271	Gasket, between Flange and Air Box Base	1		**
UFN.125/L	Nut, securing Pipe to Air Box Base	2		
FG.104/X	Spring Washer, under Nut	2		
C.25263	Hose, connecting Pipes	2		*
C.2905/8	Clip, securing Hoses	4		

PART NO.	Description.	NO. PER UNIT.	REMARKS

Cylinder Head (Continued).

PART NO.	Description.	NO. PER UNIT.	REMARKS
C.18396	Exhaust Manifold Front	1	
C.18397	Exhaust Manifold Rear	1)	NOT FOR U.S.A. or) CANADA up to Eng. No.) 7R2082 and 7R35462) Fitted to all engines after
C.28683	Exhaust Manifold Rear	1)	U.S.A. and CANADA up) to Eng.Nos.7R2082 and) 7R35462
C.2318	Gasket, Exhaust Manifold to Head	2	**
C.15848	Clip, under Manifold Nut retaining Dipstick	1)	NOT U.S.A. or) CANADA. fitted to
C.19706	Distance Piece, under Clip	1)	all Engines from) 7R2083 and 7R35463
C.28893	Clip, locating Dipstick	1)	U.S.A. and CANADA) up to Eng. Nos.) 7R2082 and 7R35462
C.2369	Stud, in Manifold Flange for Down Pipes	8	**
C.17916	Special Nut, on Studs	8	**
FW.106/T	Plain Washer, under Nuts	8	
C.18405/1	Sealing Ring, between Manifold and Down Pipes	2	**
C.29017	Mixture Housing, on Top of Rear Exhaust Manifold	1)	
C.2157	Headed Plug (Screwed)	1)	
C.2296/2	Copper Washer, on Plug	1)	FOR USA and) CANADA up to Eng.
C.28706	Gasket Mixture Housing to Manifold	1)	Nos.7R2082. Open and
C.28814	Stud, Mixture Housing to Manifold	1)	F.H.C.
C.29199	Stud, Underside of Exhaust Manifold to Mixture Housing	2)	7R35462. 2+2
UFN.131/L	Nut, on Stud	2)	
FG.105/X	Spring Washer, under Nut	2)	
C.24558	Inlet Manifold	1)	NOT U.S.A. or
C.25078	Adaptor, for Brake Vacuum Hose	1)	CANADA
C.2296/1	Copper Washer, on Adaptor	1)	
C.23232/1	Gasket, Inlet Manifold to Cyl.Head	1)	**
C.28695	Inlet Manifold	1)	For U.S.A. and
C.25078	Adaptor, for Brake Vacuum Hose	1)	CANADA up to Eng.
C.2296/1	Copper Washer, on Adaptor	1)	Nos. 7R.1837 and
C.23232/1	Gasket, Inlet Manifold to Cyl.Head	1)	7R35329 **
C.30376	Inlet Manifold	1)	For U.S.A. and
C.25078	Adaptor for Brake Vacuum Hose	1)	CANADA fitted from
C.2296/1	Copper Washer, on Adaptor	1)	Eng.No.7R1838.Open
C.23232/1	Gasket, Inlet Manifold to Cyl.Head	1)	and F.H.C. Eng. No. **
		)	7R35330. 2+2

PART NO.	Description.	NO. PER UNIT.	REMARKS

Cylinder Head (Continued).

PART NO.	Description.	NO. PER UNIT.	REMARKS
C.2496	Stud, in Inlet Manifold for Thermostat Housing	1	
C.28248	Stud, in Inlet Manifold for Thermostat and Water Outlet	2	
C.28212	Thermostat Housing	1	**
C.28374	Gasket, Thermostat Housing to Inlet Manifold	1	
C.28223	Water Outlet Pipe	1	
C.28222	Gasket, Water Outlet Pipe to Thermo Housing	1	**
C.28442	Bleed Valve	1	
C.2496	Stud, securing Water Outlet Pipe	2	
UFN.131/L	Nut, on Studs	4	
FG.105/X	Spring Washer, under Nuts	4	
C.28067	Thermostat (74° C)	1)	Fitted up to 7R5262) 7R37489
C.28067/1	Thermostat (82°C)	1)	Fitted from 7R5263 Open) and F.H.C.) 7R37490.2+2
C.18232	Stud, in Inlet Manifold for Carburetters	12)	NOT U.S.A.
UFN.131/L	Nut, on Studs	12)	OR
FG.105/X	Spring Washer, under Nuts	12)	CANADA
C.17421	Adaptor, at Rear of Inlet Manifold for Heater Water Feed	1	
C.2296/1	Copper Washer, on Adaptor	1	
11763	Sparking Plug (N.11.Y)	6	**
5520	High Tension Cable (Plug Leads)	20 ft	
C.30190/1	H.T.Lead.Coil to Distributor	1	
C.27494	Spark Plug Terminal and Suppressor	6	**
C.27856	Rubber Sleeve, for Spark Plug Terminals	6	
C.25127	Clip, retaining Spark Plug Leads to Timing Cover	1	
3204	Grommet, in Clip	1	
C.19889	Sleeve (P.V.C.) on Spark Plug Leads	1	
C.24126	Conduit, enclosing Spark Plug Leads	1	

PART NO.	Description.	NO. PER UNIT.	REMARKS

TIMING GEAR.

PART NO.	Description.	NO. PER UNIT.	REMARKS
C.24686	Sprocket, for Camshaft	2	*
C.26688	Adjusting Plate, and Coupling for Sprocket	2	*
C.30767	Circlip, retaining Coupling in Sprocket	2	*
C.2310	Setscrew, securing Coupling and Sprocket	4	
C.4128/1	Front Bracket, mounting Timing Gear	1	
C.21703	Rear Bracket, mounting Timing Gear	1	
C.2182	Stud, fixing Brackets together	4	
UFN.125/L	Nut, on Stud	4	
C.724	Shakeproof Washer, under Nut	4	
UFB.131/17R	Bolt, long, fixing Brackets to Block	4	
C.740	Shakeproof Washer, on Bolts	4	
C.26740	Idler Sprocket Assembly	1	*
C.2319/1	Bush in Idler Sprocket	1	*
C.27189	Eccentric Shaft, for Idler Sprocket	1	
C.2282	Plug, in End of Eccentric Shaft	1	
C.4404	Micro-Adjustment Plate for Upper Chain	1	*
C.3338/4	Nut, securing Adj.Plate for Eccentric Shaft	1	
C.742	Shakeproof Washer, under Nut	1	
C.4405	Plunger Pin, locking Adjustment Plate	1	*
C.2297	Spring, behind Plunger Pin	1	*
C.25275	Intermediate Sprocket Assembly, top of Lower Chain	1	*
C.2320	Bush for Intermediate Sprocket	1	
C.26608	Shaft, for Intermediate Sprocket	1	
C.16626	Shim (Shaft End Float Adjustment)	As req'd	
C.2335	Circlip, retaining Shaft	1	
C.2256	Upper Timing Chain	1	**
C.13617	R.H.Upper Chain Damper	1	**
C.13616	L.H.Upper Chain Damper	1	**
C.21734	Distance Piece, for Upper Dampers	4	
C.25819	Retainer, for Upper Chain	1	
C.2255	Lower Timing Chain	1	**
C.21815	Intermediate Damper for Lower Chain	1	**
UFS.131/5R	Setscrew, Interm.Damper to Block	2	
C.21831	Tab Washer, on Setscrews	1	
C.13614/1	Vibration Damper, for Lower Chain	1	**
UFS.131/5R	Setscrew, Vibration Damper to Block	2	
C.20397	Tab Washer, on Setscrews	1	
C.10332	Hydraulic Tensioner Assembly(Lower Chain)	1	**
6029	Tab Washer, retaining Adjuster Plug	1	
C.9766	Shim, for Adjustment of Tensioner	As req'd	
UFB.125/11R	Bolt, Tensioner to Cylinder Block	2	
C.10333	Tab Washer, retaining Bolts	1	
6265	Repair Kit, for Hydraulic Tensioner	1	*
C.13457	Filter Gauze, behind Tensioner	1	*

PART NO.	DESCRIPTION.	NO.PER UNIT.	REMARKS.

Timing Gear (Continued).

PART NO.	DESCRIPTION.	NO.PER UNIT.	REMARKS.
C.8614/1	Front Timing Cover	1)	Fitted up to Eng.Nos.
C.8615	Gasket, Timing Cover to Block	1)	7R1914 and 7R35388 **
C.28480	Front Timing Cover	1)	Fitted from Eng.
C.28658	Gasket, Timing Cover to Block	1)	No.7R1915 Open and F.H.C.
UCS.131/9R	Setscrew, Pump to Timing Cover	1)	Eng. No. 7R35389 2+2
C.24611/2	Oil Seal, Timing Cover to Oil Sump	1	**
C.2183	Stud, in Timing Cover Fixing Cylinder Head	2	
UFN.131/L	Nut, on Studs	2	
FW.105/E	Copper Washer, under Nut	2	
C.2325	Stud, in Timing Cover Fixing Sump	4	
UFN.131/L	Nut, on Studs	4	
C.725	Shakeproof Washer, under Nut	4	
UFB.131/22R	Bolt, Water Pump and Timing Cover to Block	1	NOT POWER STEERING
UCB.131/12R	Bolt, Water Pump & Timing Cover to Block	2	
UFB.131/14R	Bolt, Timing Cover to Block	1	
UFB.131/15R	Bolt, Timing Cover and Alternator Shield to Block	1	
UFB.131/9R	Bolt, Timing Cover to Block	1	
UFB.131/21R	Bolt, Water Pump and Timing Cover to Block	2	
UFB.131/26R	Bolt, Water Pump and Timing Cover to Block	2	
FG.105/X	Spring Washer, on Bolt	10	
UFB.137/11R	Bolt, Timing Cover to Block	3)	2 only required
FG.106/X	Spring Washer, on Bolts	3)	with Power Steering
C.29369	Ignition Timing Pointer on Timing Cover	1	
UFB.131/25R	Bolt, Water Pump and Link to Timing Cover	1	
C.23381	Bracket, on Timing Cover mounting Tensioner for Water Pump Belt	1	
C.20955/5	Bush, in Bracket	2	
UFB.137/13R	Bolt, Bracket and Timing Cover to Block	1	
UFB.137/14R	Bolt, Bracket and Timing Cover to Block	1	
FG.106/X	Spring Washer, on Bolts	2	
C.18447	Torsion Spring	1	**
C.21330	Carrier for Jockey Pulley	1	*
C.8737/2	Nut, securing Carrier to Bracket	1	
C.21326	Thrust Washer and Stop Under Nut	1	*
C.18733	Jockey Pulley, Tensioning Belt	1	**
C.3968/2	Nut, securing Jockey Pulley to Carrier	1	

PART NO.	Description.	NO. PER UNIT.	REMARKS

CARBURETTERS AND PETROL FILTER.
NOT FOR U.S.A. AND CANADA.

PART NO.	Description.	NO. PER UNIT.	REMARKS
C.26622	Front Carburetter Assembly	1	
10338	Body only	1	
7090	Adaptor, for Ignition Union	1	
7091	Gasket, under Adaptor	1	
5618	Screw, securing Adaptor	2	
7105	Shakeproof Washer, on Screw	2	
7106	Ignition Union	1	
8763	Suction Chamber and Piston Assembly	1	
7093	Screw, holding Jet Needle	1	
8764	Damper Assembly, in Suction Chamber	1	
7095	Washer, for Damper	1	
7871	Spring, for Piston Return	1	
7872	Skid Washer, under Spring	1	
5618	Screw, suction Chamber to Carburetter Body	4	
5980	Jet Needle. UM	1	*
7860	Jet and Diaphragm Assembly	1	*
6958	Jet Bearing	1	
6959	Nut, locking Jet Bearing	1	
8765	Spring, under Jet Diaphragm	1	
11275	Jet Housing Assembly	1	
8759	Shoe and Rod Assembly	1	
10939	Return Spring, for Shoe and Rod Assy	1	
8761	Plate. Top of Shoe and Rod Assembly	1	
7879	Screw, securing Plate	1	
7105	Shakeproof Washer, on Screw	1	
7048	Screw, in Plate for Choke/Throttle Opening	1	
7049	Spring, on Screw	1	
6993	Float Chamber Assembly	1	
7115	Bolt, securing Float Chamber	4	
7105	Shakeproof Washer, on Bolt	4	
10026	Lid, for Float Chamber	1	
1090	Float	1	*
10532	Needle & Seat Controlling Petrol Flow	1	**
10027	Lever, operating Float Needle	1	
1153	Pin, securing Lever to Lid	1	
7119	Gasket, under Float Chamber Lid	1	
5832	Cap Nut, securing Lid	1	
1298	Serrated Washer (Fibre) for Cap Nut	1	
7120	Washer (Aluminium) for Cap Nut	1	
479	Filter, in Float Chamber Lid	1	
C.11488	Banjo Bolt, securing Feed Pipe to Float Chamber Lid	1	
C.11489	Fibre Washer, on Banjo Bolt	2	
6967	Valve Slow-Running Adjustment	1	
6966	Spring, for Slow-Run Valve	1	
6968	Gland Washer, for Slow-Run Valve	1	
6969	Brass Washer, top of Gland Washer	1	

PART NO.	Description.	NO. PER UNIT.	REMARKS

Carburetters and Petrol Filter (Continued).
Not for U.S.A. and Canada.

PART NO.	Description.	NO. PER UNIT.	REMARKS
C.26623	Centre Carburetter Assembly	1	
10339	Body only	1	
8763	Suction Chamber and Piston Assy	1	
7093	Screw, holding Jet Needle	1	
8764	Damper Assembly in Suction Chamber	1	
7095	Washer, for Damper	1	
7871	Spring, for Piston Return	1	
7872	Skid Washer, under Spring	1	
5618	Screw, Suction Chamber to Carburetter Body	4	
5980	Jet Needle UM	1	
7860	Jet and Diaphragm Assembly	1	
6958	Jet Bearing	1	
6959	Nut, locking Jet Bearing	1	
8765	Spring, under Jet Diaphragm	1	
11276	Jet Housing Assembly	1	
8759	Shoe and Rod Assembly	1	
10939	Return Spring, for Shoe and Rod Assy	1	
8761	Plate, Top of Shoe and Rod Assy	1	
7879	Screw, securing Plate	1	
7105	Shakeproof Washer, on Screw	1	
7048	Screw, in Plate for Choke/Throttle Opening	1	
7049	Spring, on Screw	1	
8756	Abutment Bracket, for Choke Outer Cable	1	
8757	Cable Clamp, for Abutment Bracket	1	
5803	Bolt, securing Cable Clamp	1	
AN.102/L	Nut (2 B.A.) on Bolt	1	
5684	Spring Washer, under Nut	1	
6993	Float Chamber Assembly	1	
7115	Bolt, securing Float Chamber	4	
7105	Shakeproof Washer, on Bolts	4	
10026	Lid, for Float Chamber	1	
1090	Float	1	*
10532	Needle and Seat Controlling Petrol Flow	1	**
10027	Lever, operating Float Needle	1	
1153	Pin, securing Lever to Lid	1	
7119	Gasket, under Float Chamber Lid	1	
5832	Cap Nut, securing Lid	1	
1298	Serrated Washer (Fibre) for Cap Nut	1	
7120	Washer (Aluminium) for Cap Nut	1	
479	Filter, in Float Chamber Lid	1	
C.11488	Banjo Bolt, securing Feed Pipe to Float Chamber Lid	1	
C.11489	Fibre Washer, on Banjo Bolt	1	
6967	Valve, for Slow-Run Adjustment	1	
6966	Spring, for Slow-Run Valve	1	
6968	Gland Washer, for Slow-Run Valve	1	
6969	Brass Washer, Top of Gland Washer	1	

PART NO.	Description.	NO. PER UNIT.	REMARKS
	Carburetters and Petrol Filter (Continued). Not for U.S.A. and Canada.		
C.26624	Rear Carburetter Assembly	1	
11275	Jet Housing Assembly	1	
10025	Lid, for Float Chamber	1	
	All other items for Rear Carburetter are as for Centre Carburetter C.26623 Except that Bracket 8756 and Clamp 8757 are not fitted.		
11252	Carburetter Service Kit	3	**
8758	Choke,Connecting Rod, between Rear and Centre Carburetters	1	
C.10700	Choke,Connecting Rod, between Centre and Front Caburetters	1	
8755	Fork End, securing Rods to Carburetters	3	
AN.102/L	Nut (2 B.A.) locking Fork Ends on Rods	3	
5511	Clevis Pins, through Outer Fork Ends	2	
7966	Washer, on Clevis Pins	2	
L.102/5U	Split Pin	4	
C.18832	Adaptor, securing Choke Cable to Centre Carburetter	1	
C.18833	Screw, securing Cable in Adaptor	1	
C.14371	Lever on Carb.Spindles for Return Springs	3	
5803	Bolt, through Levers	3	
5614	Nut, on Bolts	3	
7966	Washer, under Nuts	3	
C.14366	Throttle Return Spring, for Front and Centre Carburetters	2	
C.15963	Bracket, for Return Spring on Front Carburetter	1	
C.24736	Bracket, for Return Spring on Centre Carburetter	1	
C.15587	Throttle Return Spring, for Rear Carburetter	1	
C.24737	Bracket, on Manifold Studs, for Rear Return Spring	1	
C.24927	Lever Assembly, on Carb.Spindles for Throttle Control Rods	3	
C.25148	Control Rods, Levers to Slave Shaft	3	
C.13824	Clip, securing Control Rods	3	
C.24741	Throttle Slave Shaft Assembly.Front	1	
C.24742	Throttle Slave Shaft Assembly.Rear	1	
C.19450	Pin Forward Lever of Rear Slave Shaft for Throttle Drive	1	
C.8667/17	Nut.securing Pin to Lever	1	
C.18941	Adaptor, in Manifold, supporting Front Slave Shaft	1	

PART NO.	Description.	NO. PER UNIT.	REMARKS
	Carburetters and Petrol Filter (Continued). Not for U.S.A. and Canada.		
C.18942	Adaptor, in Manifold Supporting Front and Rear Slave Shafts	1	
C.18943	Tab Washer, locking Adaptors	2	
C.17413	Insulator, Carburetters to Manifold	3	
C.7221	Gasket, each side of Insulators	6	**
C.16873	Overflow Pipe, for Front Carburetter	1	
C.16874	Overflow Pipe, for Centre Carburetter	1	
C.24738	Overflow Pipe, for Rear Carburetter	1	
C.14090	Clip, securing Overflow Pipes	1	
C.21576	Suction Pipe, Front Carburetter to Distributor	1	*
C.21573	Elbow (P.V.C.) Pipe to Distributor	1	**
C.26818	Petrol Feed Pipe. Linking Carburetters	1	*
C.26815	Petrol Pipe, Feed Pipe to Filter	1	*
C.27588	Petrol Filter Assembly	1	*
11450	Filter Casting	1	
11951	Sealing Washer, between Casing and Filter Element	1	*
C.28080	Filter Element and Sealing Washers	1	**
11950	Sealing Washer, between Casting and Glass Bowl	1	*
7300	Glass Bowl	1	
7301	Retaining Strap Assembly	1	
C.13705	Banjo Bolt, securing Pipe to Filter	1	
C.784	Fibre Washer, on Banjo Bolt	2	
C.31032	Bracket Mounting Petrol Filter	1	
UFS.131/6R	Setscrew, securing Filter to Bracket	2	
UFN.131/L	Nut, on Setscrew	2	
FG.105/X	Spring Washer, under Nuts	2	

PART NO.	Description.	NO. PER UNIT.	REMARKS

CARBURETTERS.   FOR U.S.A. AND CANADA.

PART NO.	Description.	NO. PER UNIT.	REMARKS
C.28817	Front Carburetter Assembly	1)	*
11552	Screw, securing Diaphragm retaining Ring to Piston	4)	
11553	Sealing Wire, and Lead Seal through Suction Chamber and Carburetter Body	1)	
C.28914	Jet Needle Assembly	1)	*
11555	Float and Arm Assembly	1)	*
11556	Pivot Pin, for Float Arm	1)	
12243	Needle Valve	1)	
11557	Gasket, between Float Chamber and Carburetter Body	1)	
11558	'O' Ring, in Aperture in Bottom of Float Chamber	1)	
11559	Screw, long, securing Float Chamber to Carburetter Body	4)	
11560	Screw, short, securing Float Chamber to Carburetter Body	2)	
11561	Temperature Compensator Assembly	1)	
11562	Sealing Washer, Inner, for Compensator Valve Body	1)	
11563	Sealing Washer, Outer, for Compensator Valve Body	1)	
11564	Screw, securing Compensator to Carburetter Body	2)	
11625	Throttle By-Pass Valve	1)	
11626	Gasket, for By-Pass Valve	1)	
11560	Screw, securing By-Pass Valve	3)	Fitted up to
11565	Throttle Return Spring	1)	Engine Nos.
11566	Adaptor for Throttle Spindle Connecting Rod	1)	7R1837.Open and F.H.C. 7R35329. 2+2
11567	Tab Washer, locking Adaptor to Throttle Spindle	1)	
C.28818	Rear Carburetter Assembly	1)	*
	Individual Items are as for Front Carburetter C28817 except that By-Pass Valve (11625) with Gasket and Fixing Screws, Adaptor (11566) and Tab Washer (11567) are NOT fitted.	))))	
11561	Temperature Compensator Assembly	2)	
11568	Cover (Plastic) at Side of Compensator Body	2)	
11554	Screw, securing Cover	4)	
C.28906	Coupling Spindle Assy, between Carburetters	1)	
C.28907	Spindle only	1)	
C.28908	Pick Up Lever	1)	
C.28909	Bush	1)	
C.28910	Throttle Lever	1)	
C.28911	Spacing Washer	1)	
C.28912	Tab Washer	1)	
C.28913	Extension Nut	1)	

PART NO.	Description.	NO. PER UNIT.	REMARKS

Carburetters.   For U.S.A. and Canada (Continued).

PART NO.	Description.	NO. PER UNIT.	REMARKS
C.28917	Coupling Assembly, connecting Spindle Assembly to Carburetters	2)	Fitted up to Engine Nos.
C.28918	Coupling only	2)	7R1837 Open and F.H.C.
C.28919	Screw, through Coupling	4)	7R35329. 2+2
C.28920	Nut, on Screw	4)	
C.28921	Washer, on Screw	4)	
C.21573	By-Pass Pipe Elbow (P.V.C.)	1)	
C.30338	Front Carburetter Assembly	1	Fitted from *
C.28929	Seal, in Body for Throttle Spindle	2	7R1838 Open and F.H.C.
12372	Throttle Spindle	1	7R35330. 2+2
12374	Throttle Lever and Stop Assembly	1	
12376	Bush for Lever	1	
12377	Throttle Lever	1	
11567	Tab Washer	1	
12378	Extension Nut on Spindle for Coupling	1	
11565	Return Spring	1	
12379	Pick-Up Lever on Spindle	1	
12376	Bush for Lever	1	
12380	Floating Lever, on Spindle	1	
12382	Starter Cover (Choke)	1	
12383	Starter Spindle Assy.(Choke)	1	
12385	Spring on Starter Spindle	1	
12386	'C' Washer, retaining Spring	1	
12387	Return Spring for Starter	1	
12388	Cam Lever Assembly, for Starter	1	
12389	Screw, securing Starter to Carb.	2	
12278	Clip, on Control Bracket for securing Choke Cable	1	
12368	By-Pass Valve Assembly	1	
12369	Gasket, for By-Pass Valve	1	
11560	Screw, securing By-Pass Valve	3	
12370	Temperature Compensator Assembly	1	
11562	Sealing Washer, Inner, for Compensator Valve Body	1	
11563	Sealing Washer, Outer, for Compensator Valve Body	1	
11564	Screw, securing Compensator	2	
11555	Float and Arm Assembly	1	
12390	Sealing Plug and 'O' Ring for Float Chamber	1	
11558	'O' Ring only	1	
11557	Gasket, for Float Chamber	1	
11559	Screw (long) securing Float Chamber	4	
11560	Screw (short) securing Float Chamber	2	
12294	Damper Assembly, with 'O' Ring	1	
12293	'O' Ring only for Damper	1	
C.28914	Jet Needle (B1E)	1	*
12335	Air Valve Return Spring	1	
12371	Needle Valve	1	

PART NO.	**Description.**	**NO. PER UNIT.**	**REMARKS**

<u>Carburetters. For U.S.A. and Canada (Continued).</u>

C.30339	Rear Carburetter Assembly	1	Fitted from *
12373	Throttle Spindle	1	7R1838 Open & F.H.C.
12375	Throttle Lever & Stop Assembly	1	7R35330. 2+2
12381	Floating Lever	1	
12384	Starter Spindle Assy (Choke)	1	

All other items are as for Front Carburetter
C.30338 Except that Throttle Lever (12377)
Extension Nut (12378) and Pick-Up Lever (12379)
are NOT fitted.

12370	Temperature Compensator Assembly	2	
11568	Cover (Plastic) on Compensator	2	
11554	Screw, securing Cover	4	
C.30340	Coupling Spindle Assy.between Carburetters	1	
C.30342	Coupling Clip Assembly	2	
11549	Service Pack for Carburetter (Yellow)	1	Required at * 12000 miles and 36,000 miles etc.
11791	Service Pack for Carburetter (Red)	1	Required at » 24,000 miles and 48,000 miles etc.
C.28888	Secondary Throttle Housing, on Inlet Manifold	1	Fitted up to Eng. Nos. 7R1837 and 7R35329
C.31403/1	Secondary Throttle Housing, on Inlet Manifold	1)	Fitted from) Eng. No. 7R1838 Open and
C.17421	Adaptor for Water Outlet	1)	F.H.C.
C.2296/1	Copper Washer on Adaptor	1)	Eng. No. 7R35330 2+2
C.28928	Bush for Throttle Spindle	2)	
C.28699	Gasket, Housing to Inlet Manifold	2	**
C.28701	Stud, long, securing Throttle Housing and Carburetters to Inlet Manifold	4	
C.28702	Stud, Intermediate, securing Throttle Housing to Inlet Manifold	4	
C.18232	Stud, short, securing Carburetters to Throttle Housing	4	
FG.105/X	Spring Washer, on Studs	12	
UFN.131/L	Nut, on Studs	12	
C.31012	Top Cover, on Secondary Throttle Housing	1)	Fitted from
C.31055	Gasket, between Cover and Housing	1)	Eng. No. 7R1838 Open *
UCS.831/7H	Setscrew, securing Cover	4)	and F.H.C.
FW.105/E	Copper Washer, on Setscrew	4)	Eng. No. 7R35330. 2+2
C.30923	Hose, Water Feed to Throttle Housing from Rear of Inlet Manifold	1)	Fitted from *) Eng. No.7R1838 Open
C.30643	Hose, Water Outlet from Throttle Housing to Heater Return Pipe	1)	and F.H.C. *) Eng. No. 7R35330. 2+2
C.2905/14	Clip, securing Hose	4)	

PART NO.   **Description.**   **NO. PER**   **REMARKS**
                                                     UNIT.

Carburetters.   For U.S.A. and Canada (Continued).

Part No.	Description	No. Per Unit	Remarks
C.28704	Primary Mixture Pipe, from Throttle Housing to Rear Exhaust Manifold	1)	
C.28705	Gasket, Mixture Pipe to Throttle Housing	1)	Fitted up to Engine Nos.
C.28707	Stud, Mixture Pipe to Throttle Housing	4)	7R2082. Open and F.H.C.
C.28813	Stud, long, Mixture Pipe to Exhaust Mixture Housing	2)	7R35462. 2+2
C.28707	Stud, short, Mixture Pipe to Exhaust Mixture Housing	2)	
UFN.131/L	Nut, on Studs	8)	
FW.105/E	Copper Washer, under Nuts	8)	
C.28930	Secondary Throttle Spindle in Housing	2	
C.28931	Secondary Throttle Disc	2	
C.28932	Screw, securing Disc to Spindle	4	
C.28928	Spindle Bush, in Throttle Housing	2	
C.28929	Seal Assembly	2	
C.28933	Return Spring	1	
C.28934	Return Spring	1	
C.29135	Secondary Throttle Lever Assembly for Front Throttle	1	
C.29136	Secondary Throttle Lever Assembly for Rear Throttle	1	
C.29137	Throttle Link Assembly	1	
C.28936	Link	1	
C.29139	Starlock Washer	4	
C.28940	Shakeproof Washer	2	
C.28941	Nut	2	
C.28697	Insulator, between Carburetter and Throttle Housing	2	
C.28696	Gasket, each side of Insulator	4	
C.28915	Petrol "Tee" Pipe, between Carburetters	1	
C.28916	Clip, securing "Tee" Pipe to Carburetters	2	
C.11575	Olive for "Tee" Pipe	1	
C.11576	Union Nut, for "Tee" Pipe	1	
C.26815	Petrol Pipe "Tee" Pipe to Filter	1	
C.27588	Petrol Filter Assembly	1	*
11450	Filter Casting	1	
11951	Sealing Washer, Casting to Element	1	*
C.28080	Filter Element & Sealing Washers	1	**
11950	Sealing Washer. Casting to Bowl	1	
7300	Glass Bowl	1	*
7301	Retaining Strap Assembly	1	
C.13705	Banjo Bolt, securing Pipe to Filter	1	
C.784	Fibre Washer, on Banjo Bolt	2	
C.31032 +	Bracket, mounting Petrol Filter	1	

PART NO.	Description.	NO. PER UNIT.	REMARKS

AIR CLEANER.

PART NO.	Description.	NO. PER UNIT.	REMARKS
C.26295	Air Cleaner Assembly	1	
11306	Shell Assembly, for Air Cleaner	1	
8419	Retainer Plate, for Element	1	
8417	Gasket, at Ends of Element	2	**
8416	Element, for Air Cleaner	1	**
8418	Top Plate Assembly	1	
C.17651	Bracket, mounting Air Cleaner	1	
UFS.131/4R	Setscrew, Bracket to Air Cleaner	2	
C.725	Shakeproof Washer, on Setscrew	2	
FW.105/T	Plain Washer, on Setscrew	2	
UFS.125/4R	Setscrew, Bracket to Body	2	
C.724	Shakeproof Washer, on Setscrew	2	
BD.541/20	Plain Washer, on Setscrew	2	
C.17652/1	Support Bracket, for Air Cleaner	1	
C.31973/12	Nut, (Plastic) in Support Bracket	1	
C.26364/1	Screw, securing Air Cleaner to Support Bracket	1	
UFS.131/4R	Setscrew, support Bracket to Body	2	
UFN.131/L	Nut, on Setscrews	2	
C.725	Shakeproof Washer, under Nut	2	
C.17546	Grommet (Rubber) between Air Cleaner and Air Intake Box	1	
C.17533	Air Intake Box Assembly	1) Not for	
		)	
C.25266	Base Assembly, for Air Intake Box (complete with Trumpets)	1) U.S.A. or Canada)	
C.17539	Gasket, Neoprene.Base to Air Intake Box	1)	**
C.12734	Wing Nut, Air Intake Box to Base	2) Not	
C.17544	Washer, under Wing Nut	2) for	
		) U.S.A. or	
C.7164	Gasket Base to Carburetters	3) Canada	
UFN.131/L	Nut, securing Base to Carburetters	6)	
FG.105/X	Spring Washer, under Nut	6)	
C.28712	Air Intake Box Assembly	1))	
C.28717	Base Assembly, for Air Intake Box	1)	
C.17539	Gasket.Neoprene.Base to Air Intake Box	1)	**
C.12734	Wing Nut, Air Intake Box to Base	2)	
C.17544	Washer, under Wing Nut	2))	
C.28719	Air Pipe, Base to Carburetters	2) For	
C.28728	Gasket. Base to Air Pipe	2) U.S.A.	**
C.28721	Gasket Air Pipe to Carburetter	2) and	**
UFN.131/L	Nut, securing Air Pipe to Base	6) Canada	
FG.105/X	Spring Washer, under Nut	6))	
UFS.131/6.5R	Setscrew, short.Air Pipe to Carbs.	4)	
UFS.131/8R	Setscrew, long,Air Pipe to Carbs.	2)	
FG.105/X	Spring Washer, on Setscrews	6)	

PART NO.	Description.	NO. PER UNIT.	REMARKS

ACCELERATOR CONTROLS R.H.DRIVE.

PART NO.	Description.	NO. PER UNIT.	REMARKS
C.26514	Accelerator Pedal Assembly	1	
C.26563	Return Spring, for Pedal	1	
C.17844	Housing Assembly, for Pedal	1	
C.17851	Pivot Bush.each side of Housing	2	
C.17848	Stud, securing Housing to Scuttle	3	
C.20639	Stop Plate, on Studs (Pedal Adjustment)	1	
C.8667/1	Nut, on Studs	3	
FW.104/T	Plain Washer, under Nuts	3	
C.25581	Gasket.Neoprene.Housing to Scuttle	1	
C.18302	Accelerator Pedal Lever Assembly	1	
C.3767	Ball Pin, in end of Lever	1	
UFB.137/16R	Bolt, securing Pedal and Lever in Housing	1	
C.410	Plain Washer, under Head of Bolt	1	
C.19915	Spacing Collar, on Bolt	1	
C.19914	Special Washer, on Pedal Lever Boss	1	
C.8737/3	Nut, on Bolt	1	
C.17867	Control Rod,Pedal Lever to Outer Fulcrum Lever	1	
C.17858	Outer Fulcrum Lever Assembly	1	
C.3767	Ball Pin, in ends of Lever	2	
C.24780	Bracket, Outer Fulcrum Lever to Dash	1	
UFS.125/4R	Setscrew, securing Bracket to Dash	2	
C.724	Shakeproof Washer, on Setscrew	2	
L.102.5/8U	Split Pin, retaining Fulcrum Lever on Bracket	1	
FW.104/T	Plain Washer, under Split Pin	1	
BD.1708/5	Double Coil Spring Washer, behind Plain Washer	1	
C.23915	Eccentric Sleeve, for Fulcrum Lever Stop Adjustment	1	
UFB.125/12R	Bolt, securing Eccentric Sleeve to Bracket	1	
C.724	Shakeproof Washer, on Bolt	1	
FW.104/T	Plain Washer, under Shakeproof Washer	1	
C.17868	Control Rod, linking Fulcrum Levers	1	Open and F.H.Coupe
C.30932	Control Rod, linking Fulcrum Levers	1	2+2 Models.
C.24771	Inner Fulcrum Lever Assembly	1	
C.3767	Ball Pin, in Lever	1	
C.24767	Bracket, fixing Inner Fulcrum Lever to Dash	1	Open and F.H.Coupe
C.30933	Bracket, fixing Inner Fulcrum Lever to Dash	1	2+2 Models
UFS.125/4R	Setscrew, securing Bracket	2	
C.724	Shakeproof Washer, on Setscrew	2	
FW.104/T	Plain Washer, under Setscrew	2	

PART NO.	Description.	NO. PER UNIT.	REMARKS

Accelerator Controls R.H.Drive (Continued).

PART NO.	Description.	NO. PER UNIT.	REMARKS
L.102.5/8U	Split Pin, retaining Fulcrum Lever on Bracket	1	
FW.104/T	Plain Washer, under Split Pin	1	
BD.1708/5	Double Coil Spring Washer, behind Plain Washer	1	
C.31597	Control Rod.Linking Inner Fulcrum Lever to Rear Slave Shaft	1	Open & F.H.Coupe
C.24747	Control Rod.Linking Inner Fulcrum Lever to Rear Slave Shaft	1	2+2 Models.
C.13824	Clip, securing Control Rod	2	
C.24746	Bracket, on Dash supporting End of Rear Slave Shaft	1	
C.24816	Bush in Bracket	1	
UFS.125/7R	Setscrew, securing Bracket	2	
C.724	Shakeproof Washer, on Setscrew	2	
FW.104/T	Plain Washer, under Shakeproof Washer	2	
C.24742	Rear Throttle Slave Shaft Assembly	1	
C.19450	Pin, in Forward Lever on Shaft	1	
C.8667/17	Nut, securing Pin	1	
C,24741	Front Slave Shaft Assembly	1	Std.Transmissions.
C.25802	Front Slave Shaft Assembly	1	Automatic 2+2 only
C.18941	Adaptor, in Inlet Manifold Front Boss Supporting Front Slave Shaft	1	
C.18942	Adaptor, in Inlet Manifold Rear Boss Supporting Front & Rear Slave Shafts	1	
C.18943	Tab Washer, locking Adaptors	2	
C.25148	Control Rod Linking front Shaft Levers to Carburetters	3	
C.13824	Clip, securing Control Rods	6	
C.25804	Control Rod Linking front Slave Shaft with Relay Shaft	1))	
C.13824	Clip, securing Control Rod	2)	
C.27900	Support Bracket and Relay Shaft Assembly Operating Kick-Down Cable	1))	
C.25805	Relay Shaft Assembly	1)	Automatic
C.24334	Lever on Relay Shaft	1)	Transmission
411524/08	Pin, securing Lever to Shaft	1)	2+2 only
C.25800	Support Bracket Assembly	1))	
C.26756/3	Kick-Down Cable Assembly	1)	
C.25801	Location Bracket, retaining Outer Cable	1)	

PART NO.	Description.	NO. PER UNIT.	REMARKS

ACCELERATOR CONTROLS L.H.D.

PART NO.	Description.	NO. PER UNIT.	REMARKS
C.18467	Accelerator Pedal Assembly	1	Open and F.H.Coupe
C.26592	Accelerator Pedal Assembly	1)	
C.26585	Pedal Plate Assembly	1)	
C.26590	Mounting Bracket	1)	2+2
C.6969	Fulcrum Pin.Plate to Bracket	1)	Models
C.8737/1	Nut, on Fulcrum Pin	1)	Only
FW.104/T	Plain Washer, under Nut	1)	
UFS.125/4R	Setscrew, securing Pedal to Floor	2	
C.724	Shakeproof Washer, on Setscrew	2	
C.18478	Link Assembly, between Pedal and Accelerator Drop Arm	1	
C.18482	Retainer for Link	1	
C.8667/17	Nut, securing Retainer to Link	1	
C.18476	Accelerator Drop Arm Assembly	1	
C.26564	Return Spring, for Drop Arm	1	
C.17845	Housing Assembly, for Drop Arm	1	
C.17851	Pivot Bush each Side of Housing	2	
C.17848	Stud, securing Housing to Scuttle	4	
C.8667/1	Nut, on Stud	4	
FW.104/T	Plain Washer, under Nut	4	
C.25578	Gasket, Housing to Scuttle	1	
C.29404	Connecting Lever Assembly, between Drop Arm and Control Rod	1	
C.3767	Ball Pin, in Lever	1	
UFB.137/16R	Bolt, securing Drop Arm and Lever in Housing	1	
C.410	Washer, under Head of Bolt	1	
C.19915	Spacing Collar, on Bolt	1	
C.19914	Spacing Washer, in Boss of Connecting Lever	1	
C.8737/3	Nut, on Bolt	1	
C.31596	Control Rod, between Connecting Lever and L.H.Fulcrum Lever	1	
C.17859	L.H.Fulcrum Lever Assembly	1	Not U.S.A. and CANADA
C.29075	L.H.Fulcrum Lever Assembly	1	For U.S.A. and CANADA
C.3767	Ball Pin, in Lever	2	
C.18276	Pivot Pin, for Fulcrum Lever	1	Open and F.H.Coupe
C.30938	Pivot Pin, for Fulcrum Lever	1	2+2 Models
C.30937	Packing Piece, for Fulcrum Lever	1	2+2 Models
C.18275	Eccentric Sleeve, for Fulcrum Lever Stop adjustment	2	
UFB.125/11R	Bolt, Eccentric Sleeve to Dash	2	Open and F.H.Coupe
UFB.125/14R	Bolt, Eccentric Sleeve to Dash	2	2+2 Models
C.18274	Stiffening Plate, in Pivot Pin and Bolts	1	
C.25450	Tab Washer, locking Pivot Pin and Bolts	1	

PART NO.	Description.	NO. PER UNIT.	REMARKS

Accelerator Controls L.H.D. (Continued).

PART NO.	Description.	NO. PER UNIT.	REMARKS
C.17870	Control Rod, linking Fulcrum Levers	1	Not U.S.A. and CANADA
C.17870/1	Control Rod, linking Fulcrum Levers	1	For U.S.A. and CANADA
C.24769	R.H.Fulcrum Lever Assembly	1	
C.3767	Ball Pin in Lever	1	
C.24767	Bracket Assembly, securing R.H.Fulcrum Lever to Dash	1	Open and F.H.Coupe
C.30935	Bracket Assembly, securing R.H.Fulcrum Lever to Dash	1	2+2 Models
UFS.125/4R	Setscrew, securing Bracket	2	
C.724	Shakeproof Washer, on Setscrew	2	
FW.104/T	Plain Washer, under Shakeproof Washer	2	
L.102.5/8U	Split Pin, retaining Fulcrum Lever on Bracket	1	
FW.104/T	Plain Washer, under Split Pin	1	
BD.1708/5	Double Coil Spring Washer	1	
C.31597	Control Rod.linking R.H.Fulcrum Lever to Rear Slave Shaft	1	Open and F.H.Coupe
C.24747	Control Rod.linking R.H.Fulcrum Lever to Rear Slave Shaft	1	2+2 Models
C.13824	Clip, securing Control Rod	2	*
C.24746	Bracket, on Dash, supporting End of Rear Slave Shaft	1	) NOT required for U.S.A. and) Canada up to Engine Nos.) 7R1837 and 7R35329
C.31069	Bracket, on Dash, supporting End of Rear Slave Shaft	1	) For U.S.A. and Canada) from Eng. Nos.) 7R1838 and 7R35330
C.24816	Bush, in Bracket	1	
UFS.125/4R	Setscrew, securing Bracket	2	
C.724	Shakeproof Washer, on Setscrew	2	
FW.104/T	Plain Washer, under Shakeproof Washer	2	
C.24742	Rear Slave Shaft Assembly	1	Not U.S.A. and CANADA
C.28833	Rear Slave Shaft Assembly	1	) For U.S.A. and Canada up to) Eng.Nos.7R1837 and 7R35329
C.30326	Rear Slave Shaft Assembly	1	) For U.S.A. and Canada from) Eng.Nos.7R1838 and 7R35330
C.19450	Pin, in Forward Lever of Shaft	1	
C.8667/17	Nut, securing Pin	1	
C.24741	Front Slave Shaft Assembly	1	) Standard Trans., but Not) U.S.A. and Canada.
C.28722	Front Slave Shaft Assembly	1	) Standard Trans., for U.S.A.) and Canada up to 7R1837) and 7R35329
C.25802	Front Slave Shaft Assembly	1	) Automatic 2+2 only. But) not U.S.A. and Canada
C.28831	Front Slave Shaft Assembly	1)	Automatic 2+2 only for U.S.A.) and Canada up to 7R35329

PART NO.	Description.	NO. PER UNIT.	REMARKS

Accelerator Controls L.H.D. (Continued).

PART NO.	Description.	NO. PER UNIT.	REMARKS
C.30324	Front Slave Shaft Assembly	1	) All Transmissions for U.S.A) and Canada from Eng.Nos.) 7R1838 and 7R35330
C.18941	Adaptor, in Inlet Manifold Front Boss Supporting Front Slave Shaft	1	
C.18942	Adaptor, in Inlet Manifold Rear Boss Supporting Front and Rear Slave Shafts.	1	
C.18943	Tab Washer, locking Adaptor	2	Not U.S.A. and Canada
C.25148	Control Rod, linking Front Shaft Levers to Carburetters	3	) Not for U.S.A. and) Canada
C.13824	Clip, securing Control Rods	6	) *
C.28837	Connecting Link Front Slave Shaft to Caburetters	1	) For U.S.A. and Canada) Up to Eng. Nos.
C.13824	Clip, securing Connecting Link	2	) 7R1837 and 7R35329
C.28992	Washer, for Clip	1	)
C.30330	Adjustable Link, Front Slave Shaft to Carburetters	1	) For U.S.A. and Canada) fitted from Eng. Nos.
C.13824	Clip, securing Link	2	) 7R1838 and 7R35330
C.28992	Washer, for Clip	1	)
C.25804	Control Rod, linking Front Slave Shaft with Relay Shaft	1	))
C.13824	Clip, securing Control Rod	2	) Automatic)
C.27900	Support Bracket and Relay Shaft Assembly Operating Kick-Down Cable	1	) Transmission)
C.25805	Relay Shaft Assembly	1	) 2+2 only
C.24334	Lever, on Relay Shaft	1	)
422524/08	Pin, securing Lever to Shaft	1	) Not for
C.25800	Support Bracket Assembly	1	)) U.S.A. and
C.26756/3	Kick-Down Cable Assembly	1	)) Canada
C.25801	Location Bracket, retaining Outer Cable	1	)
C.23239	Control Rod, linking Front Slave Shaft Relay Shaft	1	)) Automatic
C.13824	Clip, securing Control Rod	2	) Transmission) 2+2 only
C.28901	Support Bracket and Relay Shaft Assembly Operating Kick-Down Cable	1	) For U.S.A.) and Canada
C.28828	Relay Shaft Assembly	1	) Fitted up to
C.24334	Lever, on Relay Shaft	1	) Eng. No.
422524/08	Pin, securing Lever to Shaft	1	) 7R35329
C.28823	Support Bracket Assembly	1	)
C.26756/1	Kick-Down Cable Assembly	1	))
C.25801	Location Bracket, retaining Outer Cable	1	)

PART NO.	Description.	NO. PER UNIT.	REMARKS

Accelerator Controls L.H.D.(Continued).

PART NO.	Description.	NO. PER UNIT.	REMARKS
C.31615	Control Rod, linking Front Slave Shaft with Relay Shaft	1)	
C.13824	Clip, securing Control Rod	2)	Automatic Transmission 2+2 only
C.30352	Support Bracket and Relay Shaft Assembly operating Kick-Down Cable	1)	For U.S.A. and Canada
C.30321	Relay Shaft Assembly	1)	Fitted from
C.24334	Lever, on Relay Shaft	1)	Engine No.
422524/08	Pin, securing Lever to Shaft	1)	7R35330
C.30318	Support Bracket Assembly	1)	
C.26756/1	Kick-Down Cable Assembly	1)	
C.25801	Location Bracket, retaining Outer Cable	1)	

PART NO.	Description.	NO. PER UNIT.	REMARKS	

CLUTCH UNIT AND CONTROLS.

PART NO.	Description.	NO. PER UNIT.	REMARKS	
C.27019	Clutch Cover Assembly	1)	Fitted up to Eng. Nos.7R2587 and 7R35730	*
C.31399	Clutch Cover Assembly	1)	Fitted from Eng.Nos. 7R2588 and 7R35731	
C.25874	Clutch Driven Plate Assembly	1		*
11273	Facings Package (Linings & Rivets)	1		
C.23575/1	Release Bearing and Cup Assembly	1		**
4163	Retainer, securing Cup to Fork	2		**
C.8631	Dowel, locating Clutch Cover to Flywheel	3		
UFS.131/6.5R	Setscrew, securing Clutch to Flywheel	6		
FG.105/X	Spring Washer, on Setscrew	6		
C.23965	Balance Weight (.036" thick)	as req'd)	Selective Weights	
C.23965/2	Balance Weight (.064" thick)	as req'd)		
C.23965/3	Balance Weight (.104" thick)	as req'd)		
C.23965/4	Balance Weight (.128" thick)	as req'd)		
C.25293	Clutch Pedal	1	R.H.Drive	
C.25294	Clutch Pedal	1	L.H.Drive	
C.19154	Bush, in Clutch Pedal	2		
C.25506	Return Spring, for Clutch Pedal	1		**
C.26532	Pad (Steel) on Clutch Pedal	1		
C.8737/3	Nut, securing Pad to Pedal	1		
C.9934	Pad (Rubber) on Clutch Pedal	1		**
C.25290	Pedal Housing	1		
C.18203	Stud, securing Housing to Scuttle	2		
C.25322	Stud, securing Housing to Scuttle	3		
C.8737/2	Nut, on Stud	5		
FW.105/T	Plain Washer, under Nut	5		
C.25301	Gasket, between Housing and Scuttle	1		
C.25295	Shaft, in Housing mounting Pedals	1		
C.25297	Fibre Washer, on Shaft	2		
C.25296	Spacer, on Shaft between Pedals	1		
C.8737/4	Nut, retaining Shaft in Housing	1		
FW.107/T	Plain Washer, under Nut	1		
C.22669	Reservoir Assembly, for Clutch Fluid	1		*
C.19515	Cap, on Reservoir	1		
C.24856	Bracket R.H.side of Dash supporting Reservoir Clamps	1)		
UFS.131/4R	Setscrew, securing Bracket to Dash	2)		
C.725	Shakeproof Washer, on Setscrew	2) R.H.Drive Cars only. See also Hydraulic Brake Pipe Section.		
C.24607	Outer Clamp, mounting Reservoirs	1)		

PART NO.	Description.	NO. PER UNIT.	REMARKS

Clutch Unit and Controls (Continued).

PART NO.	Description.	NO. PER UNIT	REMARKS
C.24128	Inner Clamp, mounting Reservoirs	1)	R.H.Drive Cars only.
C.20235	Stud, through Bracket and Clamps	1)	See also Hydraulic
C.8737/1	Nut, on Stud	2)	Brake Pipe Section
C.17812	Bracket, fixing Reservoir Bracket to L. H. Side Member	2)	
UFS.125/9R	Setscrew, securing Brackets to Exhaust Heatshield Bracket	2)	
UFN.125/L	Nut, on Setscrew	2)	
C.724	Shakeproof Washer, under Nut	2)	
C.18695	Heatshield Assembly	1)	Manual Steering
C.30735	Heatshield Assembly	1)	Power Steering
UFS.131/7R	Setscrew, securing Shield and Reservoir Bracket to Fixing Bracket	4)	
C.18698	Spacer, on Setscrews	4)	Manual Steering
C.725	Shakeproof Washer, on Setscrews	4)	only. L.H.Drive
FW.105/T	Plain Washer, on Setscrews	6)	Cars only
UFN.131/L	Nut, on Lower Setscrews	2)	See also
C.21255	Captive Nut, for Upper Setscrews	2)	Hydraulic Brake Pipe Section
C.20234	Bracket, mounting Fluid Reservoirs	1)	
C.19497	Clamp, securing Reservoirs to Bracket	2)	
C.20235	Stud, through Bracket and Clamp	2)	
C.8737/1	Nut, on Studs	4)	
C.6854	Low Pressure Hose, Reservoir to Pipe	1)	*
C.15886/4	Clip, securing Hose	2)	R.H.Drive
C.27155	Pipe, Low Pressure Hose to Master Cyl.	1)	Cars only
C.20072/14	Low Pressure Hose, Reservoir to Pipe	1)	*
C.15886/4	Clip, securing Hose	2)	L.H.Drive
C.27180	Pipe, Low Pressure Hose to Master Cyl.	1)	Cars only
C.27186	Clutch Master Cylinder Assembly	1	*
12276	Push Rod	1	
12277	Return Spring	1	
C.31725	Spacer, between Master Cylinder and Pedal Housing	1	
C.27072	Stud, securing Master Cylinder to Pedal Housing	2	
C.8667/2	Nut, on Stud	2	
J.105/12S	Joint Pin, securing Master Cylinder Push Rod to Clutch Pedal	1	
L102.5/6U	Split Pin, retaining Joint Pin	1	
FW.105/T	Plain Washer, behind Split Pin	1	
12275	Repair Kit, for Clutch Master Cylinder	1	**

PART NO.	Description.	NO. PER UNIT.	REMARKS

Clutch Unit and Controls (Continued).

PART NO.	Description.	NO. PER UNIT.	REMARKS
C.27156	Pipe Assembly, Master Cylinder to Flexible Hose	1)	R.H.Drive Cars only.
C.1040/22	Clip, securing Pipe to Steering Column Bracket	1)	
C.1040/24	Clip, securing Pipe to Frame	1)	
C.27179	Pipe Assembly, Master Cylinder to Pipe Connector	1)	L.H.Drive Cars only
C.1040/24	Clip, securing Pipe to Frame	1)	
C.13187	Pipe Connector	1)	
C.25675	Pipe Assembly, Pipe Connector to Flexible Hose	1)	
C.11603	Flexible Hose, between Pipes	1	**
UFN.237/L	Nut, securing Flexible Hose	2	
C.741	Shakeproof Washer, under Nut	2	
C.17826	Bracket, on Frame, for Hose	1	
C.17828	Bracket, on Cylinder Block for Hose	1	
C.11583	Distance Piece, under Bracket	1	
C.17827	Pipe Assembly, Flexible Hose to Slave Cylinder	1	
C.29801	Slave Cylinder, for Clutch Operation	1	*
C.9858	Stud, securing Slave Cylinder to Clutch Housing	2	
FG.106/X	Spring Washer, on Stud	1	
C.723	Shakeproof Washer, on Stud	1	
UFN.137/L	Nut, on Stud	2	
8593	Repair Kit, for Slave Cylinder	1	**
C.31623	Operating Rod. Slave Cylinder to Clutch Fork	1	
C.31622	Adjuster Assembly, for operating Rod	1	
C.20954/4	Bush, for Adjuster	1	
UFN.231/L	Nut, locking Adjuster on Op. Rod	1	
C.29803	Pivot Pin, securing Adjuster to Fork	1	
C.27328/5	Clip, retaining Pivot Pin	1	
C.9797	Fork.operating Release Bearing	1	
C.9857	Shaft, in Clutch Housing holding Fork	1	
C.8011	Screw, securing Fork to Shaft	1	
UFN.125/L	Nut, locking Screw	1	
C.5120	Return Spring, for Fork	1	*
C.5178	Plate anchoring Return Spring	1	
C.22623	Clutch Housing (Bushed)	1	
C.10025	Bush for Shaft	2	

PART NO.	Description.	NO. PER UNIT.	REMARKS

Clutch Unit and Controls (Continued).

PART NO.	Description.	NO. PER UNIT.	REMARKS
UFB.143/13R	Bolt, Housing to Gearbox	6	
C.587	Plate, locking Bolts	2	
C.5073	Plate, locking Bolts	1	
C.20335	Setscrew, Housing to Gearbox	1	
C.20334	Bolt, Housing to Gearbox	1	
FW.107/T	Plain Washer, on Bolt and Setscrew	2	
C.3262	Locking Wire	As req'd	
UFB.137/23R	Bolt, Housing to Cylinder Block	8	
C.726	Shakeproof Washer, on Bolt	8	
C.11910	Cover, over Timing Aperture Housing	1	
BD.524/2	Rivet, securing Cover	1	
C.18739	Oil Seal, in Housing for Gearbox Constant Pinion Shaft	1	**
C.5072	Cover Plate, at Front of Housing	1	
UCS.125/4R	Setscrew, securing Cover Plate	4	
C.724	Shakeproof Washer, on Setscrew	4	
C.19207	Support Bracket, R.H.Side of Housing	1	
C.19206	Support Bracket, L.H.Side of Housing	1	
UFB.131/10R	Bolt, Brackets to Cylinder Block	3	
UFB.131/12R	Bolt, Bracket and Hose Bracket to Cylinder Block	1	
UFN.131/L	Nut, on Bolt	4	
FG.105/X	Spring Washer, under Nut	4	
UFB.137/23R	Bolt, Brackets to Housing	2	
UFB.137/11R	Bolt, Brackets to Housing	4	
UFN.137/L	Nut, on Bolts	6	
C.726	Shakeproof Washer, under Nuts	6	

PART NO.	Description.	NO. PER UNIT.	REMARKS

GEARBOX FOR OPEN AND F.H.COUPE ONLY.

PART NO.	Description.	NO. PER UNIT.	REMARKS
C.28642	Gearbox Assembly (KE Series)	1	Std.Ratio Gears
C.28648	Gearbox Assembly (KJ Series) PLEASE NOTE :- Gearbox Assemblies must be ordered on Service Division.	1	Close Ratio Gears
C.20019	Gearbox Case	1	
C.19543	Oil Drain Plug	1	
C.799	Oil Filler Plug	1	
C.785	Fibre Washer, on Plug	2	
C.1845/1	Ball Bearing, for Mainshaft	1	*
C.1855	Circlip, for Bearing	1	*
C.20491	Ball Bearing,for Constant Pinion Shaft	1	*
C.20492	Circlip, for Bearing	1	*
C.20494	Collar, Circlip to Gearbox Case	1	
C.920	Fibre Washer, for Countershaft	1	*
C.22837	Filter Gauze, in Rear Face of Gearbox Case	1	*
C.20658	Gasket, Gearbox to Clutch Housing	1	**
C.21306	Oil Pump Body, Rear of Gearbox	1	
C.21307	Outer Gear for Oil Pump	1	
C.21308	Inner Gear, for Oil Pump	1	
UCS.519/5H	Screw.Pump Body to Rear Cover	3	
C.21309	Pin, on Mainshaft for Oil Pump	1	
C.21299	Rear End Cover	1	
C.20020	Gasket,End Cover to Gearbox Case	1	**
UFS.131/9R	Setscrew, End Cover to Gearbox Case	7	
FG.105/X	Spring Washer, on Setscrew	7	
UCS.131/3R	Plug, at top of End Cover	1	
FW.105/E	Copper Washer, on Plug	1	
C.21310	Speedometer Driven Gear	1	**
C.21312	Bearing, for Driven Gear	1	*
C.12377/1	Oil Seal, in Bearing	1	*
C.9177	'O' Ring, around Bearing	1	**
C.21314	Screw, locking Bearing in Rear Cover	1	
FG.105/X	Spring Washer, on Screw	1	
C.21340	Oil Seal, at end of Rear Cover	1	**
C.25068	Housing, for Rear Oil Seal	1	
C.25410	Gasket, Housing to Rear End Cover	1	**
UCS.531/7H	Setscrew, Housing to Rear End Cover	4	

PART NO.	Description.	NO. PER UNIT.	REMARKS

STRIKING GEAR FOR OPEN AND F.H.COUPE ONLY.

PART NO.	Description.	NO. PER UNIT.	REMARKS
C.24915	Striking Rod, 1st/2nd Gears	1	
C.24914	Striking Rod, 3rd/Top Gears	1	
C.21478	Striking Rod, Reverse Gear	1	
C.20060	'O' Ring, on Striking Rods	3	*
C.20315	Stop, for 1st/2nd Striking Rod	1	
C.20316	Stop, for 3rd/Top Striking Rod	1	
C.21572/1	Selector Fork, 1st/2nd & 3rd/Top Gears	2	
C.21616	Selector Fork, Reverse	1	
C.22925	Locating Arm, on Reverse Striking Rod	1	
C.25468	Plunger, for Reverse Stop	1	
C.9849	Spring, for Plunger	1	*
C.1319	Ball, Locking Reverse Plunger	1	*
C.20065	Spring, for Ball	1	*
UFS.131/5R	Screw, Adjusting Spring Tension	1	
UFN.231/L	Nut, locking Screw	1	
C.20314	Dowel Screw, securing Forks and Locating Arm	4	
C.837	Wire, locking Dowel Screws	As req'd	
C.20066	Interlock Roller 1st/2nd Striking Rod	1	
C.922	Ball, between Striking Rods for Interlock	2	*
C.22628	Top Cover	1	
C.20057	Gasket.Top Cover to Gearbox Case	1	**
C.1083	Switch, in Cover for Reverse Lamp	1	**
C.4531	Gasket, for Switch	1	**
C.7379	Plug, in Top Cover	1	
C.2296/1	Copper Washer, on Plug	1	
UFB.131/13R	Bolt, Top Cover to Gearbox Case	4	
UFS.131/8R	Setscrew, Top Cover to Gearbox Case	6	
C.16816	Spring Washer, on Screws and Bolts	10	
OD.105/6H	Dowel.locating Cover on Case	2	
C.1319	Ball Engaging Reverse Striking Rod	1	**
C.13334	Plunger, holding Ball	1	**
C.845	Spring, at Top of Ball	1	**
C.26113	Welch Washer $\frac{3}{4}$" diam.	3	
C.9840	Welch Washer 7/16" diam.	1	
C.7116	Breather Elbow in Top Cover	1	
C.7125	Nut, locking Breather Elbow	1	
C.25028	Gearbox Breather, on Manifold Studs	1	*
C.20113	Hose, Breather to Gearbox Elbow	1	
C.15886/6	Clip, securing Hose	2	
C.19706	Distance Piece, on Manifold Studs	2	
C.21104	Pivot Jaw, Housing Selector Lever	1	
C.1907	Bush, in Top Cover for Pivot Jaw	1	
C.1894	Washer (Tufnol) at Front & Rear of Bush	2	
C.8737/4	Nut, securing Pivot Jaw	1	
C.1905	Spring Washer, under Nut	1	
C.1914	"D" Washer, between Spring Washer and Tufnol Washer	1	
C.20067	Selector Lever, end of C/S Lever	1	

PART NO.	Description.	NO. PER UNIT.	REMARKS

Striking Gear for Open and F.H.Coupe only (Continued).

PART NO.	Description.	NO. PER UNIT.	REMARKS
C.1906	Bush, in Selector Lever	1	*
C.1908	Washer, (Tufnol) at each Side of Lever	2	
C.1929	Spring Washer, between Jaw and Tufnol Washer	1	
C.21110	Pivot Pin, mounting Lever in Pivot Jaw	1	
C.8737/4	Nut, securing Pivot Pin	1	
C.23178	Change-Speed Lever	1	
C.23007	Knob, on Lever	1	**
C.23006	Cone, locking Knob to Lever	1	*
C.22394	Upper Bush, in Selector Lever	1	*
C.22395	Washer, at Top of Upper Bush	1	
C.21921	Lower Bush, in Selector Lever	1	*
C.8737/2	Nut, securing Change Speed Lever	1	
C.26595	Special Washer, under Nut	1	
C.21303	Flange, on Mainshaft	1	
C.840	Nut, slotted, securing Flange	1	
C.23168	Washer, under Nut	1	
L.104/12U	Split Pin, securing Slotted Nut	1	
C.19827	Bolt, securing Flange to Propshaft	4	
C.21300	Mainshaft	1	
C.21302	Speedo Driving Gear	1	
C.21301	Distance Piece, behind Speedo Driving Gear	1	
C.21098	Reverse Gear on Mainshaft	1	
C.28429	1st Speed Gear on Mainshaft	1	
C.21095	Bearing Sleeve, for 1st Speed Gear	1	
C.23109/1	Needle Roller in 1st Speed Gear	120) Selective Sizes	**
C.23109/2	Needle Roller in1st Speed Gear	120) Use Rollers of	**
C.23109/3	Needle Roller in 1st Speed Gear	120) one size in gear units	**
C.23097	Spacer, for Roller in 1st Speed Gear	1	
C.28432	Synchro Hub for 1st/2nd Speeds	1	
C.28436	Operating Sleeve for 1st/2nd Speeds	1	
C.24641	Thrust Member, between Sleeve and Hub	3	*
C.21088	Plunger, under Thrust Member	3	*
C.27491	Spring, under Plungers	3	**
C.1319	Ball, between Sleeve and Hub	3	**
C.24181	Spring, under Ball	3	**
C.22391	Synchro Ring for 1st/2nd Gears	2	
C.28430	2nd Speed Gear, on Mainshaft	1	
C.28417	3rd Speed Gear, on Mainshaft	1	Std.Ratio
C.23109/1	Needle Roller, in 2nd & 3rd Gears	212) Selective Sizes	**
C.23109/2	Needle Roller, in 2nd & 3rd Gears	212) Use Rollers of	**
C.23109/3	Needle Roller, in 2nd & 3rd Gears	212) one size in Gear Units	**
C.23098	Spacer, for Rollers in 2nd Gear	1	
C.23099	Spacer, for Rollers in 3rd Gear	1	
C.28432	Synchro Hub for 3rd/Top Gear	1	
C.28436	Operating Sleeve for 3rd/Top Gear	1	
C.24641	Thrust Member, between Sleeve and Hub	3	*
C.21088	Plunger, under Thrust Member	3	*
C.27491	Spring, under Plungers	3	**

PART NO.	Description.	NO. PER UNIT.	REMARKS	

Striking Gear for Open and F.H.Coupe only (Continued).

PART NO.	Description.	NO. PER UNIT.	REMARKS	
C.1319	Ball, between Sleeve and Hub	3		**
C.24181	Spring, under Ball	3		**
C.22391	Synchro Ring, for 3rd/Top Gears	2		
C.21617	Nut, locking Gears on Mainshaft	1		
C.21618	Tab Washer, locking Nut	1		
C.20027	Plug, in End of Mainshaft	1		
C.28415	Constant Pinion Shaft	1	Std. Ratio	
C.25424	Roller Bearing, inside Shaft	1		
C.20493	Oil Thrower, on Shaft	1		
C.21617	Nut, securing Shaft in Bearing	1		
C.21618	Tab Washer, locking Nut	1		
C.20052	Reverse Spindle	1		
C.753	Key, locking, Spindle in Gearbox Case	1		
C.20313	Reverse Idler Gear	1		
C.21198	Lever Assembly, operating Reverse Gear	1		
UFS.137/8R	Setscrew, pivoting Lever	1		
C.930	Fibre Washer, on Setscrew	1		
C.21200	Tab Washer, locking Setscrew	1		
C.866	Reverse Slipper	1		
L.103/8U	Split Pin, retaining Slipper on Lever	1		
C.25437	Countershaft	1		
C.753	Key, locking Countershaft in Casing	1		
C.28416	Gear Unit (Cluster) on Countershaft	1	Std. Ratio	
C.918/1	Needle Roller, in Gear Unit	58)	Selective Sizes	*
C.918/2	Needle Roller, in Gear Unit	58)	Use Rollers of one	*
C.918/3	Needle Roller, in Gear Unit	58)	size in Gear Units	*
C.21099	Retaining Ring, at Rear of Front Rollers and at each end of Rear Rollers	3		
C.21100	Thrust Washer, at Rear of Gear Unit	1		
C.1861	Thrust Washer, Inner, Front of Gear Unit	1		
C.1862	Thrust Washer, Outer, Front (.156")	1)	Selective Sizes	
C.1862/1	Thrust Washer, Outer, Front (.159")	1)	use as	
C.1862/2	Thrust Washer, Outer, Front (.162")	1)	necessary to	
C.1862/3	Thrust Washer, Outer, Front (.152")	1)	obtain correct	
C.1862/4	Thrust Washer, Outer, Front (.164")	1)	end float	

PART NO.	Description.	NO. PER UNIT.	REMARKS

GEARBOX FOR STANDARD TRANSMISSION 2+2 MODELS ONLY.

| C.28643 | Gearbox Assembly (KJS Series) | 1 | Std.Ratio Gears. |

PLEASE NOTE :- Gearbox Assemblies must be ordered on Service Division.

C.20019	Gearbox Case	1	
C.19543	Oil Drain Plug	1	
C.799	Oil Filler Plug	1	
C.785	Fibre Washer, on Plugs	2	
C.1845/1	Ball Bearing, for Mainshaft	1	*
C.1855	Circlip, for Bearing	1	*
C.20491	Ball Bearing, for Constant Pinion Shaft	1	*
C.20492	Circlip, for Bearing	1	*
C.20494	Collar, Circlip, Gearbox Case	1	
C.920	Fibre Washer, for Countershaft	1	*
C.22837	Filter Gauze, in Rear Face of Gearbox Case	1	*
C.20658	Gasket, Gearbox to Clutch Housing	1	**
C.21306	Oil Pump Body, Rear of Gearbox	1	
C.21307	Outer Gear, for Oil Pump	1	
C.21308	Inner Gear, for Oil Pump	1	
UCS.519/5H	Screw, Pump Body to Rear Cover	3	
C.21309	Pin, on Mainshaft for Oil Pump	1	
C.22950	Rear End Cover	1	
C.20020	Gasket, end Cover to Gearbox Case	1	**
UFS.131/9R	Setscrew, end Cover to Gearbox Case	7	
FG.105/X	Spring Washer, on Setscrew	7	
UCS.131/3R	Plug, at Top of End Cover	1	
FW.105/E	Copper Washer, on Plug	1	
C.18719	Ball Bearing, in Rear End Cover	1	*
C.23392	Speedometer Driven Gear	1	**
C.21312	Bearing, for Driven Gear	1	*
C.12377/1	Oil Seal, in Bearing	1	*
C.9177	'O' Ring, around Bearing	1	**
C.22999	Screw, locking Bearing in Rear Cover	1	
FG.105/X	Spring Washer, on Screw	1	
C.23394	Oil Seal, at End of Rear Cover	1	**

STRIKING GEAR FOR 2+2 MODELS ONLY.

C.24915	Striking Rod 1st/2nd Gears	1	
C.24914	Striking Rod 3rd/top Gears	1	
C.21478	Striking Rod Reverse Gear	1	
C.20060	'O' Ring, on Striking Rods	3	*
C.20315	Stop, for 1st/2nd Striking Rod	1	
C.20316	Stop for 3rd/Top Striking Rod	1	
C.21572/1	Selector Fork, 1st/2nd & 3rd/Top Gears	2	
C.21616	Selector Fork, Reverse	1	
C.22925	Locating Arm, on Reverse Striking Rod	1	
C.25468	Plunger, for Reverse Stop	1	
C.9849	Spring, for Plunger	1	*
C.1319	Ball, locking Reverse Plunger	1	*
C.20065	Spring, for Ball	1	*

PART NO.	Description.	NO. PER UNIT.	REMARKS

Striking Gear for 2+2 Models only (Continued).

PART NO.	Description.	NO. PER UNIT.	REMARKS
UFS.131/5R	Screw, adjusting Spring Tension	1	
UFN.231/L	Nut, locking Screw	1	
C.20314	Dowel Screw, securing Forks and locating Arm	4	
C.857	Wire, locking Dowel Screws	As req'd	
C.20066	Interlock Roller 1st/2nd Striking Rod	1	
C.922	Ball, between Striking Rods for Interlock	2	*
C.22628	Top Cover	1	
C.20057	Gasket, Top Cover to Gearbox Case	1	**
C.1083	Switch, in Cover for Reverse Lamp	1	**
C.4531	Gasket, for Switch	1	**
C.7379	Plug, in Top Cover	1	
C.2296/1	Copper Washer, on Plug	1	
UFB.131/13R	Bolt, Top Cover to Gearbox Case	4	
UFS.131/8R	Setscrew, Top Cover to Gearbox Case	6	
C.16816	Spring Washer, on Screws and Bolts	10	
OD.105/6H	Dowel.locating Cover on Case	2	
C.1319	Ball, engaging Reverse Striking Rod	1	**
C.13334	Plunger, holding Ball	1	**
C.845	Spring, at Top of Ball	1	**
C.26113	Welch Washer $\frac{1}{4}$" diam.	3	
C.9840	Welch Washer 7/16" diam.	1	
C.7116	Breather Elbow, in Top Cover	1	
C.7125	Nut, locking Breather Elbow	1	
C.25028	Gearbox Breather, on Manifold Studs	1	
C.20113	Hose, Breather to Gearbox Elbow	1	*
C.15886/6	Clip, securing Hose	2	
C.21104	Pivot Jaw,Housing Selector Lever	1	
C.1907	Bush, in Top Cover for Pivot Jaw	1	
C.1894	Washer (Tufnol) at Front & Rear of Bush	2	
C.8737/4	Nut, securing Pivot Jaw	1	
C.1905	Spring Washer, under Nut	1	
C.1914	"D" Washer, between Spring Washer and Tufnol Washer	1	
C.20067	Selector Lever, End of C/S Lever	1	
C.1906	Bush, in Selector Lever	1	*
C.1908	Washer (Tufnol) at each side of Lever	2	
C.1929	Spring Washer, between Jaw and Tufnol Washer	1	
C.21110	Pivot Pin, mounting Lever in Pivot Jaw	1	
C.8737/4	Nut, securing Pivot Pin	1	
C.23178	Change-Speed Lever	1	
C.23007	Knob, on Lever	1	**
C.23006	Cone, locking Knob to Lever	1	*
C.22394	Upper Bush, in Selector Lever	1	*
C.22395	Washer, at Top of Upper Bush	1	

PART NO.	Description.	NO. PER UNIT.	REMARKS	

Striking Gear for 2+2 Models only (Continued).

PART NO.	Description.	NO. PER UNIT.	REMARKS	
C.21921	Lower Bush, in Selector Lever	1		*
C.8737/2	Nut, securing Change Speed Lever	1		
C.26595	Special Washer, under Nut	1		
C.885	Flange, on Mainshaft	1		
C.840	Nut, slotted, securing Flange	1		
C.23168	Washer, under Nut	1		
L.104/12U	Split Pin, securing Slotted Nut	1		
C.19827	Bolt, securing Flange to Propshaft	4		
C.8737/3	Nut (self-locking) on Bolt	4		
C.22879	Mainshaft	1		
C.23337	Speedo Driving Gear	1		
C.23336	Distance Tube, between Bearing and Distance Piece	1		
C.21301	Distance Piece, between Distance Tube and Bearing	1		
C.21098	Reverse Gear, on Mainshaft	1		
C.28429	1st Speed Gear on Mainshaft	1		
C.21095	Bearing Sleeve, for 1st Speed Gear	1		
C.23109/1	Needle Roller, in 1st Speed Gear	120)	Selective Sizes	**
C.23109/2	Needle Roller, in 1st Speed Gear	120)	Use Rollers of one	**
C.23109/3	Needle Roller, in 1st Speed Gear	120)	size in gear units	**
C.23097	Spacer, for Roller in 1st Speed Gear	1		
C.28432	Synchro Hub, for 1st/2nd Speeds	1		
C.28436	Operating Sleeve for 1st/2nd Speeds	1		
C.24641	Thrust Member, between Sleeve and Hub	3		*
C.21088	Plunger, under Thrust Member	3		*
C.27491	Spring, under Plunger	3		**
C.1319	Ball, between Sleeve and Hub	3		**
C.24181	Spring, under Ball	3		**
C.22391	Synchro Ring for 1st/2nd Gears	2		
C.28430	2nd Speed Gear on Mainshaft	1		
C.28417	3rd Speed Gear on Mainshaft	1	Std.Ratio	
C.23109/1	Needle Roller, in 2nd/3rd Gears	212)	Selective Sizes	**
C.23109/2	Needle Roller, in 2nd/3rd Gears	212)	Use Rollers of one	**
C.23109/3	Needle Roller, in 2nd/3rd Gears	212)	size in Gear Units	**
C.23098	Spacer, for Rollers in 2nd Gear	1		
C.23099	Spacer, for Rollers in 3rd Gear	1		
C.28432	Synchro Hub for 3rd/Top Gear	1		
C.28436	Operating Sleeve for 3rd/Top Gear	1		
C.24641	Thrust Member, between Sleeves and Hub	3		*
C.21088	Plunger, under Thrust Member	3		*
C.27491	Spring, under Plungers	3		**
C.1319	Ball, between Sleeve and Hub	3		**
C.24181	Spring, under Ball	3		**
C.22391	Synchro Ring, for 3rd/Top Gears	2		
C.21617	Nut, locking Gears on Mainshaft	1		
C.21618	Tab Washer, locking Nut	1		
C.20027	Plug, in end of Mainshaft	1		
C.28415	Constant Pinion Shaft	1	Std.Ratio	

PART NO.	Description.	NO. PER UNIT.	REMARKS

Striking Gear for 2+2 Models only (Continued).

PART NO.	Description.	NO. PER UNIT.	REMARKS
C.25424	Roller Bearing, inside Shaft	1	
C.20493	Oil Thrower, on Shaft	1	
C.21617	Nut, securing Shaft in Bearing	1	
C.21618	Tab Washer, locking Nut	1	
C.20052	Reverse Spindle	1	
C.753	Key, locking Spindle in Gearbox Case	1	
C.20313	Reverse Idler Gear	1	
C.21198	Lever Assembly, operating Reverse Gear	1	
UFS.137/8R	Setscrew, pivoting Lever	1	
C.930	Fibre Washer, on Setscrew	1	
C.21200	Tab Washer, locking Setscrew	1	
C.866	Reverse Slipper	1	
L.103/8U	Split Pin, retaining Slipper on Lever	1	
C.25437	Countershaft	1	
C.753	Key, locking Countershaft in Casing	1	
C.28416	Gear Unit (Cluster) on Countershaft	1	Std. Ratio
C.918/1	Needle Roller, in Gear Unit	58)	Selective Sizes
C.918/2	Needle Roller, in Gear Unit	58)	Use Rollers of one
C.918/3	Needle Roller, in Gear Unit	58)	size in Gear Units
C.21099	Retaining Ring, at Rear of Front Rollers and at each end of Rear Rollers	3	
C.21100	Thrust Washer, at Rear of Gear Unit	1	
C.1861	Thrust Washer, Inner, Front of Gear Unit	1	
C.1862	Thrust Washer, Outer, Front (.156")	1)	Selective Sizes
C.1862/1	Thrust Washer, Outer, Front (.159")	1)	Use as
C.1862/2	Thrust Washer, Outer, Front (.162")	1)	necessary to
C.1862/3	Thrust Washer, Outer, Front (.152")	1)	obtain correct
C.1862/4	Thrust Washer, Outer, Front (.164")	1)	end float

PART NO.	Description.	NO. PER UNIT.	REMARKS

AUTOMATIC TRANSMISSION UNIT 2+2 MODELS ONLY.

PART NO.	Description.	NO. PER UNIT.	REMARKS
C.26900	Automatic Transmission Unit less Convertor	1)	Order on Service Division.
C.22781	Convertor Assembly	1	*
10563	Transmission Case Assembly	1	
10564	Plug Sealing Holes in Flange	2	
10565	Dowel, for Front Servo	1	
10566	Plug, for Pressure Test	1	
10567	Oil Seal, for Manual Control Shaft	1	*
10568	Screw, for Rear Servo Adjustment	1	
10569	Nut, locking Screw	1	
C.23415	Union, for Oil Outlet Pipe	1	
C.23414	Union, for Oil Return Pipe	1	
10570	Breather Assembly, on Transmission Case	1	
C.25691	Manual Control Shaft in Trans.Case	1	
C.25853	Selector Lever, on Manual Control Shaft	1	
C.8737/3	Nut, self-locking, securing Selector Lever	1	
C.25917	Spacer, under Nut	1	
10571	Lever, on Shaft, for Manual Valve Detent	1	
10572	Locknut, retaining Lever to Shaft	1	
9874	Ball, positioning Detent Lever	1	
10573	Spring, tensioning Ball	1	
10574	Link, Detent Lever to Torsion Lever	1	
9875	Clip, retaining Link	2	
9876	Torsion Lever, for Parking Brake Linkage	1	
9877	Spring, for Tension between Torsion Lever and Forked Lever	1	*
9878	Forked Lever, engaging Ball Pin in Toggle Lever	1	
9879	Clip, retaining Torsion Lever, Forked Lever and Spring	1	
9890	Washer, under Clip	1	
9880	Toggle Lever, for Parking Brake Pawl	1	
10575	Shouldered Pin, pivoting Toggle Lever	1	
10576	Plug, retaining Pin	1	
10577	Ball Pin, securing Link to Toggle Lever	1	
10578	Spring, on Ball Pin	1	
9888	Link, connecting Toggle Lever to Parking Brake Pawl	1	
10579	Pawl, for Parking Brake	1	
10580	Pivot Pin, for Parking Brake Pawl	1	
9889	Pin, securing Pawl to Link	1	
10581	Extension Case Assembly	1	
10582	Cover Plate, sealing Governor Inspection Aperture	1	
10583	Gasket, for Cover Plate	1	*
10584	Screw, and Lockwasher Assembly	2	
10586	Gasket Extension Case to 'Rear Pump Flange	1	*
10587	Bolt.Ext., Case & Rear Pump to Trans.Case	2	

PART NO.	Description.	NO. PER UNIT.	REMARKS

Automatic Transmission Unit 2+2 Models only (Continued).

PART NO.	Description	NO. PER UNIT	REMARKS
10588	Bolt.Ext Case & Rear Pump to Transmission Case	1	
C.25692	Special Stud, securing Ext., Case and Rear Pump to Transmission Case	2	
9910	Lockwasher, on Bolts and Studs	5	
10589	Bearing, Rear of Ext., Case for Mainshaft	1	
10590	Snap Ring, around Mainshaft Bearing	1	
10591	Spacing Washer, between Bearing and Oil Collector Sleeve	1	
C.22852	Housing, for Speedo.Driven Gear	1	
10592	Gasket Housing to Ext., Case	1	*
10587	Bolt, Housing to Extension Case	2	
8435	Bolt, Housing to Extension Case	3	
8427	Lockwasher, on Bolts	5	
10593	Oil Seal, at Rear of Housing	1	
C.22348	Speedometer Driven Gear	1	
C.21297	Bearing, for Speedo.Driven Gear	1	
C.12377/1	Oil Seal, at Bottom of Bearing	1	*
C.21058	'O' Ring, around Bearing	1	*
C.21073	Plate, retaining Gear in Housing	1	
UCS.125/4B	Setscrew, securing Plate	2	
FG.104/X	Spring Washer, on Setscrew	2	
C.22782	Flange, on Mainshaft	1	
10594	Nut, securing Flange to Mainshaft	1	
10595	Lockwasher, under Nut	1	
10596	Special Washer, under Lockwasher	1	
10597	Front Pump Assembly	1	
10598	Oil Seal, for Front Pump	1	
10599	Sealing Ring, between Pump and Case	1	
10600	Bolt. Front Pump to Case	4	*
10601	Front Clutch Assembly	1	
10602	Piston Assembly, for Front Clutch	1	
10603	Cylinder, for Front Clutch	1	
10604	Sealing Ring, Inner for Piston	1	
10605	Sealing Ring, Outer, for Piston	1	
10606	Split Ring, seating Clutch Spring	1	
10607	Spring, for Front Clutch	1	
10608	Snap Ring, retaining Clutch Spring	1	
N.S.S.	Pressure Plate, for Front Clutch	1	) Not supplied
N.S.S.	Clutch Plate (Drive)	3	) Separately
N.S.S.	Clutch Plate (Friction)	4	) Use Kit No.10974
10612	Hub Carrying Front Clutch Plates	1	
10613	Thrust Washer (Fibre) Hub to Input Shaft	1	
10614	Input Shaft Assembly	1	
10615	Thrust Washer, Input Shaft to Transmission Case	1	
10616	Snap Ring, retaining Input Shaft	1	

PART NO.	Description.	NO. PER UNIT.	REMARKS

Automatic Transmission Unit 2+2 Models only (Continued).

PART NO.	Description.	NO. PER UNIT.	REMARKS
11546	Rear Clutch and Front Drum Assembly	1	
11547	Front Drum Assembly	1	
11548	Piston Assembly, for Rear Clutch	1	
10620	Sealing Ring, Inner, for Piston	1	
10621	Sealing Ring, Outer, for Piston	1	
10622	Spring, for Rear Clutch	1	
10623	Seat, for Clutch Spring	1	
10624	Snap Ring, retaining Seat	1	
N.S.S.	Clutch Plate (Friction)	5)	Not supplied
N.S.S.	Clutch Plate (Drive)	5)	separately use
N.S.S.	Pressure Plate, for Clutch	1)	Kit No. 10975
10616	Snap Ring, retaining Clutch Plates in Front Drum	1	
10618	Thrust Washer (Bronze) between Front Clutch Cylinder and Front Drum	1	
10629	Thrust Washer (Steel) at Rear of Bronze Thrust Washer	1	
11547	Front Drum Assembly	1	
10630	Needle Bearing in Front Drum	1	
10631	Brake Band, for Front Drum	1	
10632	Strut (Servo) operating Brake Band	1	
10633	Front Servo Assembly	1	
10634	Body, for Front Servo	1	
10635	Lever, operating Servo Strut	1	
10636	Pivot Pin, for operating Lever	1	
9902	Roll Pin, securing Pivot Pin	1	
10637	Screw, for Servo Adjustment	1	
9904	Nut, locking Screw	1	
10638	Return Spring, for Servo Piston	1	
10639	Piston Assembly, for Servo	1	
10640	'O' Ring (Small) on Piston	1	
10641	'O' Ring (Large) on Piston	1	
10642	Piston Sleeve, for Servo	1	
10643	Sealing Ring, for Sleeve	1	
10644	Snap Ring, retaining Piston, and Sleeve in Body	1	
10587	Bolt, securing Servo to Trans. Case	1	
8427	Lockwasher, on Bolt	1	
10645	Forward Sun Gear Assembly	1	
10646	Sealing Ring, at Front of Sun Gear Shaft	2	
10647	Sealing Ring, at Centre of Sun Gear Shaft	2	
10648	Sealing Ring, at Rear of Sun Gear Shaft	2	
10649	Thrust Bearing (Needle) between Forward Sun Gear & Planetary Carrier	1	
10650	Race, for Thrust Bearing	1	
10651	Thrust Washer (Bronze) between Forward and Reverse Sun Gears	1	

PART NO.	Description.	NO. PER UNIT.	REMARKS

Automatic Transmission Unit 2+2 Models only (Continued).

PART NO.	Description.	NO. PER UNIT.	REMARKS
10652	Centre Support Assembly	1	
10653	Screw, securing Support in Trans. Case	2	
9910	Lockwasher, on Screws	2	
10654	Planetary Gears and Rear Drum Assembly	1	
10655	Outer Race, for One Way Clutch	1	
10656	Snap Ring, retaining Outer Race	1	
10657	Thrust Washer .061"/063" thick	1)	Selective
10658	Thrust Washer .067"/.069" thick	1)	Sizes to
10659	Thrust Washer .074"/.076" thick	1)	obtain
10660	Thrust Washer .081"/.083" thick	1)	correction
10661	Thrust Washer .092"/094" thick	1)	end float
10662	Thrust Washer .105"/.107" thick	1)	

The above Thrust Washer Fits between Planetary Carrier and Mainshaft.

PART NO.	Description.	NO. PER UNIT.	REMARKS
10663	One-Way Clutch Assembly, in Rear Drum	1	
10664	Brake Band, for Rear Drum	1	
10665	Strut (Servo) operating Brake Band	1	
10666	Anchor Strut, for Rear Brake Band	1	
10667	Rear Servo Assembly	1	
10668	Body Assembly, for Rear Servo	1	
10669	Lever, operating Rear Servo Strut	1	
10670	Shaft, for Lever	1	
9902	Roll Pin, securing Shaft in Body	1	
10671	Piston, for Rear Servo	1	
10672	'O' Ring, on Piston.	1	
10673	Return Spring, for Piston	1	
10674	Plate, retaining Spring	1	
10675	Snap Ring, securing Plate	1	
10676	Screw, Rear Servo to Trans., Case	1	
10677	Bolt, Rear Servo to Trans., Case	1	
10678	Lockwasher, on Screw and Bolt	2	
10679	Ring Gear Driving Mainshaft	1	
10680	Mainshaft Assembly	1	
10681	Snap Ring, retaining Mainshaft in R.Gear	1)	Selective
10682	Snap Ring, retaining Mainshaft in R.Gear	1)	Sizes
10683	Snap Ring, retaining Mainshaft in R.Gear	1)	
10684	Rear Pump Assembly	1	
10685	Plate Retaining Pump Gears	1	
10686	Screw and Lockwasher for Plate	5	
10965	Screw and Lockwasher for Plate	1	
10690	Key, in Mainshaft Driving Rear Pump	1	
10691	Gasket, Rear Pump to Trans., Case	1	
10692	Oil Inlet Tube, for Rear Pump	1	
10693	'O' Ring, on Oil Inlet Tube	1	
10694	Oil Outlet Tube, for Rear Pump	1	
10695	'O' Ring, on Oil Outlet Tube	1	

PART NO.	Description.	NO. PER UNIT.	REMARKS

Automatic Transmission Unit 2+2 Models only (Continued).

PART NO.	Description.	NO. PER UNIT.
10696	Governor Assembly	1
10697	Governor Body	1
10698	Screw, securing Body and Sleeve	2
8426	Lockwasher, on Screws	2
10699	Governor Weight	1
10700	Governor Valve	1
10701	Spring, for Governor	1
10702	Retaining Holding Spring on Weight	1
10703	Cover Plate, at Side of Governor Body	1
10704	Screw, securing Cover Plate	2
9922	Ball, locating Governor on Mainshaft	1
10705	Snap Ring, retaining Governor on Mainshaft	1
10706	Oil Collector Sleeve	1
9920	Piston Ring, on Mainshaft for Oil Collector Sleeve	4
10708	Oil Collector Tube, Front	1
10709	Oil Collector Tube, Intermediate	1
10710	Oil Collector Tube, Rear	1
C.22347	Drive Gear, for Speedometer	1
10711	Valve Bodies Assembly	1
10945	Spring, for Rear Pump Check Valve	1
10946	Spring, for Front Servo release Orifice Valve	1
10947	Spring for 1st/2nd Shift Valve	1
10948	Return Spring, for Throttle Cam	1
10949	Spring for D1/D2 Control Valve	1
10950	Spring for Transition Valve	1
10951	Spring, for Servo Orifice Control Valve	2
10952	Leaf Spring, for Throtte Valve Return	1
10953	Spring Inner for 2nd/3rd Valve	1
10955	Spring.Outer for 2nd/3rd Valve	1
10956	Spring at Inner End of Throttle Modulator Valve	1
10957	Spring at Outer End of Throttle Modulator Valve	1
10958	Spring Inner for Compensator	1
10959	Spring.Outer for Compensator	1
10960	Throttle Spring	1
10961	Bolt, for Assembly of Valve Bodies	4
8426	Lockwasher, on Bolts	4
10962	Screw and Lockwasher) for	15
10963	Screw and Lockwasher) Assembly	2
10964	Screw and Lockwasher) of	3
10965	Screw and Lockwasher) Valve	1
10704	Screw (Countersunk)) Bodies	2
10712	Bolt.Valve Bodies Assy to Trans.Case	3
8426	Lockwasher on Bolts	3
11244	Control Rod, operating Kick-Down Cable	1

PART NO.	Description.	NO. PER UNIT.	REMARKS

Automatic Transmission Unit 2+2 Models only (Continued).

PART NO.	Description.	NO. PER UNIT.	REMARKS
10714	Regulator Assembly	1	
10715	Spring for Primary Valve	1	
10716	Seat for Spring	1	
10717	Spring for Secondary Valve	1	
10718	Spacer, for Secondary Valve	1	
10719	Plate, retaining Valve Spring	1	
10720	Screw, Regulator to Trans., Case	2	
5908	Lockwasher, on Screws	2	
10721	Oil Tube, Front Brake Band Lubrication	1	
10722	Oil Tube, Rear Pump to Regulator	1	
10723	Oil Tube (Compensator) Valve Body to Regulator	1	
10724	Oil Tube (Control Pressure) Valve Body to Regulator	1	
10725	Oil Tube (Apply and Release) Valve Body to Front Servo	2	
10726	Oil Filter Assembly	1	
10727	Clip, retaining Oil Filter	1	
C.25690	Oil Pan Assembly	1	
10728	Gasket. Oil Pan to Trans. Case	1	*
10729	Bolt Assembly, Oil Pan to Trans.Case	14	
10970	Oil Seal and 'O' Ring Kit	1	*
10971	Gasket Kit	1	*
10972	Piston Ring and Metal Sealing Ring Kit	1	*
10973	Thrust Washer Kit	1	*
10974	Front Clutch Plates Kit	1	*
10975	Rear Clutch Plates Kit	1	*

PART NO.	Description.	NO. PER UNIT.	REMARKS

AUTOMATIC TRANSMISSION MOUNTING DETAILS 2+2 ONLY.

PART NO.	Description.	NO. PER UNIT.	REMARKS
C.26702	Converter Housing	1	
UFB.137/32R	Bolt, Housing to Cylinder Block	8	
C.726	Shakeproof Washer, on Bolt	8	
C.6866	Stud, Transmission Unit to Housing	4	
UFN.143/6	Nut, on Stud	4	
C.727	Shakeproof Washer, on Bolt	4	
C.22947	Stoneguard Assembly, covering Apertures in sides of Housing	2	
UCS.119/4R	Setscrew, securing Stoneguards	4	
C.723A	Shakeproof Washer, on Setscrew	4	
AW.102/T	Plain Washer, on Setscrew	4	
C.22361	Cover. Bottom of Converter Housing	1	
C.6874	Cover.Front of Converter Housing	1	
UCS.125/4R	Setscrew, securing Covers	8	
C.724	Shakeproof Washer, on Setscrews	8	
C.4795	R.H.Support Bracket	1	
C.11942	L.H.Support Bracket	1	
UFB.131/10R	Bolt.Brackets to Cylinder Block	4	
FG.105/X	Spring Washer, on Bolts	4	
UFN.131/L	Nut, on Bolts	4	
UFB.137/32R	Bolt, Brackets to Converter Housing	6	
FG.106/X	Spring Washer, on Bolts	6	
UFN.137/L	Nut, on Bolts	6	
C.25412	Flywheel and Drive Plate Assembly	1	
C.2313	Dowel Locating Drive Plate on Crankshaft	2	
C.4855	Setscrew, securing Flywheel Assembly to Crankshaft	10	
C.4810	Plate, locking Setscrews	1	
C.16682	Setscrew, Flywheel to Converter	4	
C.25446	Tab Washer, locking Setscrews	4	
C.25470	Bracket Assembly.Rear Engine Mounting	1	
C.12335	Spring Seat (Rubber) in Bracket	1	**
C.12265	Centre Bush	1	**
UFS.131/6R	Setscrew, Bracket to Body	5	
FW.105/T	Plain Washer, on Setscrew	5	
FG.105/X	Spring Washer, on Setscrew	5	
C.12299	Coil Spring, for Rear Engine Mounting	1	**
C.12335	Rubber Seat, at Top of Coil Spring	1	**
C.21932	Retainer, at Top of Coil Spring	1	
C.21336	Pin Assembly, retainer to Trans.,Unit	1	
C.25366	Oil Outlet Pipe. Trans., Unit to Flex Hose	1	

PART NO.	Description.	NO. PER UNIT.	REMARKS

Automatic Transmission Mounting Details 2+2 only(Continued).

PART NO.	Description.	NO. PER UNIT.	REMARKS
C.25367	Oil Return Pipe, Flex Hose to Trans. Unit	1	
C.25971/4	Flexible Hose. Oil Pipes to Radiator	2	**
C.2905/2	Clip, securing Hoses	4	
C.24549	Bracket, supporting Oil Pipes	2	
C.21390	Clamp, supporting Oil Pipes	1	
C.24599	Clip, holding Oil Pipes to Brackets and Clamp	3	
UFS.119/4R	Setscrew, securing Clips	3	
AG102/X	Spring Washer, on Setscrew	3	
UFN.119/L	Nut, on Setscrew	3	
C.25811	Transmission Dipstick Assembly	1	
C.25809	Tube Assembly, Housing Dipstick	1	
C.25807	Strut, for Clip on Tube	1	
C.17617	Clip, on Strut for Dipstick Tube	1	
UFS.131/5R	Setscrew, securing Clip to Strut	1	
FG.105/X	Spring Washer, on Setscrew	1	
UFN.131/L	Nut, on Setscrew	1	

PART NO.	Description.	NO. PER UNIT.	REMARKS

AUTOMATIC TRANSMISSION CONTROL 2+2 ONLY.

PART NO.	Description.	NO. PER UNIT.	REMARKS
C.25994	Selector Hand Lever Assembly	1	
C.28744	Knob, on Selector Lever	1	
BD.20892	Nut, locking Knob	1	
C.26020	Cam Plate Assembly complete with Pivot Pin	1	
UFS.519/10H	Setscrew, for Selector Lever Tension Spring	1	
C.25981	Circlip, retaining Cam Plate to Mounting Plate	1	
L.102/8U	Split Pin, retaining Selector Lever to Cam Plate	1	
FW.106/T	Plain Washer, behind Split Pin	1	
C.26644	Shim, between Plain Washer and Rubber Washer	As req'd	
C.25997	Rubber Washer, at Selector Lever Pivot	1	
C.900	Spring Tensioning Selector Lever	1	
UFN.219/L	Nut, retaining Spring	2	
C.25984	Mounting Plate and Selector Gate	1	
C.20953/3	Bush, for Pivot Pin in Cam Plate	2	
C.20952/3	Bush, for Transfer Lever Pivot	2	
UFS.125/6R	Setscrew, securing Mounting Plate	3	
C.724	Shakeproof Washer, on Setscrew	3	
FW.104/T	Plain Washer, under Shakeproof Washer	3	
C.25982	Grommet, at Mounting Plate Fixings	3	
C.25949	Distance Piece, in Grommets	3	
C.1083	Switch, on Selector Gate, operating Reverse Lamp	1	**
C.16626/3	Shim (.007) for Switch Adjustment	As req'd	
C.15896	Shim (.036) for Switch Adjustment	As req'd	
C.25463	Starter Cut-Out Switch on Selector Gate	1	
UFN.125/L	Nut, locking Switch	1	
C.25777	Lamp.Illuminating Selector Lever Indicator	1	
UCS.311/2H	Setscrew, securing Lamp	2	
C.720	Shakeproof Washer, on Setscrew	2	
C.26105	Operating Rod Assembly, from Cam Plate to Transfer Lever	1	
L.102/8U	Split Pin, retaining Rod to Cam Plate	1	
FW.104/T	Plain Washer, behind Split Pin	1	
C.25998	Transfer Lever Assembly, at Front of Mounting Plate	1	
L.102/8U	Split Pin, retaining Transfer Lever	1	
FW.105/T	Plain Washer, behind Split Pin	1	
C.16809	Ball Joint, connecting Operating Rod and Gear Control Cable to Transfer Lever	2	*
UFN.125/L	Nut, locking Ball Joints	2	

PART NO.	Description.	NO. PER UNIT.	REMARKS

Automatic Transmission Control 2+2 only (Continued).

PART NO.	Description.	NO. PER UNIT.	REMARKS
C.25756	Gear Control Cable	1	*
C.12586	Clamp, securing Outer Cable to Mounting Plate	1	
UFS.131/9R	Setscrew, through Clamp	1	
C.725	Shakeproof Washer, on Setscrew	1	
BD.28600	Pad Sealing Gear Control Cable through Transmission Cover	1	
BD.28599	Plate, retaining Pad	1	
DAZ.404/6C	Screw, securing Plate	2	
C.25794	Abutment Bracket, for Gear Cable on Transmission Unit	1	
C.25692	Stud, in Transmission Unit Fixing Abutment Bracket	2	
C.8737/3	Nut, on Studs	2	
C.12586	Clamp securing Cable to Abutment	1	
C.8737/2	Nut, securing Clamp	1	
C.25152	Adjustable Ball Joint, at Lower End of Cable	1	*
UFN.125/6	Nut, securing Ball Joint to Selector Lever on Transmission Unit	1	
C.724	Shakeproof Washer, under Nut	1	
C.28721	Cover Assembly, over Selector Mechanism	1)	State colour when ordering
UFS.419/4N	Setscrew, securing Cover to Tunnel	4	
C.723/A	Shakeproof Washer, on Setscrews	4	
AW.102/T	Plain Washer, on Setscrews	4	
BD.28667	Inscribed Indicator Plate at Top of Cover	1	
C.26337	Light Filter, under Indicator Plate	1	
BD.29233	Seal, under Indicator Plate	2	
DZJ.604/6C	Screw, self-tapping, securing Indicate Plate	2	

PART NO.	Description.	NO. PER UNIT.	REMARKS

PROPELLER SHAFT.

PART NO.	Description.	NO. PER UNIT.	REMARKS	
C.26576	Propeller Shaft Complete	1)		*
8404	Flange Yoke	2)		**
10065	Journal Assembly	2)		
9410	Sleeve Yoke	1)		
9411	Gaiter, for Sliding Joint	1)		
9412	Rubber Ring, retaining Gaiter	2)		
9413	Steel Ring, retaining Gaiter	1)	For Open	
		)		
10065	Journal Assembly, connecting Yokes to Propeller Shaft	2)	and F.H.Coupe	**
		)		
19	Circlip, retaining Journals	8)	only	
		)		
C.19827	Bolt, securing Propeller Shaft	8)		
C.8737/3	Nut, on Bolt	8)		
C.26579	Propeller Shaft Complete All details as for Propeller Shaft C.26576 above	1)))	2+2 Models	

PART NO.	Description.	NO. PER UNIT.	REMARKS

FINAL DRIVE UNIT 1ST TYPE WITH NORMAL DIFFERENTIAL.

FOR CARS EXPORTED TO ALL COUNTRIES EXCEPT AUSTRIA,
CANADA, SWITZERLAND AND U.S.A.

PART NO.	Description.	NO. PER UNIT.	REMARKS
C.25846	Final Drive Unit Assembly (3.07:1 Ratio)	1	Std. Transmission
9752	Gear Carrier Sub-Assembly	1	
6114	Setscrew, securing Bearing Caps	4	
8489	Lockwasher, on Setscrews	4	
8507	Cover, for Carrier	1	
3823	Plug, for Filler and Drain	2	
3931	Gasket, under Cover	1	
8509	Elbow, in Cover for Breather	1	
UCS.131/5R	Setscrew, securing Cover	10	
47	Lockwasher, on Setscrews	10	
11096	Differential Case Assembly	1	
3845	Roller Bearing, on Diff. Case	2	
8825	Crown Wheel and Pinion (3.07:1)	1	
6301	Setscrew, Crown Wheel to Diff Case	10	
6316	Lockstrap, securing Setscrew	5	
3844	Bearing, on Pinion, Inner	1	
3860	Shim.Inner.Adjusting Pinion (.003")	As req'd	) Selective
3861	Shim.Inner.Adjusting Pinion (.005")	As req'd	) Sizes
3862	Shim.Inner.Adjusting Pinion (.010")	As req'd	)
8029	Distance Washer, behind Outer Shims	1	
3856	Shim.Outer.Adjusting Pinion (.003")	As req'd	)
3857	Shim.Outer.Adjusting Pinion (.005")	As req'd	) Selective
3858	Shim.Outer.Adjusting Pinion (.010")	As req'd	) Sizes
3859	Shim.Outer. Adjusting Pinion(.030")	As req'd	)
3843	Bearing, on Pinion. Outer	1	
3934	Oil Slinger, on Pinion	1	
3840	Oil Seal, on Pinion	1	*
3841	Gasket, for Oil Seal	1	*
11098	Companion Flange, on Pinion	1	
11099	Nut, securing Flange to Pinion	1	
6128	Washer, under Nut	1	
11100	Drive Shaft and Flange	2	
11101	Roller Bearing, on Drive Shaft	4	
11102	Spacing Collar, between Bearings	2	
11103	Shim, Adjusting Bearings (.003")	As req'd	) Selective
11104	Shim, Adjusting Bearings (.005")	As req'd	) Sizes
11105	Shim, Adjusting Bearings (.010")	As req'd	)
11106	Housing, for Drive Shaft Bearings	2	
8950	'O' Ring, on Housing	2	*
11107	Nut, securing Drive Shafts in Bearings	2	
11108	Tab Washer, locking Nuts	2	
9754	Shim.under Bearing Housing (.003")	As req'd	)
9755	Shim.under Bearing Housing (.005")	As req'd	) Selective
9756	Shim,under Bearing Housing (.010")	As req'd	) Sizes
9757	Shim,under Bearing Housing (.030")	As req'd	)
8505	Bolt, securing Bearing Housings	4	
9758	Bolt, securing Bearing Housings	6	
8506	Lockwasher, on Bolts	10	
8436/A	Oil Seal, in Bearing Housings	2	*
8510	Bolt, in Drive Shaft Flanges for Attachment of Discs & Half Shafts	8	
C.15349	Nut, self-locking on Bolts	8	

IMPORTANT - Before ordering items from this page see notes on page 76

PART NO.	Description.	NO. PER UNIT.	REMARKS

FINAL DRIVE UNIT 1ST TYPE WITH NORMAL DIFFERENTIAL (Continued).

C.17024	Bolt, securing Drive Unit to Crossmember	4	
C.837	Wire Locking Bolts	As req'd	
C.25716	Breather, for Final Drive Unit	1	
11096	Differential Case Assembly	1	
6313	Case only	1	
3929	Gear Side	2	
3855	Thrust Washer, for Side Gear	2	
3835	Gear, Pinion Mate	2	
3854	Thrust Washer, for Mate Gear	2	
3837	Shaft, for Mate Gears	1	
3838	Pin, locking Shaft in Case	1	
C.28968	Final Drive Unit Assembly (2.88:1 Ratio)	1)	Automatic
		)	Transmission.
11093	Crown Wheel and Pinion	1	
	All other items are as for Final Drive Unit C.25846		

IMPORTANT - Before ordering items from this page see notes on page 76

PART NO.	Description.	NO. PER UNIT.	REMARKS

FINAL DRIVE UNIT 1ST TYPE WITH "POWR-LOK" DIFFERENTIAL.

FOR CARS EXPORTED TO AUSTRIA, CANADA, SWITZERLAND AND U.S.A.

PART NO.	Description.	NO. PER UNIT.	REMARKS
C.25839	Final Drive Unit Assembly (3.07:1 Ratio)	1	Std.Transmission for Austria and Switzerland
9752	Gear Carrier Sub-Assembly	1	
6114	Setscrew, securing Bearing Caps	4	
8489	Lockwasher, on Setscrews	4	
8507	Cover, for Carrier	1	
3823	Plug, for Filler and Drain	2	
3931	Gasket, under Cover	1	*
8509	Elbow, in Cover for Breather	1	
UCS.131/5R	Setscrew, securing Cover	10	
47	Lockwasher, on Setscrews	10	
11238	Differential Case Assembly	1	
3845	Roller Bearing, on Diff. Case	2	
8825	Crown Wheel and Pinion (3.07:1)	1	
6301	Setscrew, Crown Wheel to Diff Case	10	
7384	Lock Strap, securing Setscrew	5	
3844	Bearing, on Pinion Inner	1	
3860	Shim.Inner.Adjusting Pinion (.003")	As req'd) Selective	
3861	Shim.Inner.Adjusting Pinion (.005")	As req'd) Sizes	
3862	Shim.Inner.Adjusting Pinion (.010")	As req'd)	
8029	Distance Washer, behind Outer Shims	1	
3856	Shim,Outer,Adjusting Pinion (.003")	As req'd) Selective	
3857	Shim,Outer,Adjusting Pinion (.005")	As req'd) Sizes	
3858	Shim,Outer,Adjusting Pinion (.010")	As req'd)	
3859	Shim,Outer,Adjusting Pinion (.030")	As req'd)	
3843	Bearing, on Pinion, Outer	1	
3934	Oil Slinger, on Pinion	1	
3840	Oil Seal, on Pinion	1	*
3841	Gasket, for Oil Seal	1	*
11098	Companion Flange, on Pinion	1	
11099	Nut, securing Flange to Pinion	1	
6128	Washer, under Nut	1	
11100	Drive Shaft and Flange	2	
11101	Roller Bearing, on Drive Shafts	4	
11102	Spacing Collar, between Bearings	2	
11103	Shim,Adjusting Bearings (.003")	As req'd) Selective	
11104	Shim,Adjusting Bearings (.005")	As req'd) Sizes	
11105	Shim,Adjusting Bearings (.010")	As req'd)	
11106	Housing, for Drive Shaft Bearings	2	
8950	'O' Ring, on Housings	2	*
11107	Nut, securing Drive Shaft in Bearings	2	
11108	Tab Washer, locking Nuts	2	
9754	Shim, under Bearing Housings(.003")	As req'd) Selective	
9755	Shim,under Bearing Housings(.005")	As req'd) Sizes	
9756	Shim, under Bearing Housings (.010")	As req'd)	
9757	Shim, under Bearing Housings (.030")	As req'd)	
8505	Bolt, securing Bearing Housings	4	
9758	Bolt, securing Bearing Housings	6	
8506	Lockwasher, on Bolts	10	
8436/A	Oil Seal, in Bearing Housings	2	*
8510	Bolt, in Drive Shaft Flanges for Attachment of Discs & Half Shafts	8	
C.15349	Nut, self locking on Bolts	8	

IMPORTANT - Before ordering items from this page see notes on page 76

PART NO.	Description.	NO. PER UNIT.	REMARKS

FINAL DRIVE UNIT 1ST TYPE WITH "POWR-LOK" DIFFERENTIAL (Continued).

C.17014	Bolt, securing Drive Unit to Crossmember	4	
C.837	Wire Locking Bolts	As req'd	
C.25716	Breather, for Final Drive Unit	1	
11328	Differential Case Assembly	1	
7887	Case only (Prs)	1	
7683	Friction Plate (Flat)	4	
8397	Friction Plate (Dished)	2	
7684	Friction Disc	4	
11290	Ring, for Side Gears	2	
11291	Side Gear	2	
7685	Pinion Mate Gear	4	
7686	Shaft, for Mate Gears	2 halves	
7680	Bolt, securing Differential Case	8	
C.25841	Final Drive Unit Assembly (3.54:1 Ratio)	1	Standard Trans. for Canada and U.S.A.
6305	Crown Wheel and Pinion	1	
	All other items are as for Final Drive Unit C.25839		
C.25954	Final Drive Unit Assembly (2.88:1 Ratio)	1	Automatic Trans., for Austria and Switzerland
11093	Crown Wheel and Pinion	1	
	All other items are as for Final Drive Unit C.25839		
C.25840	Final Drive Unit Assembly (3.31:1 Ratio)	1	Automatic Trans., for Canada and U.S.A.
6304	Crown Wheel and Pinion	1	
	All other items as for Final Drive Unit C.25839		

IMPORTANT - Before ordering items from this page see notes on page 76

PART NO.	Description.	NO. PER UNIT.	REMARKS

FINAL DRIVE UNITS 2ND TYPE.

STANDARD TRANSMISSION.
NOT FITTED FOR CARS TO AUSTRIA, CANADA, SWITZERLAND OR U.S.A.

C.32302D	Final Drive Unit Assy (3.07:1 Ratio)	1	
12461	Crown Wheel and Pinion (3.07:1)	1	
12456	Collapsible Spacer	1	
12504	Pinion Bearing, Outer	1	

ALL OTHER ITEMS AS FOR DRIVE UNIT C.25846.
NOTE - "SHIM.OUTER.ADJUSTING PINION" IS NOT REQUIRED.

AUTOMATIC TRANSMISSION (2+2 ONLY).
NOT FITTED FOR CARS TO AUSTRIA, CANADA, SWITZERLAND OR U.S.A.

C.32302H	Final Drive Unit Assy (2.88:1 Ratio)	1	
12464	Crown Wheel and Pinion (2.88:1)	1	

ALL OTHER ITEMS AS FOR DRIVE UNIT C.32302D
NOTE - "SHIM.OUTER.ADJUSTING PINION" IS NOT REQUIRED.

STANDARD TRANSMISSION, WITH POWR-LOK DIFFERENTIAL
FOR CARS TO AUSTRIA AND SWITZERLAND.

C.32301D	Final Drive Unit Assy (3.07:1 Ratio)	1	
12461	Crown Wheel and Pinion (3.07:1)	1	
12456	Collapsible Spacer	1	
12504	Pinion Bearing, Outer	1	

ALL OTHER ITEMS AS FOR DRIVE UNIT C.25839
NOTE -"SHIM.OUTER.ADJUSTING PINION" IS NOT REQUIRED.

AUTOMATIC TRANSMISSION, WITH POWR-LOK DIFFERENTIAL
(2+2 ONLY) FOR CARS TO AUSTRIA AND SWITZERLAND.

C.32301H	Final Drive Unit Assy (2.88:1 Ratio)	1	
12464	Crown Wheel and Pinion (2.88:1)	1	

ALL OTHER ITEMS AS FOR DRIVE UNIT C.32301D
NOTE - "SHIM.OUTER.ADJUSTING PINION" IS NOT REQUIRED.

IMPORTANT - Before ordering items from this page see notes on page 76

PART NO.	Description.	NO. PER UNIT.	REMARKS

Final Drive Units 2nd Type (Continued).

STANDARD TRANSMISSION.
FOR CARS TO CANADA AND U.S.A.

C.32301A	Final Drive Unit Assy (3.54:1 Ratio)	1
12458	Crown Wheel and Pinion (3.54:1)	1
12456	Collapsible Spacer	1
12504	Pinion Bearing, Outer	1

ALL OTHER ITEMS AS FOR DRIVE UNIT C.25839
NOTE - "SHIM.OUTER.ADJUSTING PINION" IS NOT REQUIRED.

AUTOMATIC TRANSMISSION (2+2 ONLY).
FOR CARS TO CANADA AND U.S.A.

C.32301X	Final Drive Unit Assy (3.31:1 Ratio)	1
12457	Crown Wheel and Pinion (3.31:1)	1

ALL OTHER ITEMS AS FOR DRIVE UNIT C.32301A
NOTE - "SHIM.OUTER.ADJUSTING PINION" IS NOT REQUIRED.

IMPORTANT - Before ordering items from this page see notes on page 76

PART NO.	Description.	NO. PER UNIT.	REMARKS

FINAL DRIVE UNITS 3RD TYPE.

STANDARD TRANSMISSION.
NOT FITTED TO CARS FOR AUSTRIA, CANADA, SWITZERLAND OR U.S.A.

PART NO.	Description.	NO. PER UNIT.	REMARKS
C.31680D	Final Drive Unit Assembly (3.07:1 Ratio)	1	
12470	Gear Carrier Sub-Assembly	1	
6114	Setscrew, securing Bearing Caps	4	
8489	Lockwasher, on Setscrew	4	
8507	Cover, for Carrier	1	
3823	Plug, for Filler and Drain	2	
3931	Gasket, under Cover	1	
8509	Elbow, in Cover, for Breather	1	
UCS.131/5R.	Setscrew, securing Cover	10	
47	Lockwasher, on Setscrew	10	
11096	Differential Case Assembly	1	
3845	Roller Bearing, on Diff. Case	2	
3935	Shim, adjusting Bearing (.003")	As req'd)	
3936	Shim, adjusting Bearing (.005")	As req'd) Selective	
3937	Shim, adjusting Bearing (.010")	As req'd) Sizes	
3938	Shim, adjusting Bearing (.030")	As req'd)	
12461	Crown Wheel and Pinion Assy (3.07:1)	1	
12252	Bearing, on Pinion, Inner	1	
3860	Shim, Inner, adjusting Pinion (.003")	As req'd)	
3861	Shim, Inner, adjusting Pinion (.005")	As req'd) Selective	
3862	Shim, Inner, adjusting Pinion (.010")	As req'd) Sizes	
12465	Bearing, on Pinion Outer	1	
12466	Oil Slinger, on Pinion	1	
3840	Oil Seal, on Pinion	1	
3841	Gasket, on Oil Seal	1	
11098	Companion Flange, on Pinion	1	
11099	Nut, securing Flange to Pinion	1	
6128	Washer, under Nut	1	
12468	Drive Shaft Assembly, R.H.	1	
12469	Drive Shaft Assembly, L.H.	1	
12268	Bolt, for Caliper Mounting Bracket	10	
12270	Lockwasher, for Mounting Bracket	10	
12473	'O' Ring, for Drive Shaft Bearing	2	
12474	Shim, Caliper Mounting Bracket (.003")	As req'd)	
12475	Shim, Caliper Mounting Bracket (.005")	As req'd) Selective	
12476	Shim, Caliper Mounting Bracket (.010")	As req'd) Sizes	
12477	Shim, Caliper Mounting Bracket (.030")	As req'd)	

IMPORTANT - Before ordering items from this page see notes on page 76

PART NO.	Description.	NO. PER UNIT.	REMARKS

Final Drive Units 3rd Type (Continued).

11096	Differential Case Assembly	1
6313	Case only (2 halves)	1
3929	Side Gear	2
3855	Thrust Washer, for Side Gears	2
3835	Gear, Pinion Mate	2
3854	Thrust Washer, for Mate Gears	2
3837	Shaft, for Mate Gears	1
3838	Pin, locking Shaft in Diff.Case	1
12461	Crown Wheel and Pinion (3.07:1)	1
6301	Setscrew, Crown Wheel to Diff.Case	10
6316	Lockstrap, securing Setscrew	5
11099	Pinion Nut	1
12456	Collapsible Spacer	1
12468	Drive Shaft Assembly R.H.	1
12260	Drive Shaft and Flange (Studded)	1
12261	Ball Bearing, on Drive Shaft	1
12264	Nut, securing Shaft in Bearing	1
12265	Tab Washer, locking Nut	1
12471	Caliper, mounting Bracket and Oil Seal Assembly R.H.	1
C.15349	Nut, for Drive Shaft Studs	4
12469	Drive Shaft Assembly, L.H.	1
12472	Caliper Mounting Bracket and Oil Seal Assembly, L.H.	1

ALL OTHER ITEMS AS FOR DRIVE SHAFT 12468

C.25716	Breather, for Drive Unit	1
C.17024	Bolt, securing Drive Unit in Rear Suspension Crossmember	4
C.837	Wire, locking Bolts	As req'd

AUTOMATIC TRANSMISSION (2+2 ONLY).
NOT FITTED TO CARS FOR AUSTRIA, CANADA, SWITZERLAND OR U.S.A.

C.31680H	Final Drive Unit Assembly (2.88:1 Ratio)	1
12454	Crown Wheel and Pinion (2.88:1)	1

ALL OTHER ITEMS AS FOR DRIVE UNIT C.31680D

AUTOMATIC TRANSMISSION (2+2 ONLY).
FOR CARS SUPPLIED BY SPECIAL ORDER TO CANADA AND U.S.A.

C.31680X	Final Drive Unit Assembly(3.33:1Ratio)	1
12457	Crown Wheel and Pinion (3.33:1)	1

ALL OTHER ITEMS AS FOR DRIVE UNIT C.31680D

IMPORTANT - Before ordering items from this page see notes on page 76

PART NO.	Description.	NO. PER UNIT.	REMARKS

Final Drive Units 3rd Type (Continued).

STANDARD TRANSMISSION, WITH POWR-LOK DIFFERENTIAL
FOR CARS TO AUSTRIA AND SWITZERLAND.

PART NO.	Description.	NO. PER UNIT.	REMARKS
C.31681D	Final Drive Unit Assembly (3.07:1 Ratio)	1	
12470	Gear Carrier Sub-Assembly	1	
6114	Setscrew, securing Bearing Caps	4	
8489	Lockwasher, on Setscrew	4	
8507	Cover, for Carrier	1	
3823	Plug, for Filler and Drain	2	
3931	Gasket, under Cover	1	
8509	Elbow, in Cover for Breather	1	
UCS.131/5R	Setscrew, securing Cover	10	
47	Lockwasher, on Setscrew	10	
11328	Differential Case Assembly	1	
3845	Roller Bearing, on Diff.Case	2	
3835	Shim, adjusting Bearing (.003")	As req'd)	
3836	Shim, adjusting Bearing (.005")	As req'd)	Selective
3837	Shim, adjusting Bearing (.010")	As req'd)	Sizes
3838	Shim, adjusting Bearing (.030")	As req'd)	
12461	Crown Wheel and Pinion (3.07:1)	1	
12252	Roller Bearing, on Pinion Inner	1	
3860	Shim. Inner, adjusting Pinion (.003")	As req'd)	
3861	Shim. Inner, adjusting Pinion (.005")	As req'd)	Selective
3862	Shim. Inner, adjusting Pinion (.010")	As req'd)	Sizes
12465	Roller Bearing, on Pinion Outer	1	
12466	Oil Slinger, on Pinion	1	
3840	Oil Seal, on Pinion	1	
3841	Gasket, for Oil Seal	1	
11098	Companion Flange, on Pinion	1	
11099	Nut, securing Flange on Pinion	1	
6128	Washer, under Nut	1	
12468	Drive Shaft Assembly R.H.	1	
12469	Drive Shaft Assembly L.H.	1	
12268	Bolt, for Caliper Mounting Bracket	10	
12270	Lockwasher, for Mounting Bracket	10	
12473	'O' Ring, for Drive Shaft Bearing	2	
12474	Shim, Caliper Mounting Bracket(.003")	As req'd)	
12475	Shim, Caliper Mounting Bracket(.005")	As req'd)	Selective
12476	Shim, Caliper Mounting Bracket (.010")	As req'd)	Sizes
12477	Shim, Caliper Mounting Bracket (.030")	As req'd)	

IMPORTANT - Before ordering items from this page see notes on page 76

PART NO.	Description.	NO. PER UNIT.	REMARKS

Final Drive Units 3rd Type (Continued).

PART NO.	Description.	NO. PER UNIT.
11328	Differential Case Assembly	1
7887	Case only (2 halves)	1
7683	Friction Plate (Flat)	4
8397	Friction Plate (Dished)	2
7684	Friction Disc	4
11290	Ring, for Side Gear	2
11291	Side Gear	2
7685	Pinion Mate Gear	4
7686	Shaft, for Mate Gears	2
7680	Bolt, securing Diff. Case	8
12461	Crown Wheel and Pinion (3.07:1)	1
6301	Setscrew, Crown Wheel to Diff.	10
6316	Lockstrap, securing Setscrew	5
11099	Pinion Nut	1
12456	Collapsible Spacer	1
12468	Drive Shaft Assembly, R.H.	1
12260	Drive Shaft and Flange (Studded)	1
12261	Ball Bearing, on Drive Shaft	1
12264	Nut, securing Drive Shaft in Bearing	1
12265	Tab Washer, locking Nut	1
12471	Caliper, mounting Bracket and Oil Seal Assembly R.H.	1
C.15359	Nut, for Drive Shaft Studs	4
12469	Drive Shaft Assembly L.H.	1
12472	Caliper Mounting Bracket and Oil Seal Assembly	1

ALL OTHER ITEMS AS FOR DRIVE SHAFT 12468

PART NO.	Description.	NO. PER UNIT.
C.25716	Breather, for Drive Unit	1
C.17024	Bolt, securing Drive Unit in Rear Suspension Crossmember	4
C.837	Wire, locking Bolt	As req'd

AUTOMATIC TRANSMISSION (2+2 ONLY) WITH POWR-LOK DIFFERENTIAL. FOR CARS TO AUSTRIA AND SWITZERLAND.

PART NO.	Description.	NO. PER UNIT.
C.31681H	Final Drive Unit Assembly (2.88:1 Ratio)	1
12464	Crown Wheel and Pinion (2.88:1)	1

ALL OTHER ITEMS AS FOR DRIVE UNIT C.31681D

IMPORTANT - Before ordering items from this page see notes on page 76

PART NO.	Description.	NO. PER UNIT.	REMARKS

Final Drive Units 3rd Type (Continued).

STANDARD TRANSMISSION WITH POWR-LOK DIFFERENTIAL.
FOR CARS TO CANADA AND U.S.A.

C.31681A	Final Drive Unit Assembly (3.54:1Ratio)	1	
12458	Crown Wheel and Pinion (3.54:1)	1	

ALL OTHER ITEMS AS FOR DRIVE UNIT C.31681D.

AUTOMATIC TRANSMISSION WITH POWR-LOK DIFFERENTIAL.
FOR CARS TO CANADA AND U.S.A.

C.31681X	Final Drive Unit Assembly (3.31:1Ratio)	1	
12457	Crown Wheel and Pinion (3.31:1)	1	

ALL OTHER ITEMS AS FOR DRIVE UNIT C.31681D.

IMPORTANT - Before ordering items from this page see notes on page 76

PART NO.   Description.   NO. PER   REMARKS
                                           UNIT.

IDENTIFICATION OF FINAL DRIVE UNITS.

1ST TYPE.   Is as illustrated on Plate 27 of Publication J38 -
                 'E' Type 2+2 Parts Catalogue.

2ND TYPE.   This is visually identical to the first type but has the
                 suffix "C" to the Serial Number of the Unit.

3RD TYPE.   This is identified by the Drive Shaft Oil Seal
                 Container being bolted on to the Gear Carrier.

                 These Final Drive Units are interchangeable as Assemblies
                 but differ in Component Form, therefore when ordering
                 Component Parts it is essential that the Unit is
                 identified correctly.

PLEASE NOTE -   From Chassis Numbers 1R1244 R.H.D. 1R9930 L.H.D.
                 Open. 1R20335 R.H.D. 1R26576 L.H.D. F.H.C.
                 1R35418 R.H.D. 1R42445 L.H.D. 2+2. The 3rd Type
                 Final Drive Unit is fitted to all cars

PART NO.	Description.	NO. PER UNIT.	REMARKS

FRONT SUSPENSION.

PART NO.	Description.	NO. PER UNIT.	REMARKS
C.24517	Upper Wishbone Assembly R.H.	1	
C.24519	Upper Wishbone R.H.	1	
C.22966	Ball Pin, in Upper Wishbone	1	**
C.23046	Rubber Sleeve, for Ball Pin	1	**
C.24521	Socket, over Ball Pin	1	**
C.24523	Shim, for Ball Pin Adjustment	As req'd	
C.635	Spring, over Socket	1	**
C.24522	Top Cover, over Ball Pin	1	**
C.15366	Circlip, securing Top Cover	1	**
C.3044/1	Grease Nipple, in Top Cover	1	**
C.22971	Nylon Washer, under Nipple	1	**
C.22967	Gaiter, at Bottom of Ball Pin	1	**
C.22970	Insert, between Gaiter and W/Bone	1	**
C.22969	Ring, securing Gaiter to W/Bone	1	**
C.8737/5	Nut, securing Ball Pin	1	
FW.108/T	Plain Washer, under Nut	1	
C.15369	Fulcrum Shaft, for Upper Wishbone	1	
C.15371	Pinch Bolt, locking Shaft	2	
C.15379	Distance Washer, on Shaft	2	
C.8672	Rubber Bush, on Shaft	2	**
NN.750/L	Slotted Nut,	2	
C.8676/1	Washer, under Slotted Nut	2	
L.104/10U	Split Pin, retaining Slotted Nut	2	
C.24518	Upper Wishbone Assembly, L.H.	1	
C.24520	Upper Wishbone L.H.	1	
	All other items are as for Upper Wishbone Assembly C.24517		
C.15151	Mounting Bracket, for Front Upper Wishbone Fulcrum Block	2	
UFB.131/17R	Bolt, securing Mounting Bracket	2	
C.8667/2	Nut, on Bolt	2	
C.15089	Fulcrum Block, for Upper Wishbone Shafts	2	
UFB.131/10R	Bolt, Fulcrum Blocks to Mounting Brackets	6	
FG.105/X	Spring Washer, on Bolts	6	
C.15153	Shim, behind Fulcrum Blocks for Camber Angle Adjustment	As req'd	
C.15090	Fulcrum Block, Rear, for Upper W/Bone Shafts	2	
UFB.131/9R	Bolt, Fulcrum Blocks to Side Member	4	
C,15113	Washer Plate, under Bolt Head	2	
C.8667/2	Nut, on Bolt	4	
C.15154	Shim, behind Rear Fulcrum Blocks	As req'd	
C.15158	Lower Wishbone Assembly, R.H.	1	
C.15373	Lower W/Bone Lever R.H.Front	1	
C.15375	Lower W/Bone Lever Rear	1	
C.15155	Bolt, joining Levers and Fixing End of Shock Absorbers	1	
C.9326	Sleeve, on Bolt	1	
FW.110/T	Plain Washer, on Sleeve	1	
UFN.450/L	Slotted Nut, on Bolt	1	

PART NO.	Description.	NO. PER UNIT.	REMARKS

Front Suspension (Continued).

PART NO.	Description.	NO. PER UNIT.	REMARKS
C.11193	Special Washer, under Nut	1	
L.104/10U	Split Pin, retaining Nut	1	
C.15372	Fulcrum Shaft	1	
C.15376	Distance Washer, on Shaft	1	
C.8673	Rubber Bush, on Shaft	2	**
NN.756/L	Slotted Nut, securing Fulcrum Shaft in Blocks	2	
C.8693/1	Special Washer, under Nuts	2	
L.104/10U	Split Pin, retaining Nuts	2	
C.15159	Lower Wishbone Assembly L.H.	1	
C.15374	Lower W/Bone Lever L.H.Front	1	
	All other items are as Lower Wishbone Assembly C.15158		
C.15088	Fulcrum Block,Front for Lower Shaft	2	
C.15091	Fulcrum Block,Rear for Lower Shaft	2	
UFB.131/16R	Bolt, Rear Fulcrum Blocks to Side Members	4	
C.8737/2	Nut, on Bolt	4	
C.20011	Front Shock Absorber	2	*
C.3273	Bush,Bottom Eye of S/Absorber	4	**
C.9380	Bolt, securing S/Absorber at Top	2	
UFN.443/L	Nut, on Bolt	2	
C.16679	Plain Washer, under Nut	2	
L.103/10U	Split Pin, retaining Nut	2	
C.15337	Lower Ball Pin, in Stub Axle Carrier	2	**
C.22974	Spigot, over Ball Pins	2	**
C.23018	Railko Socket, supporting Ball Pin	2	**
C.15341	Shim (.002") Carrier to Cap	As req'd) Selective	
C.15342	Shim (.004") Carrier to Cap	As req'd) Sizes	
C.17175	Shim (.010") Carrier to Cap	As req'd)	
C.24514	Cap, under Lower Ball Pin	2	**
C.15344/1	Bolt, securing Cap to Stub Axle Carrier	8	
C.15343	Tab Washer, securing Bolts	4	**
C.3044/1	Grease Nipple, in Caps	2	**
C.22971	Nylon Washer, under Grease Nipple	2	**
C.22967	Gaiter, for Lower Ball Pin	2	**
C.22970	Insert, between Spigot and Gaiter	2	**
C.22969	Ring, securing Gaiter to Spigot	2	**
C.8737/6	Nut, securing Ball Pin, to Lower Wishbone Levers	2	**
C.794/1	Plain Washer, under Nut	2	
C.26849	Stub Axle Carrier(Vertical Link)	2	
C.18843/1	Water Shield, on Carriers	2	
C.30516	Shield Assembly, Upper for R.H.Front Brake Disc.	1	
C.30517	Shield Assembly, Upper for L.H.Front Brake Disc.	1	

PART NO.	Description.	NO. PER UNIT.	REMARKS
	Front Suspension (Continued).		
C.30512	Shield Assembly, Lower for R.H.Front Brake Disc	1	
C.30513	Shield Assembly, Lower, for L.H.Front Brake Disc	1	
C.19423	Stub Axle Shaft	2	
C.8667/7	Nut, securing Shaft and Tie Rod Levers to Carriers	2	
C.15350	Oil Seal, for Stub Axle Shafts	2	**
C.15351	Inner Bearing, on Shaft for Hub	2	**
C.15352	Outer Bearing, on Shaft for Hub	2	**
C.19225/1	R.H.Front Hub	1	
C.19226/1	L.H.Front Hub	1	
C.18842/1	Water Thrower, on Hubs	2	
NN.756/L	Slotted Nut, securing Hub to Shaft	2	
C.3400	"D" Washer, under Slotted Nut	2	
L.104/10U	Split Pin, retaining Slotted Nut	2	
C.3076/1	Grease Nipple, in Hubs	2	
C.28684	R.H.Hub Cap	2	**
C.28685	L.H.Hub Cap	2	**
C.28687	Tool for Removing and Fitting Hub Caps	1	**
11961	R.H.Front Brake Caliper less Friction Pads	1)	For Complete Breakdown see
11962	L.H.Front Brake Caliper less Friction Pads	1)	Front Brake Section.
C.27024	Disc (Damped) for Front Caliper	2	*
C.13546	Bolt, securing Discs to Front Hubs	10	
C.24119/4	Nut, on Bolts	10	
C.30245	R.H.Tie Rod Lever	1	
C.30246	L.H.Tie Rod Lever	1	
C.30250	Bolt, Tie Rod Lever to Stub Axle Carrier	2	
FW.107/T	Plain Washer, on Bolt	2	
FG.107/X	Spring Washer, on Bolt	2	
C.30519	Bracket, on R.H.Stub Axle Carrier for Front Brake Hose	1	
C.30520	Bracket, on L.H.Stub Axle Carrier for Front Brake Hose	1	
UFS.143/6R	Setscrew, securing Bracket	2	
FG.107/X	Spring Washer, on Setscrew	2	
C.8737/1	Nut, securing Hose Bracket to Disc Shield	2	

PART NO.	Description.	NO. PER UNIT.	REMARKS

Front Suspension (Continued).

PART NO.	Description.	NO. PER UNIT.	REMARKS
C.26932	Bolt, securing Calipers and Disc Shields to Stub Axle Carriers	4	
FG.107/X	Spring Washer, on Bolts	4	
C.31335	Plain Washer, under Spring Washer	4	
C.837	Wire, locking Bolts	As req'd	
C.16629	Anti-Roll Bar	1	
C.16633	Bush, Rubber for Anti-Roll Bar	2	**
C.15097	Bracket, holding Rubber Bush	2	
C.16631	Distance Piece, under Brackets	2	
C.21946	Plate, between Distance Piece and Bracket	2	
C.25272	Bracket, under Plate for R.H.Front Brake Hose	1	
C.25273	Bracket, under Plate for L.H.Front Brake Hose	1	
UFB.131/18R	Bolt, Upper, securing Brackets, Plates and Distance Pieces to Crossmember	2	
UFB.131/32R	Bolt, Lower, securing Brackets, Plates and Lower Fulcrum Blocks to Crossmember	2	
C.8667/2	Nut, on Bolts	4	
C.20763	Link, between Anti-Roll Bar and Lower Wishbone Levers	2	
C.10940	Bush, Rubber, in Eyes of Link	4	**
UFB.143/21R	Bolt, Link to Anti-Roll Bar	2	
UFB.143/22R	Bolt, Link to Lower W/Bone Levers	2	
C.8667/4	Nut, on Bolts	4	
FW.207/T	Bevelled Washer, under Nuts	4	
C.9331	Front Torsion Bar. R.H.	1)	Fitted to R.H.Drive)
C.9332	Front Torsion Bar. L.H.	1)	Open and F.H.Coupe Models on
C.27904	Front Torsion Bar. R.H.	1)	Fitted to all) 2+2 Models. Also Fitted to
C.27905	Front Torsion Bar. L.H.	1)	L.H.Drive Open and F.H.Coupe) Models
C.27332	Bolt, locating Torsion Bar in Wishbone Levers	2	
C.8667/17	Nut, on Bolts	2	
C.19379	Bracket, at Rear End of Torsion Bar	2	
C.20426	Bolt, securing Brackets and Re-Action Plate to Side Members	4	
C.8667/3	Nut, on Bolt	4	

PART NO.	Description.	NO. PER UNIT.	REMARKS

REAR SUSPENSION.

PART NO.	Description.	NO. PER UNIT.	REMARKS
C.30286	Rear Suspension Crossmember Assy	1	
C.17198	Rubber Mounting.Crossmember to Body	4	**
UFB.131/24R	Bolt, securing Mounting to Body	8	
C.8737/2	Nut, self-locking, on Bolt	8	
UFS.131/7R	Setscrew, securing Mountings to Crossmember	8	
C.8737/2	Nut, self-locking, on Studs of Mounting	2	
FW.105/T	Plain Washer, on Studs of Mounting	4	
C.8667/2	Nut, on Setscrews and Studs of Mounting	10	
C.17228	Packing Piece, on Bolts	8	Open and F.H.Coupe only
C.20481	Mounting for Inner Fulcrum Shaft	2	
C.17009	Setscrew, Long, Mounting to Final Drive	2	
C.17010	Setscrew, short,Mounting to Final Drive	2	
C.28427	Shim (.005") under Mounting	As req'd) Selective	
C.28428	Shim (.007") under Mounting	As req'd) Sizes	
C.837	Wire locking Setscrews	As req'd)	
C.20651	Bottom Plate, on Crossmember	1	
UFS.131/5R	Setscrew, Plate to Crossmember Flange and Fulcrum Mounting	14	
C.8737/2	Nut, on Setscrew at Flange Fixing	6	
FG.105/X	Spring Washer, on Setscrew, Mounting Fixing	8	
C.20255	Wishbone Assembly R.H.	1	
C.20256	Wishbone Assembly L.H.	1	
C.3044/1	Grease Nipple, on Inner Fork	4	
C.17008	Inner Fulcrum Shaft	2	*
C.17663/1	Distance Tube, on Fulcrum Shaft	2	*
C.17168/1	Bearing Tube, on Fulcrum Shaft	4	*
C.17167	Needle Bearing, on Tubes	8	**
C.17166	Thrust Washer, Inner, Bearing Tube Ends	8	**
C.17213	Sealing Ring, on Inner Thrust Washers	8	**
C.17936	Retainer, for Sealing Rings	8	**
C.17165	Thrust Washer, Outer, on Fulcrum Shaft	8	**
C.8667/5	Nut, self locking, on Fulcrum Shaft	4	
C.16624	Outer Fulcrum Shaft	2	*
C.16623	Sleeve, on Fulcrum Shafts	4	*
C.16626	Shim (.003") between Sleeves	As req'd) Selective	
C.16626/3	Shim (.007") between Sleeves	As req'd) Sizes	
C.16029	Bearing, Taper Roller on Fulcrum Shaft	4	*
C.16628	Seating Ring, on Shaft for Oil Seal	4	**
C.20178	Oil Seal, Felt, on Fulcrum Shaft	4	**
C.20179	Container, for Oil Seal	4	**
C.20180	Spacer, between Bearing & Seal Containers	4	*
C.20182	Retaining Washer, on Seating Ring	4	*
C.16626/1	Shim (.003") Outer on Fulcrum Shaft	As req'd) Selective	
C.16626/2	Shim (.007") Outer on Fulcrum Shaft	As req'd) Sizes.	
C.8667/7	Nut, self locking, on Fulcrum Shaft	4	

PART NO.	Description.	NO. PER UNIT.	REMARKS
	Rear Suspension (Continued).		
C.26701	Hub Carrier	2	
C.9048	Grease Nipple, in Hub Carrier	2	
C.18124	Grease Cap Top of Hub Carrier	2	
C.20889	Rear Hub Assembly R.H.	1	*
C.20890	Rear Hub Assembly L.H.	1	*
C.20813	Water Thrower on Hubs	2	*
C.28684	Hub Cap R.H.	1	*
C.28685	Hub Cap L.H.	1	*
C.28687	Hub Cap Removal Tool	1	*
C.24789	Oil Seal, Outer, for Hubs	2	**
C.24791	Seating Ring, on Hubs for Outer Seal	2	**
C.19066	Outer Bearing, for Hubs	2	**
C.15230	Inner Bearing, for Hubs	2	**
C.19110/A	Spacer (.109") on Splined Yoke(Brg.Adj't)2)		
C.19110/B	Spacer(.112") on Splined Yoke (Brg.Adj't)2)		
C.19110/C	Spacer(.115") on Splined Yoke(Brg.Adj't) 2)		
C.19110/D	Spacer(.118") on Splined Yoke(Brg.Adj't) 2)		
C.19110/E	Spacer(.121") on Splined Yoke(Brg.Adj't) 2)		
C.19110/F	Spacer(.124") on Splined Yoke(Brg.Adj't) 2)		
C.19110/G	Spacer(.127") on Splined Yoke(Brg.Adj't) 2)	Selective	
C.19110/H	Spacer(.130") on Splined Yoke(Brg.Adj't) 2)	Sizes	
C.19110/J	Spacer(.133") on Splined Yoke(Brg.Adj't) 2)		
C.19110/K	Spacer(.136") on Splined Yoke(Brg.Adj't) 2)		
C.19110/L	Spacer(.139") on Splined Yoke(Brg.Adj't) 2)		
C.19110/M	Spacer(.142") on Splined Yoke(Brg.Adj't) 2)		
C.19110/P	Spacer(.145") on Splined Yoke(Brg.Adj't) 2)		
C.19110/Q	Spacer(.148") on Splined Yoke(Brg.Adj't) 2)		
C.19110/R	Spacer(.151") on Splined Yoke'Brg.Adj't) 2)		
C.15231	Oil Seal, Inner, for Hubs	2	**
C.15232	Seating Ring, for Inner Oil Seal	2	**
C.23655/2	Half Shaft Assembly	2	*
9406	Flange Yoke	2	
9407	Splined Yoke	2	
11948	Journal Assembly	4	**
C.16621	Shim,Half Shaft to Disc(Camber Adj't)	As req'd	
C.15349	Nut,securing Half Shafts and Discs to Final Drive Unit	8	
UFN.375/L	Slotted Nut, securing Half Shafts to Hubs	2	
C.24923	Washer, under Slotted Nut	2	
L.105/13U	Split Pin, retaining Slotted Nut	2	
C.23616	Joint Cover, Outer, over Journals	2	*
C.28844	Joint Cover, Outer, with Greaser Hole	2	*
BD.1814/4	Pop Rivet, securing Covers together	8	

PART NO.	Description.	NO. PER UNIT.	REMARKS	

Rear Suspension (Continued).

PART NO.	Description.	NO. PER UNIT.	REMARKS	
C.2905/12	Clip, securing Covers to Half Shafts	2		
BD.15588/6	Plastic Plug, in Greaser Hole	2		
C.25939	Rear Suspension Coil Springs	4		*
C.25951	Rear Shock Absorber	4		*
8688	Dust Shield Assembly	4		
8689	Bush, Rubber, in S/Absorber Eyes	8		*
C.19820	Seat, for Coil Spring	4		
8687	Retainer, for Coil Spring	8		
UFB.143/16R	Bolt, securing Shock Absorber Top	4		
C.17012	Sleeve, on Bolts	4		
C.8737/4	Nut, self-locking on Bolts	4		
FW.107/T	Plain Washer, under Nuts	4		
C.17013	Shaft through Wishbones for Mounting Shock Absorbers, Bottom	2		
C.8737/4	Nut, self-locking, on Shaft	4		
C.3052	Special Washer, under Nuts	4		
C.17151	Rear Anti-Roll Bar	1)	Open and F.H.Coupe	
C.16633	Bush, Rubber, for Anti-Roll Bar	2)	Models only	**
C.25747	Rear Anti-Roll Bar	1)	2+2 Models	
C.25748	Bush, Rubber for Anti-Roll Bar	2)	only	**
C.3054	Bracket, for Rubber Bush	2		
UFS.137/7R	Setscrew, securing Brackets to Body	4		
C.726	Shakeproof Washer, on Setscrew	4		
C.20765	Link, Anti-Roll Bar to Radius Arm	2		*
C.10940	Bush, Rubber, in Eyes of Link	4		**
C.18296	Bolt, Link to Anti-Roll Bar	2		
UFB.143/15R	Bolt, Link to Radius Arm	2		
C.8667/4	Nut, on Bolts	4		
FW.107/T	Plain Washer, under Nuts	4		
C.25938	Bump Stop, on Body	2		**
C.8737/2	Nut, securing Bump Stops	4		
FW.105/T	Plain Washer, under Nuts	4		
C.23824	Radius Arm Assembly	2		*
C.23782	Rubber Bush, Front End of Arm	2		**
C.17146	Rubber Bush, Rear End of Arm	2		**
C.17149/1	Special Bolt, securing Radius Arm to Wishbone	2		
C.8737/5	Nut, on Bolt	2		
C.19031	Safety Strap Assembly	2	Open and F.H.Coupe	
C.25156	Safety Strap Assembly	2	2+2 Models.	
C.19045	Bolt, securing Radius Arm to Body	2		
C.837	Wire Locking Bolts	As req'd		
UFS.131/6R	Setscrew, Safety Strap to Body	2		
C.8667/2	Nut, on Setscrews	2		

PART NO.	Description.	NO. PER UNIT.	REMARKS
	ROAD WHEELS.		
C.28043	Wire Spoke Road Wheel (Painted) (Stoved Aluminium)	5	
7784	Long Spoke	120	
11799	Short Spoke	240	
C.5604	Nipple, for Spoke	360	
C.28044	Wire Spoke Road Wheel (Chromium Plated)	5)	Supplied
		)	to
7796	Long Spoke (C.Plated)	120)	Special
11475	Short Spoke (C.Plated)	240)	Order
C.9144	Nipple, for Spoke	360)	only.
C.29627	Tyre, for Road Wheel (185 x 15)	5	<u>Not</u> for U.S.A.
C.30607	Tyre, for Road Wheel (Whitewall)	5	For U.S.A.
C.29628	Tyre, for Road Wheel (Whitewall)	5	Special orders only but <u>NOT</u> for U.S.A.
C.24199	Tube, for Tyres (185 x 15)	5	
C.22666/1	Balance Weight for Wheel ($\frac{1}{2}$ oz.)	As req'd	
C.22666/2	Balance Weight for Wheel (1 oz)	As req'd	
C.22666/3	Balance Weight for Wheel ($1\frac{1}{2}$ oz.)	As req'd	
C.22666/4	Balance Weight for Wheel (2 oz.)	As req'd	
C.22666/5	Balance Weight for Wheel ($2\frac{1}{2}$ oz.)	As req'd	
C.22666/6	Balance Weight for Wheel (3 oz.)	As req'd	

PART NO.	Description.	NO. PER UNIT.	REMARKS

FRONT BRAKES.

PART NO.	Description.	NO. PER UNIT.	REMARKS
11961	R.H.Front Caliper Assembly, less Friction Pads	1	*
12274	Outer Piston	2	
10031	Inner Piston	1	
11368	Pin, retaining Friction Pads	2	
11369	Clip, retaining Pins	2	
11370	Bleed Screw	1	
1675	Dust Cap, on Bleed Screw	1	*
11962	L.H.Front Caliper Assembly, less Friction Pads	1	*
	Individual Items are as for 11961		
12247	Friction Pad Kit (Set of 4 Pads)	1	**
12292	Anti-Rattle Spring, for Friction Pads	4	**
12281	Seals Kit, for Front Caliper	1	**
C.26932	Special Bolt, securing Caliper and Disc Shields to Stub Axle Carrier	4	
FG.107/X	Spring Washer, on Bolts	4	
C.31335	Plain Washer, on Bolts	4	
C.837	Wire Locking Caliper Bolts	As req'd	
C.27024	Disc Assembly, for Front Caliper	2	*
C.13546	Bolt, securing Discs to Hubs	10	
C.24119/4	Nut, self-locking, on Bolts	10	

PART NO.	Description.	NO. PER UNIT.	REMARKS

REAR BRAKES.

PART NO.	Description.	NO. PER UNIT.	REMARKS
11833	R.H.Rear Caliper Assembly less Friction Pads	1	*
11372	Piston	2	
11368	Pin, retaining Friction Pad	2	
11369	Clip, retaining Pin	2	
11374	Bridge Pipe Assembly	1	
11375	Bleed Screw	1	
1675	Dust Cap, on Bleed Screw	1	*
11832	L.H.Rear Caliper Assembly less Friction Pads	1	*
	Individual Items are as for 11833		
12248	Friction Pad Kit (Set of 4 Pads)	1	**
11376	Seals Kit, for Rear Calipers	1	**
C.22817	Adaptor Plate, for Caliper R.H.	1	
C.22818	Adaptor Plate, for Caliper L.H.	1	
C.26981	Bolt, securing Caliper to Adaptor Plate	4	
FG.107/X	Spring Washer, on Bolt	4	
C.21126	Wire locking Bolts	As req'd	
C.1919/2	Distance Piece. Caliper to Adaptor Plates	4	
C.13198	Shim(.005") for Caliper Adjustment	As req'd) Selective	
C.13199	Shim(.020") for Caliper Adjustment	As req'd) Sizes	
C.22764	Handbrake Mechanism Assy R.H.	1	
10125	Pad Carrier Assy, R.H.Inner	1	
9328	Pad Carrier Assy, R.H.Outer	1	
8938	Anchor Pin, for Return Spring	1	
9330	Operating Lever Assy	1	
8940	Return Spring	1	
8836	Pawl Assembly	1	
8837	Tension Spring, for Pawl	1	
8838	Anchor Pin, for Tension Spring	1	
8980	Adjusting Nut	1	
8840	Friction Spring, on Adj. Nut	1	
8841	Hinge Pin, securing operating Lever	1	
L.102/4U	Split Pin, through Hinge Pin	1	
9334	Protection Cover Assy. Outer	1	
9335	Protection Cover Assy. Inner	1	
9336	Bolt, securing Protection Covers	1	
BD.2906/3	Shakeproof Washer, on Bolt	1	
9749	Bolt, securing Pad Carriers to operating Levers	1	
L.102.5/10U	Split Pin, retaining Bolt	1	
C.22727	Handbrake Mechanism Assy L.H.	1	
10127	Pad Carrier Assy L.H.Inner	1	
9329	Pad Carrier Assy L.H.Outer	1	
9330	Operating Lever Assembly	1	

All other items are as for Mechanism C.22764

PART NO.	Description.	NO. PER UNIT.	REMARKS
	Rear Brakes (Continued).		
8016	Bolt, securing Handbrake Mechanism to Rear Caliper	4	
9750	Retraction Plate, on Bolts	2	
9751	Tab Washer, locking Bolts	2	
10531	Handbrake Mechanism Repair Kit	1	**
C.26779	Disc Assembly, for Rear Caliper	2	**

PART NO.	Description.	NO. PER UNIT.	REMARKS

BRAKE VACUUM SERVO.

PART NO.	Description.	NO. PER UNIT.	REMARKS
C.26024	Brake Vacuum Servo Assembly	1	*
10924	End Cover Assembly	1	
10936	Diaphragm	1	
10935	Support Plate, for Diaphragm	1	
10923	Return Spring, for Diaphragm	1	
10805	Key, retaining Push Rod in Support Plate	1	
10925	Servo Shell	1	
10933	Abutment Plate	1	
10880	Screw, Servo Shell to Slave Cylinder Body	3	
10934	Plate, locking Screws	1	
10937	Gasket, Servo Shell to Slave Cylinder Body	1	
10932	Spigot, for Push Rod	1	
10931	Seal, for Push Rod.by Spigot	1	
10930	Spacer, Seal to Primary Piston	1	
10927	Push Rod	1	
10926	Primary Piston Assembly	1	
10928	Pin, Primary Piston to Push Rod	1	
10929	Clip, round Primary Piston	1	
10895	Cup, on Primary Piston	1	
10894	Slave Cylinder Body	1	
11232	Secondary Piston	1	
10895	Cup Secondary Piston, Tapered End	1	
11236	Cup Secondary Piston, by Spring Seat	1	
10912	Washer, between Cup and Piston	1	
10896	Stop Pin	1	
10920	Return Spring, Secondary Piston	1	
10922	Spring Seat	1	
11235	Inlet Union, on Slave Cylinder Body	1	
2539	Copper Washer, on Inlet Union	1	
10921	Outlet Union (Female) on Slave Cylinder Body	1	
C.11356	Washer, on Outlet Union	1	
10889	Valve Assembly, below Outlet Union	1	
10891	Spring under Valve	1	
11237	Repair Kit, for Vacuum Servo	1	**
C.8737/2	Nut, securing Servo to Toe Board	3	
FW.105/T	Plain Washer, under Nut	3	
C.26005	Washer (Polyurethane)	3	
C.24618	Bracket, supporting Slave Cylinder	1	
UFS.119/5R	Setscrew, Bracket to Front Frame	1	
C.8737/9	Nut, on Setscrew	1	
AW.102/T	Plain Washer, under Nut	1	
UFS.131/3R	Setscrew, Bracket to Slave Cylinder	1	
C.725	Shakeproof Washer, on Setscrew	1	

PART NO.	Description.	NO. PER UNIT.	REMARKS

RESERVAC TANK FOR BRAKE SERVO.

PART NO.	Description.	NO. PER UNIT.	REMARKS	
C.24099	Reservac Tank Assembly	1		*
UFS.125/4R	Setscrew, securing Tank to Body	4		
FG.104/X	Spring Washer, on Setscrew	4		
C.30758	Hose, Reservac Tank to Adaptor	1		*
C.15886/5	Clip, securing Hose	2		
C.25168	Adaptor, on Check Valve for Hose	1		
C.14693	Check Valve Assembly	1		*
C.30757	Hose, Check Valve to Manifold	1		*
C.15886/5	Clip, securing Hose	2		
C.30757/1	Hose, Check Valve to "T" Piece	1)		*
C.15886/5	Clip, securing Hose	2)		
C.23211	"T" Piece Connecting Hoses	1)		
C.30757/2	Hose "T" Piece to Rear of Reaction Valve	1)		*
C.15886/5	Clip, securing Hose	2)		
C.30757/3	Hose "T" Piece to Vacuum Pipe	1)		*
C.15886/5	Clip, securing Hose	2)		
C.26612	Vacuum Pipe, behind Dash Top Panel	1)		
C.25339	Flange fixing Pipe at R.H.End(also C25308)	1)	R.H.Drive	
C.25309/1	Flange fixing Pipe at L.H.End	1)	Cars	
C.11712/1	Rivet, securing Pipe through Flanges	5)	only	
		)		
C.31146/7	Hose, Pipe to Front of Servo	1)		*
C.15886/5	Clip, securing Hose	2)		
C.31146/5	Hose, Front of Reaction Valve to Pipe	1)		*
C.15886/5	Clip, securing Hose	2)		
C.25308	Pipe, lower, behind Dash Top Panel	1)		
C.25339	Flange fixing Pipe at R.H. End (Also C.26612)	1)		
C.25309/1	Flange fixing Pipe at L.H.End	1)		
C.11712/1	Rivet, securing Pipe through Flanges	5)		
C.31146/6	Hose, lower Pipe to Rear of Servo	1)		*
C.15886/5	Clip, securing Hose	2)	R.H.Drive	
		)	Cars	
BD.7738/4	Clip, securing Hoses (C31146/6 and C31146/7) to Frame Side Member	1)	only	
		)		
C.30759	Hose, Check Valve to Vacuum Pipe	1)		*
C.15886/5	Clip, securing Hose	2)		
C.25308	Vacuum Pipe, behind Dash Top Panel	1)		
C.25309/1	Flange fixing Vacuum Pipe	2)		
C.11712/1	Rivet, securing Pipe and Flanges to Dash	6)	L.H.Drive Cars	
C.11046	Rubber Plug, sealing Redundant Holes in Dash	2)	only	
C.30760	Hose, Pipe to "T" Piece	1)		*
C.15886/5	Clip, securing Hose	2)		
BD.7738/4	Clip, securing Hose to Frame	1)		
C.23211	"T" Piece, connecting Hoses	1)		
C.30761	Hose, "T" Piece to Rear of Reaction Valve	1)		*

PART NO.	Description.	NO. PER UNIT.	REMARKS	

Reservac Tank for Brake Servo (Continued).

PART NO.	Description.	NO. PER UNIT.	REMARKS	
C.15886/5	Clip, securing Hose	2)	L.H.Drive	
C.30760	Hose "T" Piece to Front of Servo	1)	Cars	*
C.15886/5	Clip, securing Hose	2)	only	
C.30762	Hose, Front of Reaction Valve to Rear of Servo	1)		*
C.15886/5	Clip, securing Hose	2)		

BRAKE CONTROLS.

C.25291	Brake Pedal	1	R.H.Drive	
C.25292	Brake Pedal	1	L.H.Drive	
C.19154	Bush, in Brake Pedal	2		
C.25495	Return Spring, for Brake Pedal	1		**
C.25297	Fibre Washer, between Pedals and Housing	2		
C.25296	Spacer, between Brake and Clutch Pedals	1		
C.26532	Pad (Steel) on Brake Pedal	1		
C.8737/3	Nut, securing Pad to Pedal	1		
C.9934	Pad (Rubber) on Brake Pedal	1		**
C.25865	Brake Pedal	1)		
C.19154	Bush, in Brake Pedal	2)		
C.25495	Return Spring, for Brake Pedal	1)		**
C.25297	Fibre Washer, between Pedal and Housing	1)	For cars	
C.25381	Spacer, between Pedal and Housing	1)	Fitted with Automatic	
C.26535	Pad (Steel) on Brake Pedal	1)	Transmission	
C.8737/3	Nut, securing Pad to Pedal	1)	2+2 Models only	
C.21515	Pad (Rubber) on Brake Pedal	1)		**
C.25337	Cover Plate, over Clutch Master Cylinder Aperture in Pedal Housing	1)		
UCS.131/4R	Setscrew, securing Cover Plate	2)		
C.725	Shakeproof Washer, on Setscrew	2)		
C.25290	Pedal Housing	1		
C.18203	Stud, Housing to Scuttle	2		
C.25322	Stud, Housing to Scuttle	3		
C.8737/2	Nut, on Studs	5		
FW.105/T	Plain Washer, under Nuts	5		
C.25301	Gasket, Housing to Scuttle	1		
C.25295	Shaft, mounting Brake to Pedal	1		
C.8737/4	Nut, retaining Shaft in Housing	1		
FW.107/T	Plain Washer, under Nut	1		
UCS.125/14R	Setscrew, Brake Pedal Stop	1		
UCN.225/L	Nut, locking Setscrew	1		
C.26293	Brake Master Cylinder and Reaction Valve Assembly	1		*

PART NO.	Description.	NO. PER UNIT.	REMARKS

Brake Controls (Continued).

PART NO.	Description.	NO. PER UNIT.	REMARKS
11233	Master Cylinder Assembly(less Reaction Valve)	1	
10899	Valve Housing Assembly	1	
10915	Screw, Valve Housing to Master Cylinder Body	2	
10916	Shakeproof Washer, on Screw	2	
10904	Support, for Diaphragm	1	
10892	Reaction Valve Assembly, with Cover	1	Also part of 11305.
10907	Screw, securing Valve Cover to Housing	5	
N.S.S.	Boot, Rubber, Over End of Master Cylinder	1)	Part of Repair Kit No. 10918
N.S.S.	Gasket, Valve Housing to Master Cylinder	1)	
N.S.S.	Diaphragm, for Reaction Valve	1	Part of 11305
11233	Master Cylinder Assembly (less Reaction Valve)	1	*
10874	Body only	1	
10890	Piston Assembly	1	
10882	Piston Bearing (Inner)	1	
10878	Piston Bearing (Outer)	1	
10879	Circlip, retaining Bearings	1	
10883	Return Spring, for Piston	1	
10884	Retainer, holding Return Spring	1	
10885	Circlip, securing Retainer to Piston	1	
10886	Outlet Union, at Front of Body	1	
C.11356	Copper-Washer, on Outlet Union	1	
10889	Valve Assembly, below Outlet Union	1	
10891	Spring under Valve	1	
10875	Piston, operating Reaction Valve	1	
C.26292	Banjo for Hose from Fluid Reservoir	1	
11234	Bolt, securing Banjo	1	
2539	Copper Washer, on Banjo Bolt	2	
N.S.S.	Piston Seal, in Outer Bearing	1)	Part of Repair Kit No. 10918
N.S.S.	'O' Ring around Outer Bearing	1)	
N.S.S.	Seal, on Valve Piston	1)	
N.S.S.	'O' Ring, on Valve Piston	1)	
C.25321	Stud, securing Master Cylinder to Pedal Housing	2	
C.8667/2	Nut, on Stud	2	
C.26529	Push Rod Assembly	1	
J.105/14S	Joint Pin, securing Push Rod to Pedal	1	
L.102.5/6U	Split Pin, retaining Joint Pin	1	
FW.105/T	Plain Washer, behind Split Pin	1	

PART NO.	Description.	NO. PER UNIT.	REMARKS

Brake Controls (Continued).

10918	Repair Kit, for Brake Master Cylinder Comprising - Spring Retainer for Piston Main Clip, for Piston Piston Seal, in Outer Bearing 'O' Ring, around Outer Bearing Seal, on Valve Piston 'O' Ring, on Valve Piston Boot, Rubber, over End of Master Cylinder Gasket, Valve Housing to Master Cyl.Body	1	**
11305	Repair Kit, for Reaction Valve Comprising - Reaction Valve Assy with Cover Diaphragm for Reaction Valve	1	**

PART NO.	Description.	NO. PER UNIT.	REMARKS

HYDRAULIC BRAKE PIPES R.H. DRIVE.

PART NO.	Description.	NO. PER UNIT.	REMARKS	
C.23639	Reservoir Assembly, for Brake Fluid	2		*
C.23631	Filler Cap, with Switch	2		
C.23627	Protective Cap, over Switch Plunger	2		*
C.24856	Bracket, on R.H.Side of Dash for Fluid Reservoir Clamps	1)		
UFS.131/4R	Setscrew, securing Bracket to Dash	2)		
C.725	Shakeproof Washer, on Setscrew	2)		
C.24607	Outer Clamp mounting Fluid Reservoirs	1)	Standard Transmission	
C.24128	Inner Clamp mounting Fluid Reservoirs	1)		
C.20235	Stud, through Bracket and Clamps	1)		
C.8737/1	Nut, on Stud	2)		
C.25481	Bracket, on R.H.Side of Dash for Fluid Reservoir	1)	Automatic Transmission	
UFS.131/4R	Setscrew, securing Bracket to Dash	2)	2+2	
C.725	Shakeproof Washer, on Setscrew	2)	only	
UFB.125/20R	Bolt, clamping Reservoir in Bracket	1)		
C.8737/1	Nut, on Bolt	1)		
C.24619	Clip, mounting Reservoir to L.H.Side of Scuttle	1		
UFS.125/7R	Setscrew, securing Clip	1		
C.8737/1	Nut, on Setscrew	1		
FW.104/T	Plain Washer, under Nut	1		
C.20072/7	Low Pressure Hose, from Reservoir to Master Cylinder	1)	Standard Transmission	*
C.20072/10	Low Pressure Hose, from Reservoir to Master Cylinder	1)	Automatic Transmission 2+2 only.	*
C.20072/8	Low Pressure Hose, from Reservoir to Servo	1		
C.15886/4	Clip, securing Low Pressure Hoses	4		
C.25217	Hydraulic Pipe, Master Cylinder to Pipe Connector	1		
C.3923	Pipe Connector	1		
C.25218	Hydraulic Pipe, Pipe Connector to Rear of Servo	1		
C.26095	Hydraulic Pipe, Servo to 3 Way Union	1		
C.25390	3 Way Union, on Front Frame Bolt	1		
C.25391	Distance Piece, under 3 Way Union	2		
C.25220	Hydraulic Pipe, 3 Way Union to R.H. Front Flexible Hose	1		
C.25221	Hydraulic Pipe, 3 Way Union to L.H. Front Flexible Hose	1		

PART NO.	Description.	NO. PER UNIT.	REMARKS
	<u>Hydraulic Brake Pipes R.H.Drive (Continued).</u>		
C.30752	Front Flexible Hose	2	*
UFN.237/L	Nut, securing Flexible Hoses	4	
C.741	Shakeproof Washer, under Nut	4	
C.30443	Hydraulic Pipe, Flexible Hoses to Calipers	2	
C.26096	Hydraulic Pipe, from Servo to 3 Way Union on Dash	1	
C.25519	3 Way Union on Dash	1	
C.8136	Distance Piece, under Union	1	
UFS.131/10R	Setscrew, securing Union	1	
C.725	Shakeproof Washer, on Setscrew	1	
C.26257	Hydraulic Pipe, 3 Way Union to Rear Flexible Hose	1)	Open and F.H.Coupe only
C.25715	Hydraulic Pipe, 3 Way Union to Rear Flexible Hose	1)	2+2 only
C.30753	Rear Flexible Hose	1	Open & F.H.Coupe *
C.30754	Rear Flexible Hose	1	2+2 only *
UFN.237/L	Nut, securing Hose to Body Bracket	1	
C.741	Shakeproof Washer, under Nut	1	
C.11239	Copper Gasket, between Hose and 3 Way Union	1	
C.18834	3 Way Union on Rear Crossmember	1)	Open and F.H.Coupe only.
UFS.131/5R	Setscrew, securing 3 Way Union	1)	
UFN.131/L	Nut, on Setscrew	1)	
C.740	Shakeproof Washer, under Nut	1)	
C.25390	3 Way Union, on Rear Crossmember	1)	2+2 only.
UFS.131/9R	Setscrew, securing 3 Way Union	1)	
UFN.131/L	Nut, on Setscrew	1)	
C.740	Shakeproof Washer, under Nut	1)	
C.30495	Hydraulic Pipe, 3 Way Union to R.H. Rear Caliper	1)	Open and F.H.Coupe only
C.30496	Hydraulic Pipe, 3 Way Union to L.H. Rear Caliper	1)	
C.30609	Hydraulic Pipe, 3 Way Union to R.H. Rear Caliper	1)	2+2 only
C.30610	Hydraulic Pipe, 3 Way Union to L.H. Rear Caliper	1)	

PART NO.	Description.	NO. PER UNIT.	REMARKS

HYDRAULIC BRAKE PIPES L.H. DRIVE.

PART NO.	Description.	NO. PER UNIT	REMARKS
C.23639	Reservoir Assembly, for Brake Fluid	2	*
C.23631	Filler Cap, with Switch	2	*
C.23627	Protective Cap, over Switch Plunger	2	
C.17812	Bracket, fixing Reservoir Bracket to L.H.Side Member	2	
UFS.125/9R	Setscrew, securing Bracket	2	
UFN.125/L	Nut, on Setscrew	2	
C.724	Shakeproof Washer, under Nut	2	
C.18695	Shield, Protecting Reservoirs from Exhaust Heat	1)	Manual Steering only
C.30735	Shield, Protecting Reservoirs from Exhaust Heat	1)	Power Steering
UFS.131/7R	Setscrew, securing Shield and Reservoir Brackets	4	
C.18696	Spacer, on Setscrews	4)	Manual Steering only
C.725	Shakeproof Washer, on Setscrews	4	
FW.105/T	Plain Washer, on Setscrews	6	
UFN.131/L	Nut, on Lower Setscrews	2	
C.21255	Captive Nut, for Upper Set Screws	2	
C.20234	Bracket, Mounting Reservoirs	1	
C.19497	Clamp, securing Reservoirs to Bracket	2)	Standard Transmission
C.20235	Stud, through Bracket and Clamps	2)	
C.8737/1	Nut, on Studs	4)	
C.24607	Outer Clamp mounting Reservoirs	1)	
C.24128	Inner Clamp, mounting Reservoirs	1)	Automatic
C.20235	Stud, through Bracket and Clamp	1)	Transmission 2+2
C.8737/1	Nut, on Stud	2)	only
C.20009	Low Pressure Hose, from Reservoir to Master Cylinder	1	*
C.20072/7	Low Pressure Hose, from Reservoir to Servo	1	*
C.15886/4	Clip, securing Low Pressure Hoses	4	
C.25672	Hydraulic Pipe, Master Cylinder to Rear of Servo	1	
C.26095	Hydraulic Pipe, Servo to 3 Way Union	1	
C.25390	3 Way Union on Front Frame Bolt	1	
C.25391	Distance Piece, under Union	2	
C.25220	Hydraulic Pipe, 3 Way Union to R.H. Front Flexible Hose	1	
C.25221	Hydraulic Pipe, 3 Way Union to L.H. Front Flexible Hose	1	

PART NO.	Description.	NO. PER UNIT.	REMARKS

Hydraulic Brake Pipes L.H.Drive (Continued).

PART NO.	Description.	NO. PER UNIT.	REMARKS
C.30752	Front Flexible Hose	2	*
UFN.237/L	Nut, securing Flexible Hoses	4	
C.741	Shakeproof Washer, under Nut	4	
C.30443	Hydraulic Pipe, Flexible Hoses to Calipers	2	
C.26096	Hydraulic Pipe, from Servo to 3 Way Union on Dash	1	
C.25519	3 Way Union on Dash	1	
C.8136	Distance Piece, under Union	1	
UFS.131/10R	Setscrew, securing Union	1	
C.725	Shakeproof Washer, on Setscrew	1	
C.26257	Hydraulic Pipe, 3 Way Union to Rear Flexible Hose	1))	Open and F.H.Coupe only
C.25715	Hydraulic Pipe, 3 Way Union to Rear Flexible Hose	1))	2+2 only
C.30753	Rear Flexible Hose	1	Open and F.H.Coupe *
C.30754	Rear Flexible Hose	1	2+2 only *
UFN.237/L	Nut, securing Hose to Body Bracket	1	
C.741	Shakeproof Washer, under Nut	1	
C.11239	Copper Gasket, between Hose and 3 Way Union	1	
C.18834	3 Way Union on Rear Crossmember	1)	
UFS.131/5R	Setscrew, securing Union	1)	Open and
UFN.131/L	Nut, on Setscrew	1)	F.H.Coupe
C.740	Shakeproof Washer, on Setscrew	1)	only
C.25390	3 Way Union on Rear Crossmember	1)	
UFS.131/9R	Setscrew, securing Union	1)	2+2
UFN.131/L	Nut, on Setscrew	1)	only
C.740	Shakeproof Washer, on Setscrew	1)	
C.30495	Hydraulic Pipe, 3 Way Union to R.H. Rear Carrier	1))	Open and
C.30496	Hydraulic Pipe, 3 Way Union to L.H. Rear Caliper	1))	F.H.Coupe only
C.30609	Hydraulic Pipe, 3 Way Union to R.H. Rear Caliper	1))	2+2 only
C.30610	Hydraulic Pipe, 3 Way Union to L.H. Rear Caliper	1)	

PART NO.	Description.	NO. PER UNIT.	REMARKS	

HANDBRAKE CONTROL.

PART NO.	Description.	NO. PER UNIT.	REMARKS	
C.16823	Handbrake Lever Assembly	1	Open & F.H.Coupe	*
C.25579	Handbrake Lever Assembly	1)	2+2 Manual Trans Fitted up to 1R35018 R.H.D. 1R40237 L.H.D.	*
C.30222	Handbrake Lever Assembly	1)	2+2 Manual Trans. fitted from 1R35019 R.H.D. 1R40238 L.H.D.	*
C.25579	Handbrake Lever Assembly	1)	2+2 Automatic Transmission	*
UFS.531/6R	Setscrew, securing Handbrake Lever	4)	Open and	
C.17879	Tapped Plate, at Rear Fixing	1)	F.H.Coupe only	
UFS.131/5R	Setscrew, securing Handbrake Lever to Tunnel at Side	2)		
UFS.131/6R	Setscrew, securing Handbrake Lever to Tunnel at Top	1)	2+2 Models	
C.19706	Spacer, on Top Setscrew	1)	only	
FG.105/X	Spring Washer, on Setscrew	3)		
C.25335	Rubber Seal, Handbrake Lever to Tunnel	1)		
C.16660	Switch, for Handbrake Warning Lamp	1		
UFN.225/L	Nut, securing Switch	2		
C.18737	Bracket, mounting Switch	1)	Open and	
UFS.119/8R	Setscrew, securing Bracket to Lever	1)	F.H.Coupe	
C.8667/17	Nut, on Setscrew	1)	only	
FW.102/T	Plain Washer, on Setscrew	2)		
C.18738	Spring Striker, for Switch	1)		
C.23096	Cable Abutment Bracket	1)	2+2	
UFS.131/7R	Setscrew, securing Bracket to Tunnel	2)	only	
FG.105/X	Spring Washer, on Setscrew	2)		
C.20401	Handbrake Cable Assembly	1)		*
J.105/10S	Clevis Pin, securing Cable at Ends	2)	Open and	
L.103/7U	Split Pin, retaining Clevis Pin	2)	F.H.Coupe	
FW.105/T	Plain Washer, Behind Split Pin	1)	only	
C.17432	Grommet, in Tunnel for Cable	1)		
C.30221	Handbrake Cable Assembly	1)		*
UFS.125/8R	Setscrew, securing Cable to Abutment Bracket	1)		
FG.104/X	Spring Washer, on Setscrew	1)	2+2	
J.105/9S	Clevis Pin, securing Cable at Ends	2)	only	
L.103/7U	Split Pin, retaining Clevis Pins	2)		
FW.105/T	Plain Washer, behind Split Pins	2)		

PART NO.	Description.	NO. PER UNIT.	REMARKS

Handbrake Control (Continued).

PART NO.	Description.	NO. PER UNIT	REMARKS
C.22955	Handbrake Compensator Complete	1	
UFS.131/5R	Setscrew, securing Compensator to Rear Crossmember	2	
FG.105/X	Spring Washer, on Setscrew	2	
J.105/10S	Clevis Pin, securing Compensator to Handbrake Mechanism Levers	2	
L.103/7U	Split Pin, retaining Clevis Pins	2	
FW.105/T	Plain Washer, on Clevis Pin Retaining Link	1	

POWER STEERING PUMP AND HYDRAULICS.

PART NO.	Description.	NO. PER UNIT	REMARKS
C.31435	Oil Pump Assembly	1	*
C.29833	Pulley, for Oil Pump	1	*
C.21111	Key, securing Pulley to Oil Pump	1	*
432429	Washer, at side of Pulley	1	
UCS.131/7R	Setscrew, securing Pulley to Pump	1	
FG.105/X	Spring Washer, on Setscrew	1	
C.29829	Mounting Plate Assembly for Oil Pump	1	
UFB.125/6R	Bolt, securing Pump to Mounting Plate	4	
FG.104/X	Spring Washer, on Bolt	4	
UFB.131/19R	Bolt, securing Mounting Plate to L.H. Front Engine Bracket	1	
C.740	Shakeproof Washer, on Bolt	1	
C.30620	Stud, securing Mounting Plate, Water Pump and Timing Cover to Block	1	
UFN.131/L	Nut, on Stud	1	
UFB.137/12R	Bolt, securing Mounting Plate and Timing Cover to Block	1	
C.29834	Belt, driving Water Pump and Power Steering Oil Pump	1	*
C.30795	Reservoir, for Oil Feed to Power Steering Unit	1	
C.31174	Heatshield, for Reservoir	1	R.H.Drive only
C.30732	Bracket Assembly, mounting Reservoir	1	R.H.Drive only
UFS.125/4R	Setscrew, securing Reservoir to Bracket	3	
UFN.125/L	Nut, on Setscrew	3	
C.724	Shakeproof Washer, on Setscrew	3	
C.30733	Bracket Assembly, mounting Reservoir	1	L.H.Drive only
UFS.125/6R	Setscrew, securing Reservoir to Bracket	3	
BD.27907	Spacer, on Setscrew	3	
UFN.125/L	Nut, on Setscrew	3	
C.724	Shakeproof Washer, under Nut	3	
C.17811	Clamp Plate, for Bracket	1	

PART NO.	Description.	NO. PER UNIT.	REMARKS	

Power Steering Pump and Hydraulics (Continued).

PART NO.	Description.	NO. PER UNIT.	REMARKS	
UFS.125/9R	Setscrew, through Bracket and Clamp Plate	1		
UFN.125/L	Nut, on Setscrew	1		
C.724	Shakeproof Washer, under Nut	1		
C.30597	High Pressure Hose, Pump to Rack Assembly	1)		*
C.30596	Low Pressure Hose, Rack to Reservoir	1)		*
C.2905/3	Clip, securing Hose	1)	R.H.Drive	
C.30598	Low Pressure Hose, Reservoir to Pump	1)		*
C.2905/2	Clip, securing Hose	2)		
C.29559	High Pressure Hose, Pump to Rack Assy	1)		*
C.29558	Low Pressure Hose, Rack to Reservoir	1)		*
C.2905/3	Clip, securing Hose	1)	L.H.Drive	
C.29560	Low Pressure Hose, Reservoir to Pump	1)		*
C.2905/2	Clip, securing Hose	2)		

PART NO.	Description.	NO. PER UNIT.	REMARKS

STEERING UNIT. POWER ASSISTED.

PART NO.	Description.	NO. PER UNIT.	REMARKS
C.28621	Rack and Pinion Assembly Complete	1	R.H.Drive *
12031	Housing for Rack and Pinion	1	
12032	Rack only	1	
12030	Valve Body, Valve & Pinion Assembly	1	
12033	Oil Transfer Pipe, Short	1	
12034	Oil Transfer Pipe, Long	1	
12008	Adaptor for Short Pipe	1	
12000	Air Balance Pipe	1	
12004	Air Pipe Connection (Pinion End)	1	
12005	Fibre Washer, under Connection	1	
12003	Air Pipe Connection	1	
11986	Circlip, at top of Pinion Housing	1	
11987	Seat, in Pinion Housing for High Pressure Hose	1	
11988	Seat, in Pinion Housing for Low Pressure Hose	1	
11989	Plug (Trim Screw) in Pinion Housing	1	
11990	Ball Bearing, for Pinion	1	
11991	Seal Housing, below Ball Bearing	1	
12002	Circlip, below Ball Bearing	1	
11992	Needle Bearing, at Bottom of Pinion	1	
12020	Liner, between Valve Body and Rack Housing	1	
11993	Stud, securing Valve Body to Rack Housing	3	
11999	Nut, self locking on Stud	3	
12016	Plunger, applying Friction to Rack	1	
12017	Spring, for Plunger	1	
12015	Screwed Plug, retaining Spring and Plunger	1	
11994	Grease Nipple, in Screwed Plug	1	
12018	Locknut, retaining Screwed Plug in Housing	1	
11995	Seal Housing, in Rack Tube	1	
11996	Ring Seal Housing in Rack Tube	1	
12010	Piston, on Rack	1	
12011	Ring, on Piston	1	
12009	Circlip, retaining Piston on Rack	2	
12012	Clevite Bush, in Tube for Rack	1	
11997	Special Ring Nut, on Tube	1	
11998	Circlip, on Tube for Ring Nut	1	
12035	Bush, Cylinder End for Long Oil Pipe	1	
12024	Adaptor on Ends of Rack for Tie Rods	2	
12019	Tab Washer, locking Adaptors	2	
12021	Spring, for Ball Pin Tie Rods	2	
C.7599	Socket, for Ball Pin Tie Rods	2	
12025	Shim, between Socket and Adaptor	As req'd	
12022	Packing Washer, for Ball Pin	2	
C.15418	Ball Pin Tie Rod	2	
C.10026	Housing, for Ball Pin	2	
C.15408	Tab Washer, locking Housing	2	
12014	Bellows, at Ends of Rack Housing	2	**
12013	Tie Wire, securing Bellow to Rack Housing	2	**

PART NO.	Description.	NO. PER UNIT.	REMARKS	
	Steering Unit. Power Assisted (Continued).			
C.2905/2	Clip, securing Bellows to Tie Rods	2		
C.25447	Ball Joint Assembly, at Outer End of Ball Pin Tie Rods	2		**
C.15409	Locknut, securing Ball Joint to Tie Rods	2		
12036	Mounting Plate (Pinion End)	1		
12037	Mounting Plate (Cylinder End)	1		
11983	Seals Kit, for use when Overhauling Rack and Pinion Assembly	1		**
C.25447	Ball Joint Assembly, at Outer Ends of Ball Pin Tie Rods	2		**
C.3363/1	Grease Nipple	2		**
C.22976	Washer, under Grease Nipple	2		**
C.22975	Rubber Washer, under Grease Nipple	2		**
C.22683	Gaiter, over Ball Joints	2		**
C.22685	Ring, securing Gaiters	2		**
C.8737/5	Nut, securing Ball Joint to Steering Arm	2		**
C.791	Plain Washer, under Nut	2		**
C.28622	Rack and Pinion Assembly Complete	1	L.H.Drive	*
12041	Housing, for Rack and Pinion	1		
12040	Valve Body, Valve and Pinion Assy	1		
12042	Oil Transfer Pipe, Short	1		
12043	Oil Transfer Pipe, Long	1		
12246	Mounting Plate (Pinion End)	1		
	All other items are as for Rack and Pinion Assembly C.28621			
C.26007	Rubber Mounting, for Rack and Pinion Assembly	2		**
UFS.131/6R	Setscrew, securing Rubber Mounting to Rack and Pinion Assembly	2		
UFS.131/24R	Setscrew, securing Mounting to Crossmember at Pinion End	1		
UFB.131/13R	Bolt, securing Mounting to Crossmember at Pinion End	1		
C.18901	Distance Tube, on Setscrew and Bolt	2		
C.15183	Plain Washer, on Setscrew and Bolt	2		
UFS.131/24R	Setscrew, securing Mounting to Crossmember at Cylinder End	1		
UFS.131/12R	Setscrew, securing Mounting to Crossmember at Cylinder End	1		
UFN.131/L	Nut, locking Setscrews	2		
C.725	Shakeproof Washer, on Setscrews	2		
C.15183	Plain Washer, on Setscrews	2		
C.8667/2	Nut (self-locking) on Setscrews, Bolts and Studs on Rubber Mountings	12		

PART NO.	Description.	NO. PER UNIT.	REMARKS	

STEERING UNIT. MANUAL.

PART NO.	Description.	NO. PER UNIT.	REMARKS	
C.25492	Rack and Pinion Assembly complete	1	R.H.Drive	*
C.25934	Housing for Rack and Pinion	1		
C.15093	Rack only	1		
C.25711	Pinion only	1		
C.15203	Bearing, Bottom of Pinion	1		
C.25721	Bearing, Top of Pinion	1		
C.15205	Thrust Plate, retaining Pinion	1		
C.15206	Attachment Bracket	1		
C.15208	'O' Ring, Top of Pinion	1		
C.15209	Retainer, for 'O' Ring	1		
C.20107	Stud, Top of Pinion Housing	3		
C.8737/2	Nut, on Studs	3		
C.3363/1	Grease Nipple, on Pinion Housing	1		
C.20145	Plunger, at Top of Housing	1		
C.15199	Shim (.004") Top of Plunger	As req'd) Selective		
C.15198	Shim (.010") Top of Plunger	As req'd) Sizes		
C.20146	Spring, under Cover	1		
C.20147	Cover, over Plunger, Spring and Shims	1		
C.15202	Circlip, securing Cover	1		
C.15210	Bush, in Tube for Rack	1		
C.15418	Ball Pin Tie Rod at Ends of Rack	2		
C.10026	Housing, for Ball Pins	2		
C.7599	Socket, under Ball Pins	2		
C.8472	Spring, behind Sockets	2		
C.15407	Nut, locking Ball Pin Housing to Rack	2		
C.15408	Tab Washer, locking Nuts	2		
C.15409	Nut, locking Tie Rod Ends to Tie Rods	2		
C.30119	Bellows at Ends of Housing	2		**
C.15211	Tie Wire, securing Bellows to Pinion Housing	1		
C.2905/4	Clip, securing Bellows to Rack Tube	1		
C.2905/2	Clip, securing Bellows to Tie Rods	2		
C.25447	Ball Joints Assembly, for Tie Rods	2		**
C.25493	Rack and Pinion Assembly Complete	1	L.H.Drive	*
C.25935	Housing for Rack and Pinion	1		
C.15207	Attachment Bracket	1		
	All other items are as for Rack and Pinion Assembly C.25492.			
C.25447	Ball Joint Assembly, for Tie Rods	2		** **
C.3363/1	Grease Nipple	2		**
C.22976	Washer, under Grease Nipples	2		**
C.22975	Rubber Washer, under Grease Nipple	2		**
C.22683	Gaiter, over Ball Joint	2		**
C.22685	Ring, securing Gaiters	2		**
C.8737/5	Nut, securing Ball Joint to Steering Arm	2		**
C.791	Plain Washer, under Nut	2		

PART NO.	Description.	NO. PER UNIT.	REMARKS	

Steering Unit. Manual (Continued).

PART NO.	Description.	NO. PER UNIT.	REMARKS	
C.20087	Rubber Mounting for Rack and Pinion Assembly	2	Open and F.H.Coupe	**
C.26007	Rubber Mounting for Rack and Pinion Assembly	2	2+2 Models	**
UFS.131/6R	Setscrew, Mounting to Rack and Pinion Assembly	2		
UFS.131/4R	Setscrew, securing Mounting to Crossmember at Pinion End	1		
UFB.131/13R	Bolt, securing Mounting to Crossmember at Pinion End	1		
C.18901	Distance Tube, on Setscrew and Bolt	2		
C.15183	Plain Washer, on Setscrew and Bolt	2		
UFS.131/24R	Setscrew, securing Mounting to Crossmember at Rack Tube End	1		
UFS.131/12R	Setscrew, securing Mounting to Crossmember at Rack Tube End	1		
UFN.131/L	Nut, locking Setscrews	2		
C.725	Shakeproof Washer, under Nuts	2		
C.15183	Plain Washer, on Setscrew	2		
C.8667/2	Nut, on Setscrew, Bolt and on Stud of Rubber Mountings	12		

PART NO.	Description.	NO. PER UNIT.	REMARKS

STEERING COLUMN.

PART NO.	Description.	NO. PER UNIT.	REMARKS	
C.28542	Upper Steering Column Assembly	1	R.H.Drive	*
C.28543	Upper Steering Column Assembly	1	L.H.Drive	*
C.15619	Shaft, for Steering Wheel	1		
C.16676	Stop Button	1		
C.15419	Locknut, Clamping Shaft to Inner Column	1		
C.17938	Split Collet, Inside Locknut	1		
C.18235	Circlip	1		
C.29129	Bracket, mounting Ignition and Direction Indicator Switches	1	R.H.Drive	
C.29128	Bracket, mounting Ignition and Direction Indicator Switches	1	L.H.Drive	
UCS.119/3R	Setscrew, securing Bracket to Upper Column	3		
C.723A	Shakeproof Washer, on Setscrew	3		

The above Brackets are NOT required when Combined Steering Column Lock and Ignition Switch is fitted.

PART NO.	Description.	NO. PER UNIT.	REMARKS
C.30601	Steering Column Lock and Ignition Switch Assembly	1	L.H.Drive
C.31557	Steering Column Lock and Ignition Switch Assembly	1)))	R.H.Drive fitted from 1R1058 Open 1R20095 F.H.Coupe 1R35099 2+2
C.26851	Cover (Rubber) Protecting Switch Terminals	1	
C.29134	Mounting Bracket, for Direction Indicator Switch	1	
UCS.119/3R	Setscrew, securing Bracket to Upper Column	3	
C.723A	Shakeproof Washer, on Setscrew	3	

The above Bracket is only required when Steering Column Lock is fitted.

PART NO.	Description.	NO. PER UNIT.	REMARKS	
C.28522	Ignition Switch	1		

NOT required when Steering Column Lock is fitted.

PART NO.	Description.	NO. PER UNIT.	REMARKS	
C.28489	Direction Indicator/Horn/Headlamp Flasher Switch	1		*
C.28490	Cover over Switch	1		
C.25520	Drive Clip, for Direction Indicator Striker	1		
C.14007/1	Setscrew, securing Drive Clip to Inner Column	2		
C.23008	Plain Washer, on Setscrew	2		
C.723A	Shakeproof Washer, on Setscrew	2		
C.28590	Steering Wheel	1		
C.28573	Motif in Centre of Steering Wheel	1		
C.18304	Grub Screw, in Steering Wheel Hub	3		
C.7878	Split Cone (Pairs)	1		
C.7879	Nut, locking Steering Wheel to Shaft	1		
C.15885	Plain Washer, under Nut	1		
C.11820/7	Pal-Nut locking Nut	1		

PART NO.	Description.	NO. PER UNIT.	REMARKS	

Steering Column (Continued).

PART NO.	Description.	NO. PER UNIT	REMARKS	
C.29140	Bracket Mounting Upper Column	1		
BD.21068/6	Edge Beading, for Bracket (21"long)	1		
UFS.131/5R	Setscrew, Bracket to Body	4		
FW.105/T	Plain Washer, on Setscrew	4		
FG.105/X	Spring Washer, on Setscrew	4		
UFB.137/10R	Bolt, Column to Bracket	2		
BD.541/43	Special Washer, on Bolt	4		
FW.106/T	Plain Washer, on Bolt	2		
C.8667/3	Nut, on Bolt	2		
UFS.131/6R	Setscrew, Lower Mounting to Body	2		
FW.105/T	Plain Washer, on Setscrew	2		
FG.105/X	Spring Washer, on Setscrew	2		
C.29851	Lower Steering Column Assembly	1	Manual Steering	*
C.30853	Lower Steering Column Assembly	1	Power Steering	*
C.28599	Universal Joint.Lower Column Lower	1		
UFB.131/14R	Bolt, clamping Joint to Column	1		
C.8737/2	Nut, on Bolt	1		
C.17469	Screw, securing Joint to Steering Pinion	1		
FG.104/X	Spring Washer, on Screw	1		
C.28600	Universal Joint. Lower Column Upper	1		
UFB.131/11R	Bolt, clamping Joint to Upper and Lower Columns	2		
C.8737/2	Nut, on Bolt	2		
BD.19714	Housing,for Lower Column Seal	1)		
UFS.125/5R	Setscrew, securing Housing to Dash	4)		
FW.104/T	Plain Washer, on Setscrew	4)		
UFN.125/L	Nut, on Setscrew	4)		
C.724	Shakeproof Washer, under Nut	4)	R.H.Drive	
C.25580	Gasket, under Housing	1)	Cars only	
C.20488	Seal, at Bottom of Housing	1)		
BD.19710	Retainer, for Seal	1)		
BD.27837/1	Screw, securing Retainer to Housing	3)		
C.17845	Housing for Lower Steering Column	1)		
C.17851	Pivot Bush, at Sides of Housing	2)		
C.17848	Stud, securing Housing to Scuttle	4)		
C.8667/1	Nut, on Studs	4)		
FW.104/T	Plain Washer, under Nuts	4)		
C.25578	Gasket, under Housing	1)	L.H.Drive	
C.20488	Seal, at Bottom of Housing	1)	Cars only	
BD.19710	Retainer, for Seal	1)		
UCS.413/3H	Setscrew, securing Retainer to Housing	3)		
C.721	Shakeproof Washer, on Setscrew	3)		

PART NO.	Description.	NO. PER UNIT.	REMARKS

COOLING SYSTEM.

PART NO.	Description.	NO. PER UNIT.	REMARKS
C.28274	Radiator Block Assembly	1	Manual Transmission.
C.28098	Radiator Block Assembly	1	Automatic Trans. 2+2 only
C.28365	Filler Cap, for Radiator	1	**
C.28280	Radiator Mounting Bracket R.H.	1	
C.28281	Radiator Mounting Bracket L.H.	1	
UFS.131/4R	Setscrew, Bracket to Radiator	2	
C.725	Shakeproof Washer, on Setscrew	2	
BD.31996	Pad (Polyurethane) on Top of Radiator	1	*
C.8975	Rubber Pad, for Radiator Mounting	4	*
C.18283	Distance Collar, through Pads	2	
C.8737/3	Nut, securing Radiator to Front Sub-Frame	2	
BD.541/2	Plain Washer, under Nuts	2	
C.28742	Radiator Side Tie Strut	2	
C.28743	Bracket, for Strut	2	
UFS.125/8R	Setscrew, securing Strut to Bracket	2	
C.10126	Grommet, on Setscrew	2	*
C.26484	Distance Piece, through Grommet	2	
BD.541/20	Plain Washer, on Setscrew	2	
UFN.125/L	Nut, on Setscrew	2	
C.724	Shakeproof Washer, under Nut	2	
C.2354	Drain Tap, for Radiator	1	*
C.981	Fibre Washer, on Drain Tap	As req'd	*
C.26573	Thermostatic Switch in Radiator for Fan Motors	1	Fitted up to 7R5263 7R37489
C.33598	Thermostatic Switch in Radiator for Fan Motors	1	Fitted from 7R5264 7R37490 *
C.2475	Gasket, under Switch	1	*
UFS.119/4R	Setscrew, securing Switch	3	
C.723A	Shakeproof Washer, on Setscrew	3	
C.28150	Cooling Fan Assembly	2	*
C.8667/1	Nut, securing Fan to Motor	2	
FW.104/T	Plain Washer, under Nut	2	
C.28133	Electric Motor Driving Fan	2	*
C.28151	Motor Mounting Bracket R.H.	1	
C.28152	Motor Mounting Bracket L.H.	1	
C.18110	Grommet (Rubber) in Brackets	8	*
C.8667/17	Nut, securing Motors to Brackets	8	
C.18111	Plain Washer, under Nuts	8	
UFS.119/4R	Setscrew, securing Motor Brackets to Fan Cowl	6	
C.8667/17	Nut, on Setscrews	6	
C.28130	Fan Cowl	1	
UFS.125/4R	Setscrew, securing Cowl to Radiator	6	
C.724	Shakeproof Washer, on Setscrew	6	
C.18444	Duct Shield, Bottom of Radiator to Sub-Frame Cross Tube	1	
C.1040/20	Clip, securing Shield to Sub-Frame	3	

PART NO.	Description.	NO. PER UNIT.	REMARKS

Cooling System (Continued).

PART NO.	Description.	NO. PER UNIT.	REMARKS
UFS.125/4R	Setscrew, securing Shield and Clips	5	
C.8737/1	Nut, on Setscrews	5	
FW.104/T	Plain Washer, on Screws at Clip fixing	3	
C.29050	Water Expansion Tank on Dash	1	
C.18484	Filler Cap (7 lbs)	1	
C.19798/5	Overflow Pipe (Rubber) for Tank	1	
C.28318	Bracket, on Dash, Mounting Tank	1	
UFS.419/8H	Setscrew, securing Bracket to Dash	3)	R.H.Drive
BD.18957/1	Distance Piece, on Setscrew	3)	only
C.723A	Shakeproof Washer, on Setscrew	3)	
UFS.419/4H	Setscrew, securing Bracket to Dash	3)	L.H.Drive
C.723A	Shakeproof Washer, on Setscrew	3)	only
C.28325	Mounting Pad.(Polyurethane) for Tank	1	
C.28321	Front Strap.Clamping Tank into Bracket	1	
UFS.119/7R	Setscrew, securing Front Strap to Rear Strap	2	
UFN.119/L	Nut, on Setscrew	2	
C.723/A	Shakeproof Washer, on Setscrew	2	
C.28163	Hose, Top, Radiator to Water Manifold	1	
C.2905/5	Clip securing Hose	2	
C.28328/2	Hose, Radiator to Expansion Tank	1	R.H.Drive only
C.28328/1	Hose, Radiator to Expansion Tank	1	L.H.Drive only
C.2905/1	Clip, securing Hose	2	
C.23548/2	Hose, Radiator to Thermostat Bleed	1	
C.15996/3	Clip, securing Hose	2	
C.29642	Hose.Pump to Connecting Pipe	1)	Fitted to all
C.29644	Connecting Pipe, between Hoses	1)	Cars Except
C.29643	Hose, Connecting Pipe to Radiator (Bottom)	1)	R.H.Drive Power Steering
C.2905/6	Clip, securing Hoses to Pipe and Radiator	3)	Models
C.2905/7	Clip, securing Hose to Pump	1)	
C.29850	Hose.Pump to Radiator (Bottom)	1)	R.H.Drive
C.2905/6	Clip, securing Hose to Radiator	1)	Power Steering
C.2905/7	Clip, securing Hose to Pump	1)	only

PART NO.	Description.	NO. PER UNIT.	REMARKS	

EXHAUST SYSTEM.

PART NO.	Description.	NO. PER UNIT.	REMARKS	
C.28201	Heat Shield for Exhaust Down Pipes	1		
UFS.125/6R	Setscrew, Heat Shield to Lower Bracket	1		
FW.104/T	Plain Washer, on Setscrew	2		
UFN.125/L	Nut, on Setscrew	1		
C.724	Shakeproof Washer, under Nut	1		
UFS.131/8R	Setscrew, Heat Shield to Upper Bracket	4		
UFN.131/L	Nut, on Setscrew	4		
C.725	Shakeproof Washer, under Nut	4		
FW.105/T	Plain Washer, under Shakeproof Washer	4		
BD.28582	Bracket, Lower, Mounting Heat Shield to L.H.Frame Side Member	1		
C.26490	Bracket, Upper, Mounting Heat Shield to L.H.Frame Side Member	2		
C.26530	Clamp, holding Upper Brackets to Side Member	2)	R.H.Drive Manual	
UFS.125/9R	Setscrew, securing Clamps to Brackets	2)	Steering	
UFN.125/L	Nut, on Setscrew	2)	only	
C.724	Shakeproof Washer, under Nut	2)		
C.18426	Down Pipe, Front Manifold to Silencer	1)		*
C.1759	Flexible Pipe in Down Pipe	1)	Open	**
C.18401	Flange, on Down Pipe	1)	and F.H.Coupe Models	*
		)	only	
C.18427	Down Pipe, Rear Manifold to Silencer	1)		*
C.1759	Flexible Pipe, in Down Pipe	1)		**
C.18401	Flange, on Down Pipe	1)		
C.26073	Down Pipes Assembly, Manifolds to Silencers	1)	2+2 Models	*
C.1759	Flexible Pipe, in Down Pipes	2)	only	**
C.18401	Flange, on Down Pipes	2)		
C.18405/1	Sealing Ring, Down Pipes to Manifolds	2		**
C.17916	Nut, securing Down Pipes to Manifolds	8		**
FW.106/T	Plain Washer, under Nut	8		
C.13063	Clip, securing Down Pipes to Silencers	2		*
UFB.131/22R	Bolt, through Clips	2		
UFN.131/L	Nut, on Bolt	2		
FW.105/T	Plain Washer, under Nuts	2		
C.23869	Twin Silencers Assembly	1)		*
C.23870	R.H.Silencer	1)		*
C.23871	L.H.Silencer	1)		*
C.21786	Mounting Strap, for Silencers	2)		
C.18986	Stiffener for Silencer	1)	Open and	
		)		
C.8397	Rubber Mounting, for Silencer Assembly	4)	F.H.Coupe	**
UFS.131/6R	Setscrew, securing Silencers to Mounting	4)	Models only	
FW.105/T	Plain Washer, on Setscrew	4)		
C.8667/2	Nut, on Setscrew	4)		
		)		
UFN.131/L	Nut, securing Mountings to Body	8)		
C.725	Shakeproof Washer, under Nuts	8)		

PART NO.	Description.	NO. PER UNIT.	REMARKS

Exhaust System (Continued).

C.26747	Silencer Assembly	2)	*
C.27323	Strap, supporting Silencers at Front	1)	
C.27324	Clamp, holding Silencers to Front Strap	1)	
UFS.125/13R	Setscrew, Strap to Clamp (between Silencers)	1)	
UFS.125/5R	Setscrew, Strap to Clamp (Outside Silencers)	2)	
C.8737/1	Nut, on Setscrew	3)	
C.26153	Strap, supporting Silencers at Rear	1)	
C.26152	Clamp, holding Silencers to Rear Strap	1)	
UFS.125/13R	Setscrew, Strap to Clamp (Between Silencers)	1)	
UFS.125/9R	Setscrew, Strap to Clamp (Outside Silencers)	2)	2+2 Models only
C.26158	Special Washer, on Outer Setscrews	4)	
C.8737/1	Nut, on Setscrews	3)	
C.26150	Rubber Mounting, securing Silencers to Body	4)	**
C.8737/1	Nut, securing Mountings to Body	8)	
C.26151	Washer Plate, under Nuts	4)	
UFS.125/6R	Setscrew, securing Silencer Straps to Mounting	8)	
FW.104/T	Plain Washer, on Setscrews	8)	
C.26151	Washer Plate, on Setscrews	4)	
C.8737/1	Nut, on Setscrews	8)	
C.18433	Exhaust Tail Pipe	2	
C.27423	Strap, linking Tail Pipes together	1	
C.18196	Clip, securing Tail Pipes to Silencers	2	*
UFB.131/22R	Bolt, through Clips	2	
FW.105/T	Plain Washer, on Bolts	2	
UFN.131/L	Nut, on Bolt	2	
C.13063	Clip, securing Tail Pipes to Mufflers	2	*
UFB.131/22R	Bolt, through Clip	2	
FW.105/T	Plain Washer, on Bolt	2	
UFN.131/L	Nut, on Bolt	2	
C.30821	R.H.Muffler Assembly	1	*
C.30822	L.H.Muffler Assembly	1	*
C.18975	Tie Plate, between Mufflers	1	Open and F.H.Coupe
C.26159	Tie Plate, and Ring, between Mufflers	1	2+2 Models
UFS.125/5R	Setscrew, securing Tie Plate to Mufflers	2	
C.8667/1	Nut, on Setscrew	2	

PART NO.	Description.	NO. PER UNIT.	REMARKS

Exhaust System (Continued).

1363	Rubber Mounting for Mufflers	1)	**
UFS.131/6R	Setscrew, securing Mountings to Tie Plate	1)	
UFN.131/L	Nut, on setscrew	1)	
C.725	Shakeproof Washer, under Nut	1)	Open
		)	and
C.17462	Bracket, on Body for Rubber Mounting	1)	F.H.Coupe
C.8667/2	Nut, securing Bracket to Body	2)	Models
UFS.131/5R	Setscrew, securing Mounting to Bracket	2)	only
UFN.131/L	Nut, on Setscrew	2)	
C.725	Shakeproof Washer, under Nut	2)	
		)	
C.19018	Hooked Safety Bracket, on Setscrews	1)	
C.25020	Rubber Mounting, for Mufflers	1)	**
C.26160	Mounting Bar for Mufflers	1)	2+2 only
UFS.131/7R	Setscrew, securing Bar to Body	2)	
C.8737/2	Nut, on Setscrew	2)	

PART NO.	Description.	NO. PER UNIT.	REMARKS

FUEL SYSTEM.

PART NO.	Description.	NO. PER UNIT.	REMARKS
C.24760	Petrol Tank Assembly	1	
C.19302	Sump Assembly, at Bottom of Petrol Tank	1	
C.26310	Washer, on Sump	1	
UFS.137/4R	Setscrew, in Sump (To assist Petrol Tank Drainage)	1	
C.26311	Washer (Aluminium) on Setscrew	1	
C.15150/1	Ventilation Hose, Tank to Filler Box	1	
C.15886/6	Clip, securing Hose	2	
C.18906	Pad (Rubber) under Petrol Tank	1	
C.23601/1	Petrol Filler Cap Assembly	1	
C.23603	Sealing Ring, in Filler Cap	1	
C.23604	Spring Clip, retaining Cap to Tank	1	
UCS.819/3H	Setscrew, securing Clip to Cap	1	
AG102/X	Spring Washer, on Setscrew	1	
AW.102/T	Plain Washer, on Setscrew	1	
C.18936	Hose, Tank to Petrol Filler Box	1	*
C.2905/7	Clip, securing Hose	2	
C.20429	Petrol Gauge Element in Tank	1	*
C.15789	Lucar Blade, for Element	1	
C.937	Gasket, under Element	1	
UFS.313/3H	Setscrew, securing Element to Tank	6	
C.2296/9	Copper Washer, on Setscrews	12	
C.22458	Petrol Pump Assembly	1	*
C.22547	Clip, around Petrol Pump	1	
C.23361	Rubber Packing, inside Clip	1	
UFB.125/11R	Bolt, through Clip	1	
C.8667/1	Nut, on Bolt	1	
C.24759	Bracket, on Pump Body	1	
FS.105/3R	Setscrew, securing Bracket to Pump	2	
C.725	Shakeproof Washer, on Setscrew	2	
C.24792	Rubber Mounting, securing Clip and Bracket to Body	3	*
UFN.125/L	Nut, securing Rubber Mountings	5	
C.724	Shakeproof Washer, under Nuts	5	
FW.104/T	Plain Washer, under Shakeproof Washers	2	
C.21900	Filter Assembly, on Feed Pipe to Pump	1	
C.11576	Union Nut, securing Filter to Feed Pipe	1	
C.11575	Olive, on Pipe for Union Nut	1	
C.24542	Cover Plate Assembly, on Petrol Tank	1	
C.22226	Gasket, under Cover Plate	1	*
UFS.119/4R	Setscrew, securing Cover Plate	8	
AW.102/E	Copper Washer, on Setscrews	8	

PART NO.	Description.	NO. PER UNIT.	REMARKS

Fuel System (Continued).

PART NO.	Description.	NO. PER UNIT.	REMARKS
BD.16008	Bracket Assembly, for Forward Mounting of Petrol Tank	1	
BD.16553	Reinforcement Plate, for Bracket	1	
UFN.131/L	Nut, securing Bracket to Bulkhead	4	
C.725	Shakeproof Washer, under Nuts	4	
C.19846	Rubber Pad, at Petrol Tank Mountings	6	
C.6390	Distance Tube, through Rubber Pads	3	
C.11920	Bolt, securing Petrol Tank	3	
FG.106/X	Spring Washer, on Bolts	3	
C.410	Plain Washer, on Bolts	3	
C.24755	Petrol Pipe, Tank to Pump	1	
C.11488	Banjo Bolt, securing Pipe to Tank and Pump	2	
C.25402	Washer, Aluminium at each Side of Banjos	4	
C.24757	Petrol Pipe, Pump to Bulkhead Connector	1	
C.11488	Banjo Bolt, securing Pipe to Pump and Connector	2	
C.25402	Washer, Aluminium at each side of Banjos	4	
C.17630	Bulkhead Connector at Top of Boot Floor	1)	
C.18254	Mounting Plate, for Bulkhead Connector	1)	
C.3729	Nut, securing Connector to Mounting Plate	1)	
C.10267	Washer, under Nut	1)	
UFS.125/4R	Setscrew, securing Mounting Plate to Bulkhead	2)	Open and F.H.Coupe
C.724	Shakeproof Washer, on Setscrews	2)	Models only
C.25617	Petrol Pipe, Connector to Double Ended Union	1)	
C.3727	Clip, securing Pipe to Wheel Arch	2)	
C.1040/6	Clip, securing Pipe to Underframe Channel	5)	
DZZ.410/6C	Screw, securing Clip	5)	
C.21747	Double Ended Union	1)	
C.24723	Petrol Pipe, Double Ended Union to Filter	1)	Open and F.H.Coupe
C.1040/6	Clip, securing Pipe to Dash	1)	Models only
DZZ.410/6C	Screw, securing Clip	1)	
C.25299	Petrol Pipe (Rear) Bulkhead to Double Ended Union	1)	
C.26509	Gasket, between Pipe Flange and Bulkhead	1)	
UFS.125/4R	Setscrew, securing Flange to Bulkhead	2)	2+2
C.724	Shakeproof Washer, on Setscrew	2)	Models only.
C.1040/6	Clip, securing Pipe to Underframe	2)	
DZZ.410/6C	Screw, securing Clip	2)	
C.21747	Double Ended Union	1)	

PART NO.	Description.	NO. PER UNIT.	REMARKS

Fuel System (Continued).

PART NO.	Description.	NO. PER UNIT	REMARKS
C.25723	Petrol Pipe (Intermediate) Double Ended Union to Double Ended Union	1)	)
C.26676	Spring Clip, securing Pipe to R.H.Side Member	4)	) 2+2) Models) only)
C.21747	Double Ended Union	1)	)
C.25722	Petrol Pipe, Front Double Ended Union to Filter	1)	)
C.1040/6	Clip, securing Pipe to Dash	1)	)
DZZ.410/6C	Screw, securing Clip	1)	
C.27588	Petrol Filter Assembly	1	*
11450	Filter Casting	1	
11951	Sealing Gasket, Small	1	*
C.28080	Filter Element, with Sealing Gaskets	1	**
11950	Sealing Gasket, large	1	*
7300	Glass Bowl	1	
7301	Retaining Strap Assembly	1	
C.31032	Bracket Mounting Petrol Filter	1	
UFS.131/6R	Setscrew, securing Filter to Bracket	2	
UFN.131/L	Nut, on Setscrew	2	
FG.105/X	Spring Washer, under Nut	2	
C.26815	Petrol Pipe, Filter to Engine	1	
C.13705	Banjo Bolt, securing Pipe to Filter	1	
C.784	Fibre Washer, at each side of Banjo	2	

PART NO.	Description.	NO. PER UNIT.	REMARKS

BODY SHELL.

PART NO.	Description.	NO. PER UNIT.
BD.35765	Body Shell Assembly Complete (Body in White)	1
BD.35767	Body Underframe Assembly	1
BD.36788	Bonnet and Front Wings Assembly	1
C.20352	Front Sub-Frame Assembly	1
C.28922	Front Cross Member Assembly	1
C.15029	R.H.Side Member Assembly	1
C.15030	L.H.Side Member Assembly	1
C.19326	Bonnet Hinge	2
BD.33722	R.H.Door Shell Assembly	1
BD.33723	L.H.Door Shell Assembly	1
BD.15495	Hinge Assembly, for R.H.Door	1
BD.15496	Hinge Assembly,for L.H.Door	1
BD.22662	Check Arm Assembly, for Doors	2
BD.20957	Scuttle Top Panel Assembly	1
BD.15180	Exterior Panel Assembly, R.H.Dash Side	1
BD.15181	Exterior Panel Assembly, L.H.Dash Side	1
BD.16547	R.H.Windscreen Pillar Assembly	1
BD.16548	L.H.Windscreen Pillar Assembly	1
BD.15217	Filler Panel, at bottom of R.H. Windscreen Pillar	1
BD.15218	Filler Panel, at bottom of L.H. Windscreen Pillar	1
BD.15467	Closing Panel, under R.H.Windscreen Pillar	1
BD.15468	Closing Panel, under L.H.Windscreen Pillar	1
BD.17069	R.H.Corner Panel, Dash to Scuttle Top	1
BD.17070	L.H.Corner Panel, Dash to Scuttle Top	1
BD.15133	R.H.Sill Outer Panel	1
BD.15134	L.H.Sill Outer Panel	1
BD.15184	End Plate, at front of R.H.Sill	1
BD.15187	Bracket Assembly, at front of R.H.Sill mounting Air Cleaner	2
BD.15185	End Plate Assembly, at front of L.H.Sill	1
BD.15186	Bracket Assembly, at front of L.H.Sill mounting Battery Tray	1
BD.19586	Bracket Assembly, for Jack Location	2
BD.35604	Panel Assembly, lower rear	1
BD.35511	R.H.Rear Wing Assembly	1
BD.35512	L.H.Rear Wing Assembly	1
BD.18872	R.H.Top Quarter Panel Assembly	1
BD.18873	L.H.Top Quarter Panel Assembly	1
BD.15189	Tonneau Top Panel	1
BD.18801	Tonneau Support Panel Assembly	1
BD.35502	Tonneau Rear Panel Assembly	1
BD.28911	Boot Lid Shell Assembly	1
BD.20622	R.H.Hinge Assembly, for Boot Lid	1
BD.20623	L.H.Hinge Assembly, for Boot Lid	1

PART NO.	Description.	NO. PER UNIT.	REMARKS

Body Shell (Continued).

PART NO.	Description.	NO. PER UNIT.	REMARKS
BD.15933	Petrol Filler Box Assembly	1	Fitted from Chassis No. 1R.1001 to 1R.1392 1R.7001 to 1R.11051
BD.37605	Petrol Filler Box Assembly	1	Fitted to Chassis No. 1R.1392 onwards 1R.11052 onwards
BD.15934	Lid Assembly, for Petrol Filler Box	1	
BD.15932	Hinge Assembly, for Petrol Filler Lid	1	
BD.15930	Spring, for Petrol Filler Lid	1	
BD.28612	Bracket Assembly, for attachment of Rear Bumpers	2	
BD.19132	Bracket Assembly, for Rear Suspension Bump Stops	2	
BD.1814/6	Pop Rivets, securing Bumper Bracket to Body	4	

PART NO.	Description.	NO. PER UNIT.	REMARKS

BODY SHELL.

PART NO.	Description.	NO. PER UNIT.
BD.35771	Body Shell Assembly, complete (Body in White)	1
BD.35773	Body Underframe Assembly	1
BD.36788	Bonnet and Front Wings Assembly	1
C.20352	Front Sub-Frame Assembly	1
C.28922	Front Cross Member Assembly	1
C.15029	R.H.Side Member Assembly	1
C.15030	L.H.Side Member Assembly	1
C.19326	Bonnet Hinge	2
BD.33728	R.H.Door Shell Assembly	1
BD.33729	L.H.Door Shell Assembly	1
BD.15495	Hinge Assembly, for R.H.Door	1
BD.15496	Hinge Assembly, for L.H.Door	1
BD.22662	Check Arm Assembly, for Doors	2
BD.20957	Scuttle Top Panel Assembly	1
BD.15180	Exterior Panel Assembly, R.H.Dash Side	1
BD.15181	Exterior Panel Assembly, L.H.Dash Side	1
BD.23913	R.H.Windscreen Pillar Assembly	1
BD.23914	L.H.Windscreen Pillar Assembly	1
BD.20203	Reinforcement Channel, at top of R.H. Windscreen Pillar	1
BD.20202	Reinforcement Channel, at top of L.H. Windscreen Pillar	1
BD.15217	Filler Panel, at bottom of R.H.Windscreen Pillar	1
BD.15218	Filler Panel, at bottom of L.H.Windscreen Pillar	1
BD.24065	Drip Angle, on R.H.Windscreen Pillar	1
BD.24066	Drip Angle, on L.H.Windscreen Pillar	1
BD.15467	Closing Panel, under R.H.Windscreen Pillar	1
BD.15468	Closing Panel, under L.H.Windscreen Pillar	1
BD.17069	R.H.Corner Panel,Dash to Scuttle Top	1
BD.17070	L.H.Corner Panel,Dash to Scuttle Top	1
BD.15133	R.H.Sill Outer Panel	1
BD.15134	L.H.Sill Outer Panel	1
BD.15184	End Plate, at front of R.H.Sill	1
BD.15187	Bracket Assembly, at front of R.H.Sill mounting Air Cleaner	1
BD.15185	End Plate Assembly, at front of L.H.Sill	1
BD.15186	Bracket Assembly, at front of L.H.Sill mounting Battery Tray	1
BD.19586	Bracket Assembly, for Jack Location	1
BD.35602	Panel Assembly, lower rear	1
BD.36079	Roof Panel Assembly	1
BD.36100	R.H.Rear Wing Assembly	1
BD.36101	L.H.Rear Wing Assembly	1
BD.32491	Extension Assembly, at top of Rear Number Plate Panel	1
BD.19968	Reinforcement Panel, between Extension and R.H.Support Panel	1
BD.19969	Reinforcement Panel, between Extension and L.H.Support Panel	1
BD.26730	Retainer, for R.H.Quarter Light Seal	1
BD.26731	Retainer, for L.H.Quarter Light Seal	1

PART NO.	Description.	NO. PER UNIT.	REMARKS

Body Shell (Continued).

PART NO.	Description.	NO. PER UNIT.	REMARKS
BD.1814/2	Pop Rivet, securing Retainers	20	
BD.19635/1	Drain Tube, for Back Door Aperture	1	
BD.19544	Back Door Shell Assembly	1	
BD.19626	Support Panel Assembly, at R.H.Side of Back Door Aperture	1	
BD.19627	Support Panel Assembly, at L.H.Side of Back Door Aperture	1	
BD.20261	Hinge Assembly, for Back Door	2	
BD.19339	Petrol Filler Box Assembly	1	Fitted from Chassis No. 1R.20001 to 1R.20485 1R.25001 to 1R.27050
BD.37581	Petrol Filler Box Assembly	1	Fitted to Chassis No. 1R.20486 onwards 1R.27051 onwards
BD.22242	Lid Assembly, for Petrol Filler Box	1	
BD.19552	Hinge Assembly, for Back Door	1	
BD.15930	Spring, for Petrol Filler Lid	1	
BD.28612	Bracket Assembly, for attachment of Rear Bumpers	2	
BD.1814/6	Pop Rivet, securing Bumper Brackets to Body	4	
BD.19132	Bracket Assembly, for Rear Suspension Bump Stops	2	

PART NO.	Description.	NO. PER UNIT.	REMARKS

BODY SHELL.

PART NO.	Description.	NO. PER UNIT.	REMARKS
BD.35759	Body Shell Assembly complete (Body in White)	1	For Standard Transmission only
BD.35761	Body Underframe Assembly	1	
BD.36788	Bonnet and Front Wings Assembly	1	
C.20352	Front Sub-Frame Assembly	1	
C.28922	Front Cross Member Assembly	1	
C.15029	R.H.Side Member Assembly	1	
C.15030	L.H.Side Member Assembly	1	
C.19326	Bonnet Hinge	2	
BD.33734	R.H.Door Shell Assembly	1	
BD.33735	L.H.Door Shell Assembly	1	
BD.27680	Hinge Assembly, for R.H.Door	1	
BD.27681	Hinge Assembly, for L.H.Door	1	
BD.27794	Check Arm Assembly, for Doors	2	
BD.35811	Scuttle Top Panel Assembly	1	
BD.28003	Exterior Panel Assembly, R.H.Dash Side	1	
BD.28004	Exterior Panel Assembly, L.H.Dash Side	1	
BD.35567	R.H.Windscreen Pillar Assembly	1	
BD.35568	L.H.Windscreen Pillar Assembly	1	
BD.28102	Reinforcement Channel at top of R.H. Windscreen Pillar	1	
BD.28103	Reinforcement Channel at top of L.H. Windscreen Pillar	1	
BD.30438	Drain Tray Assembly, at bottom of R.H. Windscreen Pillar	1	
BD.30439	Drain Tray Assembly, at bottom of L.H. Windscreen Pillar	1	
BD.27676	Closing Panel, under R.H.Windscreen Pillar	1	
BD.27677	Closing Panel, under L.H.Windscreen Pillar	1	
BD.27770	Retainer, on R.H.Shut Pillar for Door Seal	1	
BD.27771	Retainer, on L.H.Shut Pillar for Door Seal	1	
BD.28237	Retainer, on R.H.Cantrail and Windscreen Pillar for Door Seal	1	
BD.28238	Retainer, on L.H.Cantrail and Windscreen Pillar for Door Seal	1	
BD.29158	Retainer, on R.H.Hinge Pillar for Door Seal	1	
BD.29159	Retainer, on L.H.Hinge Pillar for Door Seal	1	
BD.1814/2	Pop Rivet, securing Retainers	46	
BD.35597	R.H.Corner Panel, Dash to Scuttle Top	1	
BD.35598	L.H.Corner Panel, Dash to Scuttle Top	1	
BD.27639	R.H.Sill Outer Panel	1	
BD.27640	L.H.Sill Outer Panel	1	
BD.15184	End Plate, at front of R.H.Sill	1	
BD.15187	Bracket Assembly, at front of R.H.Sill mounting Air Cleaner	1	
BD.15185	End Plate Assembly, at front of L.H.Sill	1	
BD.15186	Bracket Assembly, at front of L.H.Sill mounting Battery Tray	1	
BD.35602	Panel Assembly, lower rear	1	
BD.36081	Roof Panel Assembly	1	

PART NO.	Description.	NO. PER UNIT.	REMARKS

Body Shell (Continued).

PART NO.	Description.	NO. PER UNIT.	REMARKS
BD.35519	R.H.Rear Wing Assembly	1	
BD.35520	L.H.Rear Wing Assembly	1	
BD.28160	Extension Assembly, at top of Rear Number Plate Panel	1	
BD.28052	Reinforcement Panel, between Extension and R.H.Support Panel	1	
BD.28053	Reinforcement Panel, between Extension and L.H.Support Panel	1	
BD.28235	Retainer, for R.H.Quarter Light Seal	1	
BD.28236	Retainer, for L.H.Quarter Light Seal	1	
BD.1814/2	Pop Rivet, securing Retainers	20	
BD.19635/1	Drain Tube, for Back Door Aperture ($6\frac{1}{4}$" long)	1	
BD.19544	Back Door Shell Assembly	1	
BD.20261	Hinge Assembly, for Back Door	2	
BD.19339	Petrol Filler Box Assembly	1	Fitted from Chassis No. 1R.35001 to 1R.35642 1R.40001 to 1R.42849
BD.37581	Petrol Filler Box Assembly	1	Fitted to Chassis No. 1R.35643 onwards 1R.42850 onwards
BD.22242	Lid Assembly, for Petrol Filler Box	1	
BD.19552	Hinge Assembly, for Petrol Filler Lid	1	
BD.15930	Spring, for Petrol Filler Lid	1	
BD.28612	Bracket Assembly, for attachment of Rear Bumpers	2	
BD.19132	Bracket Assembly, for attachment of Bump Stops	2	
BD.1814/6	Pop Rivets, securing Bumper Brackets to Body	4	
BD.35753	Body Shell Assembly complete (Body in White)	1	For Automatic Transmission only
BD.35755	Body Underframe Assembly	1	

PART NO.	Description.	NO. PER UNIT.	REMARKS

FRONT FRAME.

PART NO.	Description.	NO. PER UNIT.	REMARKS
C.20352	Front Sub-Frame Assembly	1	(Fitted from Chassis No. (1R.1001 to 1R.1187 (1R.7001 to 1R.9569 (1R.20001 to 1R.20269 (1R.25001 to 1R.26386 (1R.35001 to 1R.35352 (1R.40001 to 1R.42117 (EXCEPTION (Not fitted to Chassis (No.40940
C.31815	Front Sub-Frame Assembly	1	(Fitted to Chassis No. (1R.1188 onwards (1R.9570 onwards (1R.20270 onwards (1R.26387 onwards (1R.35353 onwards (1R.42118 onwards (EXCEPTION (Also fitted to Chassis N (1R.40940
C.32176	Bracket on Sub Frame Anchoring Strut	1	(
C.31816	Bolt, securing Bracket and L.H.Front Shock Absorber to Sub-Frame	1	(
FW.107/T	Plain Washer, on Bolt	1	(
UFN.443/I	Slotted Nut, on Bolt	1	(
C.28922	Front Cross Member Assembly	1	
C.15029	R.H.Side Member Assembly	1	
C.15030	L.H.Side Member Assembly	1	
UFB.131/20R	Bolt, securing Upper Front Fulcrum Blocks Side Members, Front Sub-Frame to Cross Member Top	8	
UFB.131/32R	Bolt, Lower Front Fulcrum Blocks, Side Members, Front Sub-Frame, Anti-Roll Bar Brackets to Cross Member Bottom	2	
UFB.131/19R	Bolt, Lower Front Fulcrum Blocks, Side Members, Front Sub-Frame to Cross Member Bottom	6	
UFB.131/18R	Bolt, Side Members and Front Sub-Frame Cross Member, Bottom	4	3 only for 2+2
UFB.131/26R	Bolt, Side Member, Front Sub-Frame to Cross Member Bottom also fixing 3 Way Union	1	2+2 only
C.15045	Packing Plate, Side Members to Lower Rail of Cross Member	2	
C.8667/2	Nut, on Bolts	20	
UFS.131/7R	Setscrew, securing Side Members to Dash	24	
C.8667/2	Nut, on Setscrews	12	
FW.105/T	Plain Washer, under Nuts	12	

PART NO.	Description.	NO. PER UNIT.	REMARKS

Front Frame (Continued).

PART NO.	Description.	NO. PER UNIT.	REMARKS
C.11919	Bolt, securing Side Members to Body Underframe Channels.	2	
C.8667/3	Nut, on Bolt	2	
FW.106/T	Plain Washer, under Nut	2	Open & F.H.Coupe
C.410	Plain Washer, under Nut	2	2+2 only
C.19326	Bonnet Hinge	2	
C.16804	Bush (Nylon) for Bonnet Hinge	4	
C.19330	Bearing (Steel) for Bonnet Hinge	2	
UFB.137/18R	Bolt, Hinges to Front Sub-Frame	2	
FG.106/X	Spring Washer, on Bolts	2	
C.19179	Reaction Plate Assembly	1	
C.8060	Bolt, securing Reaction Plate to Body Underframe, Channels through Side Members	2)	Open and F.H.Coupe only
UFB.150/26R	Bolt, securing Reaction Plate to Body Underframe Channels through Side Members	2)	2+2 only
C.11193	Plain Washer, on Bolt	2)	
C.8667/5	Nut, on Bolts	2	

PART NO.	Description.	NO. PER UNIT.	REMARKS

BODY UNDERFRAME AND PANELS.

PART NO.	Description.	NO. PER UNIT.	REMARKS
BD.35767	Body Underframe Assembly	1	
BD.35768	Dash Assembly	1	
BD.27374	Floor Assembly	1	
BD.32546	Rear End Assembly	1	
BD.35768	Dash Assembly	1	
BD.35774	Dash Bulkhead Assembly	1	
BD.32739	Pedal Mounting Panel Assembly R.H.	1	
BD.32438	Pedal Mounting Panel Assembly L.H.	1	

For other items see Catalogue J.37

PART NO.	Description.	NO. PER UNIT.	REMARKS
BD.35774	Dash Bulkhead Assembly	1	

For other items see Catalogue J.37

PART NO.	Description.	NO. PER UNIT.	REMARKS
BD.32546	Rear End Assembly	1	
BD.28567	Tunnel Assembly	1	
BD.32256	R.H.Shut Pillar Assembly	1	
BD.32257	L.H.Shut Pillar Assembly	1	
BD.22809	Floor Panel Assembly Rear	1	
BD.28148	Top Panel Assembly, above Rear Floor	1	
BD.27834	Panel Assembly, for Front of Spare Wheel Compartment	1	

For other items see Catalogue J.37

PART NO.	Description.	NO. PER UNIT.	REMARKS
BD.33722	R.H.Front Door Shell	1	Plate B.5
BD.29079	Drain Tray Assembly R.H.Door	1	
BD.16792	Sealing Strip, for Drain Tray	1	
BD.11712/2	Pop Rivet, securing Drain Tray to Door	4	
BD.21180	Drain Tube (Rubber) for Drain Tray	1	
BD.25213	Clip, securing Drain Tube	1	
BD.33723	L.H.Front Door Shell	1	Plate B.6
BD.29080	Drain Tray Assembly L.H.Door	1	

All other items are as for L.H.Front Door
Shell BD.33722

PART NO.	Description.	NO. PER UNIT.	REMARKS
BD.35511	R.H.Rear Wing Assembly	1	Plate B.7
BD.35512	L.H.Rear Wing Assembly	1	Plate B.8
BD.35502	Tonneau Rear Panel Assembly	1	Plate B.9
BD.35604	Panel Assembly, lower rear	1	
BD.36105	Lower Centre Panel Assembly	1	Plate B.10
BD.35595/2	Lower Centre Panel R.H.	1	Plate B.11
BD.35595/3	Lower Outer Panel L.H.	1	Plate B.12
BD.21110	Drain Tube, in R.H.Lower Outer Panel	1	
BD.21114	Drain Tube Assembly, in L.H.Lower Outer Panel	1	

PART NO.	Description.	NO. PER UNIT.	REMARKS

Body Underframe and Panels (Continued).

PART NO.	Description.	NO. PER UNIT.	REMARKS
BD.36107	Panel Assembly, mounting Rear Number Plate	1	
BD.15244/1	Support, R.H.for Floor Assembly covering Spare Wheel	1	
BD.15245	Support, L.H. for Floor Assembly covering Petrol Tank	1	
BD.35562	Closing Panel, rear	1	
BD.35573	Corner Plate, rear R.H.	1	
BD.3554	Corner Plate, rear L.H.	1	
BD.35790	Stiffener, at top of Number Plate Panel	1	
BD.35592	Mounting Plate Assembly, for Lock Mounting Bracket	1	
BD.16201	Bracket Assembly, mounting Boot Lid Lock	1	
BD.35620	Bracket, mounting R.H. Tail/Flasher Lamp	1	
BD.35621	Bracket, mounting L.H. Tail/Flasher Lamp	1	
BD.35638	Bonnet and Front Wings Assembly	1	
BD.35639	Centre Panel Assembly	1	Plate B.13
BD.35651	Front Under Panel Assembly	1	B.14
BD.35641	R.H.Front Wing Assembly	1	B.15
BD.35642	L.H.Front Wing Assembly	1	B.16
BD.35632	R.H.Valance and Air Duct Assembly	1	
BD.35633	L.H.Valance and Air Duct Assembly	1	
BD.28460	R.H.Front Diaphragm Assembly	1	
BD.28461	L.H.Front Diaphragm Assembly	1	
BD.18739	Reinforcement Angle, for R.H.Front Diaphragm	1	
BD.18738	Reinforcement Angle, for L.H.Front Diaphragm	1	
BD.28376	L.H.Rear Diaphragm Assembly	1	

For other items see Catalogue J.37

PART NO.	Description.	NO. PER UNIT.	REMARKS
BD.15180	Exterior Panel Assembly, for R.H.Side of Dash	1	Plate B.1
BD.15181	Exterior Panel Assembly, for L.H.Side of Dash	1	Plate B.2
BD.15133	R.H.Outer Sill Panel	1	Plate B.3
BD.15134	L.H.Outer Sill Panel	1	Plate B.4.

PART NO.	Description.	NO. PER UNIT.	REMARKS

BODY UNDERFRAME AND PANELS.

PART NO.	Description.	NO. PER UNIT.	REMARKS
BD.35773	Body Underframe Assembly	1	
BD.35768	Dash Assembly	1	
BD.27374	Floor Assembly	1	
BD.32496	Rear End Assembly	1	
BD.35768	Dash Assembly	1	
BD.35774	Dash Bulkhead Assembly	1	
BD.32739	Pedal Mounting Panel Assembly R.H.	1	
BD.32438	Pedal Mounting Panel Assembly L.H.	1	
	For other items see Catalogue J.37		
BD.35774	Dash Bulkhead Assembly	1	
	For other items see Catalogue J37		
BD.32496	Rear End Assembly	1	
BD.28567	Tunnel Assembly	1	
BD.32258	R.H.Shut Pillar Assembly	1	
BD.32259	L.H.Shut Pillar Assembly	1	
BD.31699	Support Panel Assembly for R.H. Rear Quarter including Safety Harness Anchor Point	1	
BD.31700	Support Panel Assembly for L.H. Rear Quarter including Safety Harness Anchor Point	1	
BD.27654	Floor Panel Assembly, Rear	1	
	For other items see Catalogue J.37		
BD.33728	R.H.Front Door Shell	1	Plate A.5
BD.29079	Drain Tray Assembly R.H.Door	1	
BD.16792	Sealing Strip for Drain Tray	1	
BD.11712/2	Pop Rivet, securing Drain Tray to Door	4	
BD.21180	Drain Tube (Rubber) for Drain Tray	1	
BD.25213	Clip, securing Drain Tube	1	
BD.33729	L.H.Front Door Shell	1	Plate A.6
BD.29080	Drain Tray Assembly L.H.Door	1	
	All other items are as for R.H.Front Door Shell BD.33726		
BD.36100	R.H.Rear Wing Assembly	1	Plate A.7
BD.36101	L.H.Rear Wing Assembly	1	Plate A.8
BD.36709	Roof Panel Assembly	1	Plate A.9
BD.32927	Windscreen Header Panel Assembly	1	
	For other items see Catalogue J.37		

PART NO.	Description.	NO. PER UNIT.	REMARKS

Body Underframe and Panels (Continued).

PART NO.	Description.	NO. PER UNIT.	REMARKS
BD.35602	Panel Assembly, lower rear	1	
BD.36105	Lower Centre Panel Assembly	1	Plate A.10
BD.35595/2	Lower Outer Panel R.H.	1	Plate A.11
BD.35595/3	Lower Outer Panel L.H.	1	Plate A.12
BD.19032	Drain Tube, for Petrol Overflow in L.H.Lower Outer Panel	1	
BD.19635/1	Drain Tube, in Back Door Drain Channel	1	
BD.36106	Panel Assembly, mounting Rear Number Plate	1	
BD.15244/1	Support R.H., for Floor Assembly covering Spare Wheel	1	
BD.15245	Support Assembly L.H., for Floor Assembly covering Petrol Tank	1	
BD.35562	Closing Panel, rear	1	
BD.35573	Corner Plate, rear R.H.	1	
BD.35574	Corner Plate, rear L.H.	1	
BD.32491	Extension Panel Assembly, at top of rear Number Plate Panel	1	
BD.35620	Bracket, mounting R.H.Tail/Flasher Lamp	1	
BD.35621	Bracket, mounting L.H.Tail/Flasher Lamp	1	
BD.36788	Bonnet and Front Wings Assembly	1	
BD.35662	Centre Panel Assembly	1	Plate A.13
BD.35651	Front Under Panel Assembly	1	Plate A.14
BD.35655	Air Duct Lower Panel Assembly	1	
BD.35641	R.H.Front Wing Assembly	1	Plate A.15
BD.35642	L.H.Front Wing Assembly	1	Plate A.16
BD.35632	R.H.Valance and Air Duct Assembly	1	
BD.36722	L.H.Valance and Air Duct Assembly	1	
BD.36577	R.H.Front Diaphragm Assembly	1	
BD.36578	L.H.Front Diaphragm Assembly	1	
BD.18739	Reinforcing Angle for R.H.Front Diaphragm	1	
BD.18738	Reinforcing Angle for L.H.Front Diaphragm	1	
BD.22749	Sealing Panel, for R.H.Front Diaphragm	1	
BD.22750	Sealing Panel, for L.H.Front Diaphragm	1	
BD.16381	R.H.Rear Diaphragm	1	
BD.28376	L.H.Rear Diaphragm	1	
BD.18767	Reinforcing Angle, Wings to Centre Panel	2	

PART NO.	Description.	NO. PER UNIT.	REMARKS

Body Underframe and Panels (Continued).

PART NO.	Description.	NO. PER UNIT.	REMARKS
BD.15180	Exterior Panel Assembly, for R.H.Side of Dash	1	Plate A.1
BD.15181	Exterior Panel Assembly, for L.H.Side of Dash	1	Plate A.2
BD.15133	R.H.Outer Sill Panel	1	Plate A.3
BD.15134	L.H.Outer Sill Panel	1	Plate A.4

PART NO.	Description.	NO. PER UNIT.	REMARKS

BODY   UNDERFRAME   AND   PANELS.

PART NO.	Description.	NO. PER UNIT.	REMARKS
BD.35761	Body Underframe Assembly	1	For Standard Transmission only
BD.35762	Dash Assembly	1	
BD.35619	Reinforcement Assembly, at top of R.H.Hinge Pillar	1	
BD.35618	Reinforcement Assembly, at top of L.H.Hinge Pillar	1	
	For other items see Catalogue J.38		
BD.35755	Body Underframe Assembly	1	For Automatic Transmission only
BD.35756	Dash Assembly	1	
BD.27759	Main Floor Assembly	1	
BD.27510	Transmission Cover Panel Assembly	1	
	All other items are as for Body Underframe Assembly BD.35761		
BD.35762	Dash Assembly	1	For Standard Transmission only
BD.35697	Dash Bulkhead Assembly	1	
BD.32739	Pedal Mounting Panel Assembly, R.H.	1	
BD.32438	Pedal Mounting Panel Assembly, L.H.	1	
	For other items see Catalogue J.38		
BD.35756	Dash Assembly	1	For Automatic Transmission only
BD.27660	Dash Centre Panel	1	
BD.27468	Panel Assembly, R.H.Side of Converter Housing	1	
BD.27469	Panel Assembly, at L.H.Side of Converter Housing	1	
	All other items are as for Dash Assembly BD.35762		
BD.35697	Dash Bulkhead Assembly	1	
	For other items see Catalogue J.38		
BD.33734	R.H.Door Shell Assembly	1	Plate A.5
BD.33735	L.H.Door Shell Assembly	1	Plate A.6
BD.32944	R.H.Shut Pillar Assembly	1	
BD.32945	L.H.Shut Pillar Assembly	1	
BD.35519	R.H.Rear Wing Assembly	1	Plate A.7
BD.35520	L.H.Rear Wing Assembly	1	Plate A.8

PART NO.	Description.	NO. PER UNIT.	REMARKS
	Body Underframe and Panels (Continued).		
BD.36081	Roof Panel Assembly	1	Plate A9
BD.32928	Windscreen Header Panel Assembly	1	
BD.23171/1	Joint Plate, from Cantrail to Reinforcement Rail	2	
	For other items see Catalogue J.38.		
BD.35602	Panel Assembly, lower rear	1	
BD.36105	Lower Centre Panel Assembly	1	Plate A10
BD.35595/2	Lower Outer Panel R.H.	1	Plate A11
BD.35595/3	Lower Outer Panel L.H.	1	Plate A12
BD.19032	Drain Tube for Petrol Overflow in L.H.Lower Outer Panel	1	
BD.19635/1	Drain Tube, in Back Door Drain Channel	1	
BD.36106	Panel Assembly,mounting Rear Number Plate	1	
BD.15244/1	Support R.H.for Floor Assembly Covering Spare Wheel	1	
BD.15245	Support Assembly L.H. for Floor Assembly covering Petrol Tank	1	
BD.35562	Closing Panel, rear	1	
BD.35573	Corner Plate, rear R.H.	1	
BD.35574	Corner Plate, rear L.H.	1	
BD.35620	Bracket,mounting R.H.Tail/Flasher Lamp	1	
BD.35621	Bracket,mounting L.H.Tail/Flasher Lamp	1	
	For other items see Catalogue J.38		
BD.36788	Bonnet and Front Wings Assembly	1	
BD.35662	Centre Panel Assembly	1	Plate A13.
BD.35651	Front Under Panel Assembly	1	Plate A14.
BD.35655	Air Duct Lower Panel Assembly	1	
BD.35641	R.H.Front Wing Assembly	1	Plate A15.
	L.H.Front Wing Assembly	1	Plate A16.
BD.35632	R.H.Valance and Air Duct Assembly	1	
BD.36722	L.H.Valance and Air Duct Assembly	1	
BD.36577	R.H.Front Diaphragm Assembly	1	
BD.36578	L.H.Front Diaphragm Assembly	1	
BD.18739	Reinforcing Angle for R.H.Front Diaphragm	1	
BD.18738	Reinforcing Angle for L.H.Front Diaphragm	1	
BD.22749	Sealing Panel for R.H.Front Diaphragm	1	
BD.22750	Sealing Panel for L.H.Front Diaphragm	1	
BD.16381	R.H.Rear Diaphragm	1	
BD.16382	L.H.Rear Diaphragm	1	
BD.18767	Reinforcing Angle, Wings to Centre Panel	2	
BD.35584	Bracket Assembly, inner,mounting Front Bumpers	2	
BD.35585	Bracket Assembly,outer,mounting Front Bumpers.	2	

PART NO.	Description.	NO. PER UNIT.	REMARKS
	Body Underframe and Panels (Continued).		
BD.35811	Scuttle Top Panel	1	
BD.35567	R.H.Windscreen Pillar Assembly	1	
BD.35568	L.H.Windscreen Pillar Assembly	1	
	For other items see Catalogue J.38		
BD.35597	R.H.Corner Panel, Dash to Scuttle Top Panel	1	
BD.35598	L.H.Corner Panel, Dash to Scuttle Top Panel	1	
BD.28003	Exterior Panel Assembly,for R.H.Side of Dash	1	Plate A1
BD.28004	Exterior Panel Assembly, for L.H.Side of Dash	1	Plate A2
BD.27639	R.H.Outer Sill Panel	1	Plate A3
BD.27640	L.H.Outer Sill Panel	1	Plate A4

FOR ALL MODELS UNLESS OTHERWISE STATED

PART NO.	Description.	NO. PER UNIT.	REMARKS

BODY FITTINGS.

PART NO.	Description.	NO. PER UNIT.	REMARKS
BD.35576	Bar Assembly only,for R.H.Front Bumper	1	*
BD.35577	Bar Assembly only, for L.H.Front Bumper	1	*
BD.35600	Over-Rider Assembly,on R.H.Front Bumper	1	*
BD.35601	Over-Rider Assembly,on L.H.Front Bumper	1	*
209	Beading(P.V.C.)between Over-Rider and Bumper	4	*
UFB.137/20R	Bolt, securing Over-Rider to Front Bumper	2	
FG.106/X	Washer, Spring, on Bolt	2	
FW.106/T	Washer, Plain, under Spring Washer	2	
BD.9604/4	Setscrew,securing Bumpers to Bonnet	4	
FG.106/X	Washer, Spring, on Setscrew	4	
FW.106/T	Washer, Plain, under Spring Washer	4	
BD.28523	Seal (Canvas/Rubber) between Bumper Brackets and Bonnet	4	
BD.18947/3	Seal (Rubber) between Bumper and Bonnet	2	
BD.10313	Clip, securing Rubber Seals	4	
BD.35500	Motif Bar, in Air Intake Aperture	1	
BD.9604/3	Screw, Set, securing Motif Bar to Bumper Bars	2	
FG.106/X	Washer, Spring, on Setscrews	2	
FW.106/T	Washer, Plain, under Spring Washers	2	
BD.28520	Motif	1	
BD.28518	Backing Piece, behind Motif	1	
BD.28519	Spring Clip, retaining Motif	1	
BD.11501	Screw, self-tapping, securing Spring Clip	2	
BD.35668	Chrome Finisher,Outer around R.H.Headlamp Aperture	1	
BD.35670	Chrome Finisher,Inner around R.H. Headlamp Aperture	1	
BD.35694	Chrome Motif Assembly, above R.H. Headlamp Aperture	1	
BD.35669	Chrome Finisher,Outer around L.H. Headlamp Aperture	1	
BD.35671	Chrome Finisher,Inner around L.H. Headlamp Aperture	1	
BD.35695	Chrome Motif Assembly above L.H. Headlamp Aperture	1	
DAZ.806/6C	Screw, self-tapping, securing Motif Assemblies	4	
BD.35729	Finisher Bead (P.V.C.) under R.H.Chrome Finisher	1	
BD.35730	Finisher Bead (P.V.C.) under L.H.Chrome Finisher	1	
BD.37862	Painted Finisher,Outer around R.H.Headlamp Aperture	1)	
BD.37864	Painted Finisher,Inner around R.H.Headlamp Aperture	1)	For Australia only
BD.37860	Painted Motif Assembly,above R.H.Headlamp Aperture	1)	
BD.37863	Painted Finisher, Outer around L.H. Headlamp Aperture	1)	

Always quote colour when ordering Trimmed Parts.

FOR ALL MODELS UNLESS OTHERWISE STATED

PART NO.	Description.	NO. PER UNIT.	REMARKS

Body Fittings (Continued).

PART NO.	Description.	NO. PER UNIT	REMARKS
BD.37865	Painted Finisher, Inner around L.H. Headlamp Aperture	1)	) For Australia only
BD.37861	Painted Motif Assembly above L.H. Headlamp Aperture	1)	)
BD.31129	Joint Finisher (Chrome) for Headlamp Apertures	2	Not for Australia
BD.37866	Joint Finisher (Painted) for Headlamp Apertures	2	For Australia only
DA.008/8S	Screw, self-tapping (Stainless) securing Joint Finishers.	2	
BD.31095/2	Rivet Clip,securing Chrome Finishers	12	
BD.31095/1	Rivet Clip,securing Chrome Finishers	2	
AW.105/T	Washer Plain, under Rivet Clips	14	
BD.19029/4	Chrome Beading,in Bonnet Joint at rear of Motif Assemblies	2)	) Not for Australia
BD.37967	Painted Beading, in Bonnet Joint at rear of Motif Assemblies	2)	) For Australia only
BD.19030	Clip (Brass)securing Chrome Beadings	14	
BD.35645	Finisher Panel Assembly, in R.H.Headlamp Recess	1	
BD.35646	Finisher Panel Assembly, in L.H.Headlamp Recess	1	
BD.28539	Drain Tube (P.V.C.) for Finisher Panels	2	
BD.1814/2	Pop Rivet, securing Finisher Panels	4	
BD.35677	Carrier Bracket Assembly for Front Number Plate	1)	) Fitted as Standard) Equipment for certain) countries. Also supplied) as Special Equipment) if required.
BD.31984	Stoneguard Assembly,behind bonnet air intake aperture	1	
BD.31976	Frame Assembly, for Stoneguard	1	
BD.36893	Operating Strut (Gas Filled) Assisting opening of Bonnet	1)	) Fitted to Chassis Nos.) 1R.1188 onwards) 1R.9570 onwards
BD.36431	Joint Pin, securing Operating Strut to Bonnet and Sub Frame.	2)	) 1R.20270 onwards) 1R.26387 onwards) 1R.35353 onwards
C.1221	Split Pin, retaining Joint Pin	2)	) 1R.42118 onwards)
BD.15654	Washer, under Split Pin	2)	) EXCEPTION.) Also fitted to Chassis) No.40940
BD.35935	Grille, for air outlet at rear edge of Bonnet.	1	

Always quote colour when ordering Trimmed Parts.

FOR ALL MODELS UNLESS OTHERWISE STATED

PART NO.	Description.	NO. PER UNIT.	REMARKS

Body Fittings (Continued).

PART NO.	Description.	NO. PER UNIT.	REMARKS
BD.35736	Bracket, receiving Safety Catch	1	For 2+2 Model only
BD.20664	R.H.Mudshield Assembly	1)	
BD.28723	L.H.Mudshield Assembly	1)	For all
BD.28668	Shield Assembly, protecting Air Cleaner Intake Tubes	1)	Models
BD.25587	Cover and Bracket Assembly, supporting	1)	For all R.H.Drive Models
BD.35664	Windscreen Glass (Clear)	1)	
BD.35664/1	Windscreen Glass (Sundym)	)	
BD.35664/2	Windscreen Glass (Shaded Sundym)	1)	
BD.35665	Seal (Rubber) around Windscreen Glass	1)	
BD.35742	Insert (Rubber) for Seal	1)	For 2+2 Model only
BD.35658	Chrome Finisher at bottom edge of Windscreen	1)	
BD.20563	Chrome Finisher at top edge of Windscreen	1)	
BD.35656	Chrome Finisher at R.H.edge of Windscreen	1)	
BD.35657	Chrome Finisher at L.H.edge of Windscreen	1)	
BD.32351	Windscreen Glass (Clear)	1)	
BD.32351/1	Windscreen Glass (Sundym)	1)	For F.H.C.Models only
BD.32351/2	Windscreen Glass (Shaded Sundym)	1)	

For all other items see Catalogue J.37

PART NO.	Description.	NO. PER UNIT.	REMARKS
BD.32640	Windscreen Glass (Clear)	1)	
BD.32640/1	Windscreen Glass (Sundym)	1)	For Open Model only
BD.33326/1	Everseal Strip (54" long) under top Chrome Finisher	1)	

For all other items see Catalogue J.37.

NOTE :- All Windscreens are supplied complete with Mounting Boss for Rear View Mirror.

PART NO.	Description.	NO. PER UNIT.	REMARKS
C.28516	Rear View Mirror	1	
BD.32397	Boss on Windscreen for Mirror	1	
C.28475	Plastic Screw, securing Mirror to Boss	1	
BD.33021	Sun Visor only	2)	
BD.35816	R.H.Inner Arm	1)	For all Open Cars
BD.35817	L.H.Inner Arm	1)	
BD.28881	R.H.Outer Arm	1)	Fitted from Chassis No.
BD.28882	L.H.Outer Arm	1)	1R.1001 to 1R.1348
UFN.225/L	Locknut	2)	1R.7001 to 1R.10522
BD.36699	R.H.Outer Arm	1)	Fitted to Chassis No.
BD.36700	L.H.Outer Arm	1)	1R.1349 onwards
UFN.225/L	Locknut	2)	1R.10523 onwards

Always quote colour when ordering Trimmed Parts.

PART NO.	Description.	NO. PER UNIT.	REMARKS

Body Fittings (Continued).

PART NO.	Description.	NO. PER UNIT	REMARKS
BD.32750	R.H.Outer Bracket	1)	
BD.32751	L.H.Outer Bracket	1)	
BD.19259	Dome Nut	2)	For all Open Cars
BD.21516/6	Shakeproof Washer	2)	
BD.22728/5	Setscrew (Cone Point) securing Sun Visors and Brackets to Body	4)	
BD.21368	Sun Visor only	2	For F.H.C. Cars only
BD.28634	L.H.Sun Visor with Mirror	1 (	(Supplied to Special Order only, for R.H.Drive F.H.C. Cars
BD.33538	Sun Visor only	2	For all 2+2 Cars
BD.33627	L.H.Sun Visor, with Mirror	1 (	(Supplied to Special Order only, for R.H.Drive 2+2 Cars
BD.21130	R.H.Friction Arm Assembly	1)	
BD.21129	L.H.Friction Arm Assembly	1)	
BD.21012	Base, for Friction Arms	2)	
BD.9635	Spring, on Arm inside Base	2)	For F.H.C. and
BD.541/32	Special Washer, at each side of Spring	4)	2+2 cars only
C.8737/1	Nut, self-locking, securing Arm in Base	2)	
BD.24593	End Cap, on Visors	2)	
BD.22728/5	Setscrew (Cone Point) securing Sun Visors and Brackets to Body	4)	
Ref (See (Heater/ (Demister(	Screen Rail Facia Assembly	1)	For 2+2 Model only
	Screen Rail Facia Assembly	1)	For F.H.C. & Open Models.
BD.32649	L.H.Facia Panel Assembly	1)	Fitted from Chassis No.
BD.32648	R.H.Facia Panel Assembly	1)	1R.1001 to 1R.1392 1R.20001 to 1R.20485 1R.35001 to 1R.35643 R.H.Drive.
BD.32516	R.H.Facia Panel Assembly	1)	Fitted from Chassis No.
BD.32517	L.H.Facia Panel Assembly	1)	1R.7001 to 1R.11051 1R.25001 to 1R.27050 1R.40001 to 1R.42849 L.H.Drive.
BD.37575	L.H.Facia Panel Assembly	1)	Fitted to Chassis No.
BD.37574	R.H.Facia Panel Assembly	1)	1R.1392 onwards 1R.20486 onwards 1R.35643 onwards R.H.Drive.

Always quote colour required when ordering Trimmed Parts.

FOR ALL MODELS UNLESS OTHERWISE STATED

PART NO.	Description.	NO. PER UNIT.	REMARKS

Body Fittings (Continued).

BD.37570	R.H.Facia Panel Assembly	1)	Fitted to Chassis No.
BD.37571	L.H.Facia Panel Assembly	1)	1R.11052 onwards
		)	1R.27051 onwards
		)	1R.42850 onwards
			L.H.Drive
BD.27499	L.H.Cubby Box	1)	For all R.H.
BD.28260	Lid for L.H.Cubby Box	1)	Drive Models.
BD.27498	R.H.Cubby Box	1)	For all L.H.
BD.28266	Lid for R.H.Cubby Box	1)	Drive Models

For all other items see Catalogue J. 38.

BD.35699	Chrome Finisher, between R.H.Facia Panel and Windscreen Pillar	1)	For 2+2
BD.35700	Chrome Finisher, between L.H.Facia Panel and Windscreen Pillar	1)	Model only
BD.29462	R.H.Scuttle Top Casing Assembly	1)	For R.H.
BD.29460	L.H.Scuttle Top Casing Assembly	1)	Drive. Open and
BD.29468	Centre Scuttle Top Casing Assembly	1)	F.H.C.Models only
BD.33104	R.H.Scuttle Top Casing Assembly	1)	For L.H.Drive
BD.33106	L.H.Scuttle Top Casing Assembly	1)	Open and F.H.C.
BD.33105	Centre Scuttle Top Casing Assembly	1)	Models only
BD.29547	R.H.Scuttle Top Casing	1)	
BD.29572	L.H.Scuttle Top Casing	1)	For L.H.Drive
BD.29549	Centre Scuttle Top Casing	1)	2+2 Model only
BD.30254	Parcel Tray Assembly R.H.	1)	For R.H.Drive
BD.30256	Parcel Tray Assembly L.H.	1)	2+2 Model only
BD.30255	Parcel Tray Assembly R.H.	1)	For L.H.Drive
BD.30257	Parcel Tray Assembly L.H.	1)	2+2 Model only

For other items see Catalogue J.38

BD.30263	Crash Roll Assembly R.H.	1)	For
BD.30264	Crash Roll Assembly L.H.	1)	2+2
BD.26308	Acorn Nut, securing Crash Roll to Tray	8)	Model only
AW.104/T	Washer, Plain, under Acorn Nut	8)	
BD.34719	Radio Panel Assembly above Gearbox Tunnel	1)	For F.H.C. and
		)	Open Models only
BD.32506	Face Panel Assembly for Radio Panel	1	
BD.12709	Spire Nut, securing Face Panel	4	
BD.32445	Mounting Panel, for Speakers	2	
BD.25350	Grille in Mounting Panels	2	
BD.26854	Gasket (Fibre) behind Grilles	2	

Always quote colour required when ordering Trimmed Parts.

FOR ALL MODELS UNLESS OTHERWISE STATED

PART NO.	Description.	NO. PER UNIT.	REMARKS

Body Fittings (Continued).

PART NO.	Description.	NO. PER UNIT	REMARKS
BD.37871	Distance Piece on Studs	8	
UCN.116/L	Nut, securing Mounting Panel and Grille	8	
C.722	Washer, Shakeproof, under Nuts	8	
AW.102/T	Washer, Plain, under Shakeproof Washer	8	
BD.34717	Radio Panel Assembly, above Gearbox Tunnel	1)	For 2+2 Models only
	All other items are as for BD.34719 Radio Panel Assembly.		
BD.30786	Trim Panel Assembly, in Radio Aperture	1	
BD.17354	Base Plate (Chrome) under Trim Panel	1	
BD.32761	Tunnel Finisher Assembly complete	1	For 2+2 Model only
BD.28707	Finisher Assembly (Trimmed) for Tunnel	1	
BD.32492	Ash Tray Assembly	1	
BD.33799	Gauntlet Panel Assembly complete	1	
BD.32762	Top Finisher Assembly (Trimmed)	1	
BD.32765	Tunnel Finisher Assembly complete	1	For F.H.C. & Open Models only
BD.32492	Ash Tray Assembly	1	
BD.33799	Gauntlet Panel Assembly complete	1	
BD.32766	Insert Panel Assembly (trimmed)	1	
BD.24989	Armrest and Stowage Compartments	1	
BD.35705	R.H.Front Seat Assembly (trimmed) less Slides	1)	Fitted from Chassis No.
BD.35707	Squab Assembly (trimmed)	1)	1R.1001 to 1R.1137
BD.32678	Base (Cushion) Assembly (trimmed)	1)	1R.7001 to 1R.8869
BD.33250	Reclining Mechanism	1)	1R.20001 to 1R.20211
BD.33278	Torque Spring R.H. on Reclining Mechanism	1)	1R.25001 to 1R.26004
		)	1R.35001 to 1R.35222
		)	1R.40001 to 1R.41501
BD.33279	Torque Spring L.H.on Reclining Mechanism	1)	
BD.32688	Lever,operating Reclining Mechanism	1)	Not required on Cars
BD.36814 +	Pivot Cover, R.H.	1)	exported to Canada,
BD.36815 +	Pivot Cover, L.H.	1)	Japan or U.S.A.
		)	
BD.35706	L.H.Front Seat Assembly (trimmed) less Slides	1)	
		)	NOTE – Headrests cannot
BD.32679	Base (cushion) Assembly (trimmed)	1)	be fitted to these
		)	seats.
	All other items are as for BD.35705 R.H.Seat	)	

NOTE:– Trim Cover Assemblies can be obtained for BD.35705)
R.H.Seat or BD.35706 L.H.Seat as follows)

BD.27782	Base (Cushion) Trim Cover for R.H.Seat	1)	
BD.27783	Base (Cushion) Trim Cover for L.H.Seat	1)	
BD.32903	Squab Trim Cover Assembly, R.H.or L.H.Seat	1)	

Always quote colour required when ordering Trimmed Parts.

FOR ALL MODELS UNLESS OTHERWISE STATED

PART NO.	Description.	NO. PER UNIT.	REMARKS

Body Fittings (Continued).

BD.37422	R.H.Front Seat Assembly (Trimmed) less slides	1)	Fitted from Chassis No.
BD.37424	Squab Assembly (Trimmed)	1)	1R.1138 to 1R.1301.
BD.36780	Base (Cushion) Assembly Trimmed	1)	1R.8869 to 1R.10152
BD.33250	Reclining Mechanism	1)	1R.20212 to 1R.20365
BD.33278	Torque Spring R.H. on Mechanism	1)	1R.26005 to 1R.26683
BD.33279	Torque Spring L.H. on Mechanism	1)	1R.35223 to 1R.35457
BD.35545	Lever,operating Reclining Mechanism	1)	1R.41502 to 1R.42559
BD.33255	Setscrew, securing Lever to Seat	1)	
C.723A	Shakeproof Washer, on Screw	1)	Not required
BD.36814	Pivot Cover R.H.	1)	on Cars exported to
BD.36815	Pivot Cover L.H.	1)	Canada, Japan,
DAB.806/4C	Screw, securing Pivot Covers	4)	Sweden or U.S.A.
BD.33677	Washer, on Screw	4)	
DAB.004/8C	Screw, securing Pivot Covers	2)	NOTE - Headrests cannot
		)	be fitted to these
BD.37423	L.H.Front Seat Assembly (Trimmed) less slides	1)	seats.
BD.36781	Base (Cushion) Assembly (Trimmed)	1)	
BD.35546	Lever, operating Reclining Mechanism	1)	

All other items are as for BD.37422 R.H.Seat.)

NOTE :- Trim Cover Assemblies can be obtained for BD.37422)
     R.H.Seat or BD.37423 L.H.Seat as follows)

BD.36739	Base (Cushion) Trim Cover for R.H.Seat	1)	
BD.36740	Base (Cushion) Trim Cover for L.H.Seat	1)	
BD.37425	Squab Trim Cover for R.H.or L.H.Seat	1)	

BD.36607	R.H.Front Seat Assembly (Trimmed) less slides	1)	Fitted from Chassis No.
BD.37353	Squab Assembly (Trimmed)	1)	1R.1302 onwards.
BD.36780	Base (Cushion) Assembly (Trimmed)	1)	1R.10152 onwards.
BD.33250	Reclining Mechanism	1)	1R.20366 onwards.
BD.33278	Torque Spring R.H. on Mechanism	1)	1R.26684 onwards.
BD.33279	Torque Spring L.H. on Mechanism	1)	1R.35458 onwards.
BD.35545	Lever,operating Reclining Mechanism	1)	1R.42560 onwards.
BD.33255	Setscrew, securing Lever to Seat	1)	
C.723A	Shakeproof Washer, on Setscrew	1)	
BD.36814	Cover R.H. on Reclining Mechanism	1)	
BD.36815	Cover L.H. on Reclining Mechanism	1)	
DAB.804/4C	Screw, securing Covers	2)	
AW.106/T	Washer, on Screw	2)	
DAB.004/8C	Screw, securing Covers	2)	

Always quote colour when ordering Trimmed Parts.

PART NO.	Description.	NO. PER UNIT.	REMARKS

Body Fittings (Continued).

BD.36608	L.H.Front Seat Assembly (Trimmed) less slides	1)	Fitted from Chassis No. 1R.10152 onwards.
BD.36781	Base (Cushion) Assembly (Trimmed)	1)	1R.1302 onwards.
BD.35546	Lever, operating Reclining Mechanism	1)	1R.20366 onwards.
		)	1R.26684 onwards.
	All other items are as for BD.36608 R.H.Seat	)	1R.35458 onwards.
		)	1R.42560 onwards.
BD.36610	Plug in Head Rest Aperture in Squab	2)	
		)	
BD.36585	Headrest Assembly, for Front Seats	2)	Supplied to Special
BD.36715	Retention Spring, retaining Headrest in Front Seats	2)	order for Front Seat Assemblies (BD.36607 R.H. and BD.36608 L.H.)

NOTE :- Trim Cover Assemblies can be obtained for BD.36607)
R.H.Seat or BD.36608 L.H.Seat as follows)

BD.36739	Base (Cushion) Trim Cover for R.H.Seat	1)	
BD.36740	Base (Cushion) Trim Cover for L.H.Seat	1)	
BD.36741	Squab Trim Cover for R.H.or L.H.Seat	1)	
BD.35712	R.H.Front Seat Assembly (Trimmed) less slides	1)	Fitted from Chassis No. 1R.1001 to 1R.1137
BD.36433	Squab Assembly (Trimmed)	1)	1R.7001 to 1R.8869
BD.35715	Head Rest Assembly (Trimmed)	1)	1R.20001 to 1R.20211
BD.32678	Base (Cushion) Assembly (Trimmed)	1)	1R.25001 to 1R.26004
BD.33250	Reclining Mechanism	1)	1R.35001 to 1R.35222
BD.33278	Torque Spring, R.H.on Reclining Mechanism	1)	1R.40001 to 1R.41501
BD.33279	Torque Spring, L.H. on Reclining Mechanism	1)	For cars exported to Canada, Japan and
BD.32688	Lever, operating Reclining Mechanism	1)	U.S.A.
BD.36814 +	Pivot Cover R.H.	1)	
BD.36815 +	Pivot Cover L.H.	1)	
		)	
BD.35713	L.H.Front Seat Assembly (Trimmed) less slides	1)	
BD.32679	Base (Cushion) Assembly (Trimmed)	1)	
	All other items are as for BD.35712 R.H. Seat	)	

NOTE :- Trim Cover Assemblies can be obtained for BD.35712)
R.H.Seat or BD.35713 L.H.Seat as follows)

BD.27782	Base (Cushion) Trim Cover for R.H.Seat	1)	
BD.27783	Base (Cushion) Trim Cover for L.H.Seat	1)	
BD.35726	Squab Trim Cover, R.H. or L.H.Seat	1)	
BD.35551	Head Rest Trim Cover, R.H. or L.H.Seat	1)	

Always quote colour when ordering Trimmed Parts.

PART NO.	Description.	NO. PER UNIT.	REMARKS

Body Fittings (Continued).

PART NO.	Description.	NO. PER UNIT.	REMARKS
BD.36600	R.H.Front Seat Assembly (Trimmed) with Headrest but less slides	1	) Fitted to Chassis No.
BD.36671	Squab Assembly, with Headrest (Trimmed)	1	) 1R.1138 onwards
BD.36780	Base (Cushion) Assembly (Trimmed)	1	) 1R.8869 onwards
BD.33250	Reclining Mechanism	1	) 1R.20212 onwards
BD.33278	Torque Spring R.H. on Mechanism	1	) 1R.26005 onwards
BD.33279	Torque Spring L.H. on Mechanism	1	) 1R.35223 onwards.
BD.35545	Lever,operating Reclining Mechanism	1	) 1R.41502 onwards.
BD.33255	Setscrew, securing Lever to Seat	1	)
C.723A	Shakeproof Washer, on Setscrew	1	) For cars exported to
BD.36814	Pivot Cover R.H.	1	) Canada, Japan,
BD.36815	Pivot Cover L.H.	1	) Sweden and U.S.A.
DAB.806/4C	Screw, securing Pivot Covers	4	)
BD.33677	Washer, on Screws	4	)
DAB.004/8C	Screw, securing Pivot Covers	2	)
			)
BD.36601	L.H.Front Seat Assembly (Trimmed) with Headrest but less slides	1	)
BD.36781	Base (Cushion) Assembly (Trimmed)	1	)
BD.35546	Lever, operating Reclining Mechanism	1	)
			)
	All other items are as for BD.36600 R.H.Seat		)
BD.36671	Squab Assembly, with Headrest (Trimmed)	2	
BD.37353	Squab Assembly, (Trimmed)	2	
BD.36585	Headrest (Trimmed)	2	
BD.36715	Spring retaining Headrest in Squab	2	

NOTE :- Trim Cover Assemblies can be obtained for BD.36600
        R.H.Seat or BD.36601 L.H.Seat as follows

PART NO.	Description.	NO. PER UNIT.
BD.36739	Base (Cushion) Trim Cover for R.H.Seat	1
BD.36740	Base (Cushion) Trim Cover for L.H.Seat	1
BD.36741	Squab Trim Cover for R.H. or L.H.Seat	1
BD.36587	Headrest Trim Cover for R.H. or L.H. Seat	1
BD.33497/4	Screw, Set, securing Reclining Mechanism to Squab	8
BD.2906/11	Washer, Shakeproof on Setscrews	8
UFS.125/4R	Screw, Set, securing Reclining Mechanism to Seat Pan	8
C.724	Washer, Shakeproof, on Setscrews	8

Always quote colour when ordering Trimmed Parts.

PART NO.	Description.	NO. PER UNIT.	REMARKS

Body Fittings (Continued).

IMPORTANT :- The following cars were fitted with Seat Assemblies
BD.35705 R.H. and BD.35706 L.H.

```
1R8870:  1R8871:  1R8873:  1R8874:  1R8875:  1R8876:  1R8877 )
1R8878:  1R8879:  1R8880:  1R8881:  1R8882:  1R8883:  1R9029 ) L.H.Drive.
1R9042:  1R9069:  1R9070:  1R9077:  1R9147:  1R9169:  1R9172 ) Open
1R9174:  1R9185:  1R9195:  1R9255:  1R9328:  1R9244:  1R9350 ) Model.
1R9396:  1R9419:

1R26002: 1R26007: 1R26010: 1R26022: 1R26023 ) L.H.Drive
1R26025: 1R26028: 1R26033: 1R26051: 1R26053 ) F.H.Coupe
1R26057: 1R26069: 1R26078:                   ) Model

1R41503: 1R41504: 1R41505: 1R41506: 1R41507 )
1R41508: 1R41509: 1R41510: 1R41511: 1R41512 )
1R41513: 1R41514: 1R41515: 1R41516: 1R41517 )
1R41518: 1R41519: 1R41521: 1R41522: 1R41523 ) L.H.Drive
1R41533: 1R41541: 1R41547: 1R41548: 1R41556 ) 2+2 Model
1R41634: 1R41635: 1R41642: 1R41676: 1R41677 )
1R41678: 1R41683: 1R41696: 1R41697  1R41705 )
1R41706: 1R41715: 1R41716:
```

PART NO.	Description.	NO. PER UNIT.	REMARKS
BD.32707	Outer Slide (locking) for R.H.Seat	1)	
BD.27432	Inner Slide (locking for R.H.Seat	1)	
		)	
BD.32706	Outer Slide (locking) for L.H.Seat	1)	
BD.27431	Inner Slide (locking) for L.H.Seat	1) For Open and F.H.C.	
12528	Plastic Sleeve, on end of Slide Operating Levers	2) Models	
		)	
BD.32693	Tie Wire, connecting Outer Slide Locks to Inner Slide Locks	2)	
BD.32694	Keeper, securing Tie Wire to Locks	4)	
	For Slide Fixings see Catalogue J.37.	)	
		)	
BD.32705	Outer Slide (locking) for R.H.Seat	1)	
BD.28418	Inner Slide (locking) for R.H.Seat	1)	
		) For 2+2 Models only	
BD.32704	Outer Slide (locking) for L.H.Seat	1)	
BD.28417	Inner Slide (locking) for L.H.Seat	1)	
12528	Plastic Sleeve, on end of Slide Operating Levers	2)	
		)	
BD.32693	Tie Wire,connecting Outer Slide Locks to Inner Slide Locks.	2)	
BD.32694	Keeper,securing Tie Wire to Slide Locks	4)	
BD.27434	Fixing Boss,locating Seat Slides at front	4)	
BD.21509/6	Screw,Set securing Fixing Bosses to Floor	4)	
BD.2906/10	Washer,Shakeproof, on Setscrews	4)	
BD.27546/3	Screw,Set,securing Slides to Floor at rear	4)	
BD.27546/4	Screw,Set,securing Slides to Seats	8)	
C.724	Washer,Shakeproof, on Setscrews	8)	
BD.13529	Packing Piece,under Fixing Bosses at front and seat slides at rear	8)	

Always quote colour when ordering Trimmed Parts.

PART NO.	Description.	NO. PER UNIT.	REMARKS

Body Fittings (Continued).

PART NO.	Description.	NO. PER UNIT.	REMARKS
BD.28371	Rear Seat Cushion Assembly (Trimmed)	1)	Fitted from Chassis No.
		)	1R.1001 to 1R.1137
BD.28729	Rear Squab Assembly, (Trimmed) Lower	1)	1R.7001 to 1R.8868
		)	1R.20001 to 1R.20211
BD.30238	Rear Squab Assembly, (Trimmed) Upper	1)	1R.25001 to 1R.26004
BD.30226	Bracket and Links Assembly, R.H. mounting Upper Squab to Body	1)	1R.35001 to 1R.35222
		)	1R.45001 to 1R.41502
BD.30227	Bracket and Links Assembly, L.H. mounting Upper Squab to Body	1)	
BD.30178	Torsion Bar Assembly, connecting Forward Links of Mounting Brackets	1)	For 2+2 Models only.
C.8667/1	Nut, self-locking, securing Torsion Bar to Forward Links and Rear Links to Squab Side Panels	4)	
BD.541/33	Washer (Brass) under Self-Locking Nuts	4)	
BD.541/40	Washer (Brass) between Forward Links and Rear Squab Side Panels	2)	
BD.541/19	Washer (Brass) between Rear Links and Rear Squab Side Panels	2)	
BD.28886	Cover Assembly (Leather) for Upper Rear Squab	1)	
BD.29325	Chrome Finisher at bottom of Side Panel Trim Rolls	2)	
DAC.504/6C	Screw, self-tapping, securing Chrome Finishers	2)	
		)	
		)	
BD.28729	Rear Seat Squab Assembly, Lower	1)	
BD.28887	Cover Assembly (Leather) for Lower Rear Squab	1)	

Always quote colour required when ordering Trimmed Parts.

FOR ALL MODELS UNLESS OTHERWISE STATED

PART NO.	Description.	NO. PER UNIT.	REMARKS

Body Fittings (Continued).

PART NO.	Description.	NO. PER UNIT.	REMARKS
BD.36737	Rear Seat Cushion Assembly (Trimmed)	1)	Fitted to Chassis Nos.
		)	1R.1138 onwards
BD.36735	Rear Squab Assembly, (Trimmed) Lower	1)	1R.8869 onwards
		)	1R.20212 onwards
BD.36770	Rear Squab Assembly (Trimmed) Upper	1)	1R.26005 onwards
BD.30226	Bracket and Links Assembly R.H.	1)	1R.35223 onwards
	Mounting Upper Squab to Body	)	1R.41502 onwards
BD.30227	Bracket and Links Assembly L.H.	1)	
	Mounting Upper Squab to Body	)	
BD.30178	Torsion Bar Assembly, connecting	1)	
	Forward Link of Mounting Brackets	)	
C.8667/1	Nut, securing Torsion Bar to forward	4)	
	Links and Rear Links to Squab	)	
	Side Panels	)	
BD.541/33	Brass Washer, under Nuts	4)	
BD.541/40	Brass Washer, between Forward	2)	
	Links and Squab Side Panels	)	
BD.541/19	Brass Washer, between Rear Links	2)	
	and Squab Side Panels	)	2+2
BD.29360/1	Finisher Bead, at top of Upper Squab	1)	only
BD.29334/1	Clip and Rivet Assembly, securing Bead	5)	
BD.28872	Trim Panel Assembly, at back of Upper	1)	
	Squab	)	
BD.604/7	Beading (Rubber) on Trim Panel	5)	
BD.29251/1	Retainer for Beading	5)	
BD.1814/6	Pop Rivet, securing Retainer to Trim	10)	
	Panel	)	
BD.29112	Trim Panel Assembly, on Upper Squab	1)	
	Base	)	
BD.604/11	Beading (Rubber) on Trim Panel	5)	
BD.29250/1	Retainer for Beading	5)	
BD.1814/6	Pop Rivet, securing Retainers	10)	
BD.28944	Trim Panel Assembly, on R.H.Side Panel	1)	
	of Upper Squab	)	
BD.28945	Trim Panel Assembly, on L.H.Side Panel	1)	
	of Upper Squab	)	
BD.29326	Trim Roll Assembly, at edge of R.H.	1)	
	Side Panel	)	
BD.29327	Trim Roll Assembly, at edge of L.H.	1)	
	Side Panel	)	
BD.29325	C.P.Finisher, at bottom of Trim Rolls	2)	
DAC.504/6C	Screw, securing C.P.Finishers	2)	
		)	
UFS.125/5R	Setscrew, securing Upper Rear Squab to	6)	
	Floor	)	
C.724	Shakeproof Washer, on Setscrew	6)	
BD.541/9	Washer, under Shakeproof Washer	6)	

Always quote colour when ordering Trimmed Parts.

FOR ALL MODELS UNLESS OTHERWISE STATED

PART NO.	Description.	NO. PER UNIT.	REMARKS

Body Fittings (Continued).

NOTE :-	Trim Cover Assemblies can be obtained for Rear Seats to the following Part Numbers	)))	
BD.36738	Trim Cover Assembly for Rear Cushion	)	2+2
BD.36736	Trim Cover Assembly for Rear Squab Lower	)	only
BD.36734	Trim Cover Assembly for Rear Squab Upper	)	
BD.32366	Lock Assembly, on R.H.Door	1)	
BD.32367	Lock Assembly, on L.H.Door	1)	
BD.19445	Link, between Lock and Outside Handle	2)	For Open and F.H.C.
BD.23473	Spring Clip, retaining Links	4)	Models
BD.1708/9	Washer,Spring, for Link Fixing at Locks	2)	
BD.32618	Lock Assembly, on R.H.Door	1)	
BD.32619	Lock Assembly, on L.H.Door	1)	
BD.32626	Link, between Lock and Outside Handle	2)	For 2+2 Model only
BD.23473	Spring Clip, retaining Links	4)	
BD.1708/9	Washer,Spring, for Link Fixing at Locks	2)	
BD.19245	Outside Handle, on R.H. Door	1)	For all models.
BD.19246	Outside Handle, on L.H.Door	1)	
	For other items see Catalogue J. 37		
BD.32368	Remote Control and Links Assembly, operating Door Locks	2))	For Open and F.H.C. Models.
BD.32620	Remote Control and Link Assembly, operating Door Locks	2))	For 2+2 Models only
BD.32365	Inside Door Handle	2	
C.22234/1	Screw (Wedglok) securing Inside Door Handle	2	
BD.32364	Handle, operating Window Regulators	2	
BD.34996/2	Screw (Wedglok) securing Regulator Handles	2	
BD.32354	Escutcheon, for Regulator Handles	2	
BD.32362	Window Regulator Assembly in R.H.Door	1)	
BD.32363	Window Regulator Assembly in L.H.Door	1)	For Open and F.H.C.
BD.29101	Thrust Pad (Rubber) around Regulator Spindle	1))	Models.
BD.32616	Window Regulator Assembly in R.H.Door	1)	
BD.32617	Window Regulator Assembly in L.H.Door	1)	For 2+2 Model only.
BD.29101	Thrust Pad (Rubber) around Regulator Spin Spindle.	1)	
BD.20801	Glass (Clear) for Door Windows	2)	For Open model only
BD.20801/1	Glass (Sundym) for Door Windows	1)	
BD.28759	Glass (Clear) for Door Windows	2)	For F.H.C. model only
BD.29273	Glass (Sundym) for Door Windows	2)	

Always quote colour required when ordering Trimmed Parts.

FOR ALL MODELS UNLESS OTHERWISE STATED

PART NO.	Description.	NO. PER UNIT.	REMARKS

Body Fittings (Continued).

PART NO.	Description.	NO. PER UNIT.	REMARKS
BD.27812	Glass (Clear) for Door Windows	2)	For 2+2 Models only
BD.29098	Glass (Sundym) for Door Windows	1)	
BD.29562	Regulator Channel for R.H.Door Glass	1)	
BD.29563	Regulator Channel for L.H.Door Glass	1)	
		)	For F.H.C.Model only
BD.28704	Run Channel,Front(Rubber)for R.H.Door Glass	1)	
BD.28705	Run Channel,Front(Rubber)for L.H.Door Glass	1)	
BD.28209/2	Run Channel,Rear (Rubber) for Rear Doors	2)	
BD.33708	Casing Assembly on R.H.Door	1)	For Open Model only
BD.33709	Casing Assembly on L.H.Door	1)	
BD.33712	Casing Assembly on R.H.Door	1)	For F.H.C.Model only
BD.33713	Casing Assembly on L.H.Door	1)	
BD.33716	Casing Assembly on R.H.Door	1)	
BD.33717	Casing Assembly on L.H.Door	1)	
		)	
BD.32614	Chrome Finisher, lower front, on Casings	2)	
BD.33747	Chrome Finisher, lower rear, on Casings	2)	
BD.33744	Escutcheon, for recess in R.H.Casing	1)	
BD.33745	Escutcheon, for recess in L.H.Casing	1)	
BD.26706/1	Rivet Clip, securing Chrome Finishers to Casings	12)	
AW.105/T	Washer, plain, on Rivet Clips	12)	
BD.11546	Clip, securing Front Chrome Finishers to Casings	2)	For 2+2 Model only
BD.1814/6	Pop Rivet, securing Escutcheons to Casings	2)	
BD.32792	Door Liner Panel (Plastic) on R.H.Inner Door Panel, behind Casing	1)	
BD.32793	Door Liner Panel (Plastic) on L.H.Inner Door Panel, behind Casing	1)	
BD.32386	Chrome Finisher, lower front, on casings	2)	
BD.33746	Chrome Finisher, lower rear, on casings	2)	
BD.33744	Escutcheon, for recess in R.H.Casing	1)	
BD.33745	Escutcheon, for recess in L.H.Casing	1)	
BD.26706/1	Rivet Clip, securing front Chrome Finishers to casings	12)	
AW.105/T	Washer, Plain, on Rivet Clips	12)	
BD.11546	Clip, securing Front Chrome Finishers to Casings	2)	For F.H.C. and Open Models only
BD.1814/6	Pop Rivet, securing Escutcheons to Casings	2)	
BD.33788	Door Liner Panel (Plastic) on R.H.Inner Door Panel, behind Casing	1)	
BD.33789	Door Liner Panel (Plastic) on L.H.Inner Door Panel, behind Casing	1)	

Always quote colour required when ordering Trimmed Parts.

FOR ALL MODELS UNLESS OTHERWISE STATED

PART NO.	Description.	NO. PER UNIT.	REMARKS

Body Fittings (Continued).

Part No.	Description	No. per Unit	Remarks
BD.36016	Armrest Assembly, on R.H.Door	1	Fitted to Chassis No.
BD.36017	Armrest Assembly, on L.H.Door	1	1R.1326 onwards) Open
BD.23470/7	Setscrew, securing Armrests to Doors	4	1R.10335 onwards)
C.723/A	Washer, Shakeproof on Setscrew	4	
			1R.20391 onwards) F.H.C.
			1R.26756 onwards)
			1R.35547 onwards) 2+2
			1R.42583 onwards)
			Not fitted to Chassis No. 1R.42586
BD.32370	Striker, for R.H.Door Lock	1	
BD.32371	Striker, for L.H.Door Lock	1	
BD.19295	Packing, under Striker	A/R	Maximum 4 off
BD.25316	Seal and Retainer, for R.H. 'A' Post and Cantrail	1)	For Open Model only
BD.25317	Seal and Retainer, for L.H. 'A' Post and Cantrail	1)	
BD.25720	Seal and Retainer, for R.H. 'A' Post and Cantrail	1)	For F.H.C. Model only
BD.25721	Seal and Retainer, for L.H. 'A' Post and Cantrail	1)	
BD.20757	Glass Assembly (Clear) for R.H. Quarter Light	1)	
BD.20758	Glass Assembly (Clear) for L.H. Quarter Light	1)	
BD.29274	Glass Assembly (Sundym) for R.H. Quarter Light	1)	
BD.29275	Glass Assembly (Sundym) for L.H. Quarter Light	1)	
BD.31889	Casing Assembly, below R.H.Quarter Light	1)	
BD.31890	Casing Assembly, below L.H.Quarter Light	1)	For F.H.C.Model only
BD.31695	Crash Roll Assembly, at top of R.H. Quarter Casing	1)	
BD.28794	Chrome Bead, on R.H.Crash Roll	1)	
BD.21358	Clip, securing Chrome Bead	2)	
BD.24834	Chrome Finisher, on R.H.Crash Roll	1)	
BD.1814/1	Pop Rivet, securing Bead and Finisher to R.H.Crash Roll	3)	
BD.31696	Crash Roll Assembly, at top of L.H. Quarter Casing	1)	
BD.28795	Chrome Bead, on L.H.Crash Roll	1)	
BD.28435	Chrome Finisher, on L.H.Crash Roll	1)	

All other items are as for BD.31695 Crash Roll Assembly.

Always quote colour required when ordering Trimmed Parts.

FOR ALL MODELS UNLESS OTHERWISE STATED

PART NO.	Description.	NO. PER UNIT.	REMARKS

Body Fittings (Continued).

Part No.	Description	No. per Unit	Remarks
BD.35785	Crash Roll Assembly, on R.H.Cantrail	1)	
BD.28757	Chrome Bead, on R.H.Crash Roll	1)	
BD.21358	Clip, securing Chrome Bead	1)	
BD.1814/1	Pop Rivet, securing Clip	2)	For 2+2 Model only
BD.35786	Crash Roll Assembly, on L.H.Cantrail	1)	
BD.28758	Chrome Bead, on L.H.Crash Roll	1)	
BD.21358	Clip, securing Chrome Bead	1)	
BD.1814/1	Pop Rivet, securing Clip	1)	
DAZ.404/10C	Screw, self-tapping securing Crash Rolls to Body	10	
DAC.606/16C	Screw, self-tapping, securing Crash Rolls to Body	2	
BD.29631	Escutcheon, at Safety Harness points	2)	For 2+2 and F.H.C.
BD.24484	Screw, special, securing Escutcheons	2)	Models, not req'd when safety harness is fitted.
BD.33543	Headlining	1)	For 2+2 Model only
BD.33544	Trim Panel Assembly, for Windscreen Header Rail	)	
DAC.006/8C	Screw, self-tapping, securing Trim Header Panel	2)	
BD.543/3	Cup Washer, on Self-Tapping Screw	2)	
BD.33545	Facing Assembly (Headlining) R.H.Cantrail	1)	
BD.33546	Facing Assembly (Headlining) L.H.Cantrail	1)	
BD.29627	Facing Assembly, on R.H.Quarter and Rear Wheel Arch	1)	For 2+2 Model only
BD.29628	Facing Assembly, on L.H.Quarter and Rear Wheel Arch	1)	
BD.10313	Clip, securing Facings to Body	4)	
BD.31885	Casing Assembly, at R.H.Side of Back Door Aperture	1)	
BD.31886	Casing Assembly, at L.H.Side of Back Door Aperture	1)	
BD.28169	Facing Assembly (P.V.C.) sealing aperture in R.H.Rear Wheel Arch	1)	For F.H.C. Model only
BD.28170	Facing Assembly (P.V.C.) sealing aperture in L.H.Rear Wheel Arch	1)	
BD.29245	Trim Panel Assembly, below Back Door Aperture	1)	
BD.11309	Clip, securing Trim Panel	4)	

Always quote colour required when ordering Trimmed Parts.

FOR ALL MODELS UNLESS OTHERWISE STATED

PART NO.	Description.	NO. PER UNIT.	REMARKS

REAR BUMPER ASSEMBLIES.

PART NO.	Description.	NO. PER UNIT.
BD.35587	R.H.Bar Assembly	1
BD.35588	L.H.Bar Assembly	1
BD.35611	Centre Bar Assembly	1
UFS.137/6R	Screw, Set, securing Centre Bar to R.H. and L.H. Bars	2
FG.106/X	Washer, Spring, on Setscrews	2
FW.106/T	Washer, Plain, under Spring Washers	2
BD.35593	R.H.Over Rider Assembly	1
BD.35594	L.H.Over Rider Assembly	1
209	Beading (P.V.C.) between Over Riders and Bumper Bars	4
UFB.137/23R	Bolt, securing Over Riders to Bumper Assembly	2
FG.106/X	Washer, Spring on Bolts	2
FW.106/T	Washer, Plain, under Spring Washers	2
UFS.137/8R	Screw, Set, securing Bumper Assembly to Body at Rear	2
FG.106/X	Washer, Spring, on Setscrew	2
BD.33118	Washer, Plate, behind Spring Washers	2
UFN.137/L	Nut, securing Bumper Assembly to Body at side	2
FG.106/X	Washer, Spring, under Nuts	2
FW.106/T	Washer, Plain, under Spring Washers	2
UFS.131/6R	Screw, Set, securing Bumper Assembly to Rear Wings	2
FG.105/X	Washer, Spring, on Setscrews	2
FW.105/T	Washer, Plain, under Spring Washers	2
BD.35977/1	Seal (Rubber) between Rear Bumper and Body (113$\frac{1}{4}$" long)	1
BD.35627	Rear Number Plate Carrier on Panel	1
BD.11712/1	Pop Rivet, securing Carrier to Panel	6
BD.35962	Finisher (Stainless) on Rear Number Plate Panel	1
BD.1814/1	Pop Rivet, securing Finisher to Panel	2
DAC.806/8C	Screw, Self-Tapping, securing Finisher to Rear Closing Panel and Tail/Flasher Lamp Mounting Panel	4
BD.35683	Mounting Panel Assembly, for R.H. Tail/Flasher Lamp	1
BD.35684	Mounting Panel Assembly, for L.H. Tail/Flasher Lamp	1
UFS.819/3H	Screw,Set,securing Mounting Panel to Rear Number Plate Panel and Mounting Brackets	8

Always quote colour required when ordering Trimmed Parts.

FOR ALL MODELS UNLESS OTHERWISE STATED

PART NO.	Description.	NO. PER UNIT.	REMARKS

Rear Bumper Assemblies (Continued).

UFN.119/L	Nut, on Setscrews at Mounting Brackets	4	
C.723/A	Washer, Shakeproof, under Nuts and on Setscrews at Rear Number Plate Panel	8	
AW.102/T	Washer, Plain, under Nuts	4	
BD.35740	Tail Finisher, behind R.H.Mounting Panel	1	
BD.35741	Tail Finisher, behind L.H.Mounting Panel	1	
UFB.131/28R	Bolt, securing Tail Finishers	2	
FG.105/X	Washer, Spring, on Bolts	2	
FW.105/T	Washer, Plain, under Shakeproof Washers	2	
BD.35780	Reinforcing Washer, under Plain Washers	2	
BD.25318/1	Finisher Seal (Rubber) between Tail Finishers and Body	2	
BD.28852	Hinged Extension Board Assembly, for Luggage Floor	1)	
BD.28832	Chrome Strip, at forward edge of Extension Board	1)	
BD.28833	Chrome Capping, at R.H.End of Chrome Strip	1)	For F.H.C.Model only
BD.28834	Chrome Capping, at L.H.End of Chrome Strip	1)	
DAC.406/6C	Screw, Self-Tapping, securing Strip and Cappings to Board	9)	
BD.29251/1	Retainer, for Rubber Beadings	3)	

HOOD AND TONNEAU COVER.

BD.32851	Hood Sticks Assembly	1)	
BD.33434/1	Bolt, securing No.1 Link to Canopy	4)	
	For other items see Catalogue J.37	)	
BD.32073	Hood Cloth Assembly, complete	1)	
	For Tacking Strips see Catalogue J.37	)	
BD.32776	Outer Toggle Clamp Assembly, securing Hood at Windscreen	2)	
BD.15912	Hook, for Toggle Clamp	2)	For Open Model only
BD.20892	Locknut, for Hook	2)	
BD.28908	Chrome Capping and Socket receiving R.H. Outer Clamp	1)	
BD.28909	Chrome Capping and Socket receiving L.H. Outer Clamp	1)	
BD.32773	Centre Toggle Clamp Assembly, securing Hood at Windscreen	1)	
BD.32948	Stabiliser Rod, between Socket at top of Windscreen and Bracket on Dash	1)	
BD.31290	Tonneau Cover Assembly Supplied to Special order only.	1	For R.H.Drive Open Model
BD.31291	Tonneau Cover Assembly Supplied to Special order only.	1	For L.H.Drive Open Model

Always quote colour required when ordering Trimmed Parts.

FOR ALL MODELS UNLESS OTHERWISE STATED

PART NO.	Description.	NO. PER UNIT.	REMARKS

CARPETS FOR F.H.C. AND OPEN MODELS.

PART NO.	Description.	NO. PER UNIT.	REMARKS
BD.34912	Carpet Assembly, on Toeboards	2	
BD.34909	Carpet Assembly, on R.H.Front Floor	1	
BD.34910	Carpet Assembly, on L.H.Front Floor	1	For R.H.D.Cars only.
BD.34911	Carpet Assembly, on L.H.Front Floor	1	For L.H.D.Cars only.
BD.34913	Carpet Assembly, at R.H.Side of Clutch Housing	1	
BD.34914	Carpet Assembly, at L.H.Side of Clutch Housing	1	
BD.34915	Carpet Assembly, at R.H.Side of Gearbox Tunnel	1	
BD.34916	Carpet Assembly, at L.H.Side of Gearbox Tunnel	1	
BD.34917	Carpet Assembly, for R.H.Side of Cross Member	1	
BD.34918	Carpet Assembly, for L.H.Side of Cross Member	1	
BD.34860	Carpet Assembly, on Bulkhead at Rear Panel	1	For Open Model only
BD.36547	Carpet, in Luggage Floor Extension Well	1	For F.H.C.Model only
BD.24925	Footrest Board Assembly, on L.H.Toeboard	1)	For R.H.Drive F.H.C.
BD.24927	Mat Assembly,on L.H.Footrest Board	1)	& Open Models only
BD.24926	Footrest Board Assembly, on R.H.Toeboard	1)	For L.H.Drive
BD.24928	Mat Assembly, on R.H. Footrest Board	1)	F.H.C. & Open) Models only.

See Catalogue J.37 for Hardura Mats, Insulating
Felts, Anti-Drum Material, and Interior Trimming.

CARPETS FOR 2+2 MODEL.

PART NO.	Description.	NO. PER UNIT.	REMARKS
BD.35830	Carpet Assembly, on R.H.Toe Board	1	
BD.35831	Carpet Assembly, on L.H.Toe Board	1	
BD.34919	Carpet Assembly, on R.H.Front Floor	1	
BD.34920	Carpet Assembly, on L.H.Front Floor	1	
BD.34921	Carpet Assembly, at R.H.Side of Clutch Housing	1	
BD.34922	Carpet Assembly, at L.H.Side of Clutch Housing	1	
BD.34923	Carpet Assembly,at R.H.Side of Gear Box Cover	1	
BD.34924	Carpet Assembly,at L.H.Side of Gear Box Cover	1	
BD.35834	Carpet Assembly,at R.H.Side of Cross Member	1	
BD.35835	Carpet Assembly,at L.H.Side of Cross Member	1	
BD.35832	Carpet Assembly, on R.H.Rear Floor	1	
BD.35833	Carpet Assembly, on L.H.Rear Floor	1	
BD.34925	Carpet,on Propeller Shaft Tunnel	1	
BD.35836	Carpet Assembly,R.H.for Rear Cushion Valance	1	
BD.35837	Carpet Assembly, L.H. for Rear Cushion Valance	1	

Always quote colour required when ordering Trimmed Parts.

PART NO.	Description.	NO. PER UNIT.	REMARKS

BODY FITTINGS, AUTOMATIC TRANSMISSION FOR 2 + 2 MODELS.

BD.34718	Radio Panel Assembly, above Gearbox Tunnel	1	
BD.32509	Face Panel Assembly, for Radio Panel	1	

All other items are as for BD.34719
Radio Panel Assembly (for Standard Transmission).

BD.32763	Tunnel Finisher Assembly, complete	1	
BD.28710	Finisher Assembly (trimmed) for Tunnel	1	
BD.32492	Ash Tray Assembly	1	
BD.32764	Insert Panel Assembly (trimmed)	1	
BD.35824	Carpet Assembly, on R.H.Front Floor	1	
BD.35825	Carpet Assembly, on L.H.Front Floor	1	
BD.35826	Carpet Assembly, at R.H.Side of Converter Housing	1	
BD.35827	Carpet Assembly, at L.H.Side of Converter Housing	1	
BD.35828	Carpet Assembly, at R.H.Side of Transmission Unit Cover	1	
BD.35829	Carpet Assembly, at L.H.Side of Transmission Unit Cover	1	

All other Carpets are as for Standard Transmission

BD.33101	Hardura Mat Assembly, under L.H. Side of Scuttle	1)	For L.H.Drive) Model only.

See Catalogue J.38 for Hardura Mats,
Insulating Felts, Anti-Drum Material
and Interior Trimming.

Always quote colour required when ordering Trimmed Parts.

FOR ALL MODELS UNLESS OTHERWISE STATED

PART NO.	Description.	NO. PER UNIT.	REMARKS

HEATER AND DEMISTER INSTALLATION.

PART NO.	Description.	NO. PER UNIT.	REMARKS
400542	Spring, operating Air Flap	1	
BD.28378	Seal (Rubber) between Bonnet and Heater Air Intake	1	
C.17771	R.H.Feed Pipe Assembly, behind Dash Top Panel, between Hose and Water Valve	1)	Open and F.H.Coupe
C.31242	R.H.Feed Pipe Assembly, behind Dash Top Panel, between Hose and Water Valve	1)	2+2 only
C.28924	Hose, between Adaptor and R.H.Feed Pipe	1)	For U.S.A. and Canada
C.2905/14	Clip, securing Hose	2)	on Open and F.H.Coupe only
C.31059	Hose, between Adaptor and R.H.Feed Pipe	1)	2+2 only But Not for
C.2905/14	Clip, securing Hose	2)	U.S.A. and Canada.
C.31060	Hose, between Adaptor and R.H.Feed Pipe	1)	2+2 only
C.2905/14	Clip, securing Hose	2)	For U.S.A. and Canada
BD.33487	L.H.Control Arm, operating Air Flap in Heater Case	1	
BD.33483	Knob, on Control Arm	1	
UCS.413/2H	Screw, securing Knob to Arm	1	
BD.33488	R.H.Control Arm, operating Water Control Valve	1	
BD.33482	Knob, on Control Arm	1	
UCS.413/2H	Screw, securing Knob to Arm	1	
C.30078	Bolt, pivoting Control Arms	1	
AW.102/T	Washer, on Bolt, between Arms	3	
C.8737/9	Nut, on Bolt	1	
BD.33112	Heater Operation Plate	1	
BD.33017/1	Hammer Drive Screw, securing Operation Plate to Facia	2	
C.16794/2	Inner Cable, operating Air Flap	1)	Open and F.H.Coupe only
C.15714/6	Outer Cable, on Air Flap Cable	1)	
C.16794/10	Inner Cable, operating Air Flap	1)	2+2 only
C.15714/7	Outer Cable, on Air Flap Cable	1)	
C.16794/9	Inner Cable, operating Water Valve	1	
C.15714/2	Outer Cable, on Water Valve Cable	1	

FOR ALL MODELS UNLESS OTHERWISE STATED

PART NO.	Description.	NO. PER UNIT.	REMARKS

Heater and Demister Installation (Continued).

PART NO.	Description.	NO. PER UNIT.	REMARKS
BD.34741	R.H.Remote Control Assembly, operating Vanes in Air Director Boxes	1	
BD.34742	L.H.Remote Control Assembly, operating Vanes in Air Director Boxes	1	
BD.14607	Rubber Elbow, Centre on Heater Box	1)	
BD.23569	Rubber Elbow, Outer on Heater Box	2)	
BD.25205	Flex Hose, from Outer Elbow to "Y" Piece	2)	
BD.23077	"Y" Piece for Demister Hoses	3)	
BD.30775	Flexible Hose, to Inner Demister Nozzles	4)	
BD.30776	Flexible Hose, to Outer Demister Nozzles	2)	Open and F.H.Coupe only
BD.32264	Screen Rail Facia Assembly	1)	
BD.32205	Demister Bezel, Centre	1)	
BD.20591	Demister Bezel, Straight	2)	
DAJ.606/12C	Screw, securing Bezels	7)	
BD.20592	Demister Bezel, Curved	2)	
DAJ.606/10C	Screw, securing Bezel	4)	
BD.37342 +	Angled Elbow, in Heater Box Top at L.H.	1)	
BD.35659	Rubber Grommet, in Heater Box.Top	4)	
BD.23569	Rubber Elbow on Heater Box, Rear	2)	
BD.30775	Flexible Hose, from Grommets to Demister Nozzles on Front Facia	4)	
BD.35748	Flexible Hose, from Elbows to Demister Nozzles on Rear Facia	2)	
BD.35675	Front Screen Rail Facia Assembly	1)	
BD.32205	Demister Bezel.Centre	1)	2+2 only
BD.20591	Demister Bezel.Straight	2)	
DAJ.606/10C	Screw, securing Bezels	7)	
BD.35691	Rear Screen Rail Facia Assembly	1)	
BD.20592	Demister Bezel.Curved	2)	
DAJ.606/10C	Screw, securing Bezels	4)	
BD.30916/6	Beading, between Facias (60"long)	1)	

All other items as for Heater and Demister Installation
in Catalogue J.38.

PART NO.	Description.	NO. PER UNIT.	REMARKS

ELECTRICAL EQUIPMENT.

PART NO.	Description.	NO. PER UNIT.	REMARKS
C.29168	Alternator	1	Fitted up to *
			1R1012 RHD) Open
			1R7442 LHD)
			1R20006 RHD) F.H.C.
			1R25283 LHD)
			1R35010 RHD) 2+2
			1R40207 LHD)
			NOT AIR CONDITIONING
C.31081	Alternator	1	Fitted from *
12346	Bracket, Drive End	1	1R1013 RHD) Open
12347	Bearing Kit, Drive End	1	1R7443 LHD)
12348	Rotor and Slip Ring Assembly	1	1R20007 RHD) F.H.C.
12349	Stator	1	1R25284 LHD)
12325	Heatsink with Cathode Base Diodes	1	1R35011 RHD) 2+2
12350	Heatsink with Anode Base Diodes	1	1R40208 LHD)
12351	Brushbox Assembly, Complete	1	NOT AIR CONDITIONING
12352	Bracket Assembly, Slip Ring End	1	
12353	Through Bolt	3	
12354	Sleeve.Slip Ring End	1	
12355	Collar.Distance.Driving End	1	
C.29779	Cooling Fan for Alternator	1	*
C.28162	Alternator	1) Air Conditioning	*
C.28041	Cooling Fan, for Alternator	1) only	*
C.31181	Heat Shield, for Alternator	1	
C.19706	Distance Piece, at Shield Fixing	2	
C.23123	Alternator Pulley	1	*
C.30615	Bracket, Mounting Alternator	1	
UFS.143/6R	Setscrew, securing Bracket to Block	2	
C.727	Shakeproof Washer, on Setscrew	2	
UFB.131/9R	Bolt, Alternator to Mounting Bracket	1	
UFB.131/11R	Bolt, Alternator to Mounting Bracket	1	
FW.205/T	Washer, on Bolts	2	
C.29847	Adjusting Link, for Alternator	1	
UCS.131/9R	Setscrew, securing Link to Alternator	1	
C.8667/10	Nut, on Setscrew	1	
FW.105/T	Plain Washer, under Nut	1	
C.29849	Belt, Driving Alternator	1	**
C.24158	Relay for Alternator	1	**

PART NO.	Description.	NO. PER UNIT.	REMARKS

Electrical Equipment (Continued).

PART NO.	Description.	NO. PER UNIT.	REMARKS
C.27178	Starter Motor	1	
11042	Bolt, through Fixing	2	
2804	Brush Set	1	
11043	Bracket, Commutator End	1	
11044	Bushing Commutator End	1	
11045	Spring Set, for Brush Tension	1	
11046	Pivot Pin	1	
11047	Drive.Roller Clutch	1	
11048	Bracket, Driving End	1	
11049	Bushing, Driving End	1	
11050	Bracket, Intermediate	1	
11051	Bushing Intermediate	1	
11460	Thrust Washer Drive End	1	
11320	Thrust Washer.Steel Com,End	1	
11321	Thrust Washer, Fibre Com.End	1	
11053	Armature	1	
11054	Solenoid	1	
11055	Bush	1	
11056	Spacing Collar	1	
11057	Field Coils. Set	1	
C.31052	Relay for Starter Solenoid	1	
C.22488	Spigot Plate for Starter Motor	1	
C.22489	Ring Dowel, locating Spigot Plate	2	
UFB.137/13R	Bolt, securing Starter Motor and Spigot Plate to Clutch Housing	2	
FG.106/X	Spring Washer, on Bolts	2	
C.30120	Ignition Coil	1	*
C.30121	Ferrule for H.T.Lead	1	
C.28854	Rubber Sleeve for H.T.Lead	1	
C.18525	Extension Bracket.Mounting Coil	1	
C.6558	Stud, in Breather Housing for Bracket	1	
UFN.125/L	Nut, on Stud	1	
C.724	Shakeproof Washer, under Nut	1	
FW.104/T	Plain Washer, under Shakeproof Washer	1	
C.8047	Bracket for Coil	1	
UFN.125/L	Nut, securing Coil to Bracket	2	
C.724	Shakeproof Washer, under Nut	2	
FW.104/T	Plain Washer, under Shakeproof Washer	2	

PART NO.	Description.	NO. PER UNIT.	REMARKS	
	Electrical Equipment (Continued).			
C.25285	Distributor (8:1 and 9:1 CR)	1	Not for U.S.A. or Canada	*
C.11906	Nut for H.T.Leads	7		
C.5452	Copper Washer	7		
6476	Clamping Plate	1		
6477	Screw, for Clamping Plate	1		
9930	Cap	1		
6479	Brush and Spring Inside Cap	1		
6060	Rotor	1		**
9931	Contact Set	1		**
6487	Insulating Bush for C/B Lever	1		
C.11991	Condenser	1		**
C.25287	Waterproof Cover	1		
9934	Earth Lead	1		
9968	Spring Set.Auto-Advance	1		
10520	Weight.Auto-Advance	1		
6497	Return Spring for Vacuum Unit	1		
9969	Vacuum Unit	1		
9938	'O' Ring, on Distributor Spigot	1		
9253	Driving Dog	1		
C.28481	Distributor (9:1 CR)	1	For U.S.A. &Canada	*
11569	Spring Set, Auto-Advance	1		
9936	Weight.Auto-Advance	1		
	All other items as for Distributor C.25285 Except that Vacuum Unit is NOT required.			
C.2607	Rubber Sleeve, on Distributor Leads	7		
C.27405	Suppressor, on Distributor Cap	6)	Fitted only to	
BD.28607	'O' Ring, in Distributor Cap	6)	Cars exported to	
		)	Denmark.	

PART NO.	Description.	NO. PER UNIT.	REMARKS

Electrical Equipment (Continued).

PART NO.	Description.	NO. PER UNIT.	REMARKS
C.22458	Petrol Pump	1	**
10202	Coil Housing	1	
9100	Rocker and Blade Assembly	1	*
1145	Terminal Screw	1	
7664	Condenser	1	
7665	Spring Clip, holding Condenser	1	
10203	End Cover	1	
10204	Breather Elbow on Cover	1	
10205	Cap for Breather	1	
10206	Ball, under Cap	1	
C.18916	Lucar Blade	2	
10199	Diaphragm Assembly	1	
10201	Roller, for Diaphragm	11	
9320	Spring, for Diaphragm	1	
10200	Gasket, under Diaphragm	1	
AS.302/4D	Setscrew, securing Diaphragm and Coil Housing	6	
10186	Valve Assembly	2	
10188	Filter, for Inlet Valve	1	
10767	Sealing Washer, for Valves and Filter	3	
10189	Cover, for Valves	2	
10190	Plate, retaining Valves	1	
10191	Screw, securing Plate	2	
10193	Cover, End of Valve Housing	1	
10192	Cork Gasket, under Cover	1	
5803	Screw, securing Cover	1	
5648	Spring Washer, on Screw	1	
10194	Dished Washer, under Spring Washer	1	
10195	Anti-Surge Diaphragm	1	
10198	Sealing Washer, under Diaphragm Plate	1	
10196	Rubber Backing for Anti-Surge Diaphragm	1	
10197	'O' Ring, under Diaphragm Cover	1	
AS.304/3D	Setscrew, securing Diaphragm Cover	4	
C.22253	Control Box	1	
C.25838	Bracket Assembly, mounting Control Box and Terminal Post	1	
UFN.119/L	Nut, securing Bracket to Body	4	
C.723/A	Shakeproof Washer, under Nut	4	
UFS.319/4H	Setscrew, securing Control Box to Bracket	2	
C.16053	Fuse Box	3	
C.5638	Fuse (35 amp)	12	**
8576	Terminal Screw	3	
C.21996	Fuse Box	1	
C.5638	Fuse (35 amp)	2	**
C.13932	Fuse (50 amp)	2	**
UFS.319/4H	Setscrew, securing Fuse Boxes to Dash	4	

PART NO.	Description.	NO. PER UNIT.	REMARKS

Electrical Equipment (Continued).

PART NO.	Description.	NO. PER UNIT.
C.23532	Connector Block	1
UCN.113/L	Nut, securing Connector Block	2
C.721	Shakeproof Washer, under Nut	2
C.28506	Instrument Panel (Trimmed Black)	1
C.28509	Fuse Indicator Plate	1
C.27398	Fixing Screw, for Instrument Panel	2
BD.5453	Fibre Washer, on Fixing Screw	2
C.16258	Pivot Screw, for Instrument Panel	2
C.782	Fibre Washer, under Pivot Screw Head	2
C.16318	Nylon Bush, on Pivot Screw	2
UFS.419/2H	Setscrew, fixing Cable Clips to Panel	3
C.723A	Shakeproof Washer, on Setscrews	3
C.28503	Bulbholder, Instrument Panel	3
BD.1814/1	Pop Rivets, securing Bulb Holder	6

PART NO.	Description.	NO. PER UNIT.	REMARKS
	Electrical Equipment (Continued).		
C.30889	Panel and Switches Assembly (Cluster)	1	
C.30888	Panel and Switches Assembly (Cluster)	1	For use with heated backlight
C.30899	Wiper Switch	1	*
C.28577	Switch, for Screen Washer	1	*
C.28578	Switch, for Heater Fan	1	*
C.28579	Switch, for Rear Window	1	For heated backlight *
	(This switch is also fitted to cars without heated backlight but is inoperative)		
C.28579	Switch for Headlamps	1	*
C.28580	Switch for Hazard Warning	1	*
C.28579	Switch for Map Light	1	*
C.28581	Switch for Panel Light	1	*
C.28579	Switch for Interior Light	1	*
C.28617	Switch for Sidelamps	1	*
C.28616	Panel for Switches	1	
C.28583	Switch Indicator Strip	1	
C.28582	Switch Indicator Strip	1	For heated backlight only
BD.32187/1	Screw, securing Switch Panel Assembly	14	
BD.33097	Finisher (Trimmed Black) between Switch Panel and Radio Panel	1	
BD.22686	Drive Fastener, securing Finisher	4	
C.28522	Ignition Switch	1	Not req'd when steering * column lock is fitted
BD.10610	Locking Barrel for Ignition Switch	1	
C.24169	Control Unit, for Ignition Warning Light	1	*
C.28607	Battery Indicator	1	*
C.28496	Petrol Gauge	1	*
C.20429	Element, in Tank for Petrol Gauge	1	*
C.937	Gasket, between Element and Tank	1	*
C.28495	Oil Pressure Gauge	1	*
C.15474	Element, for Oil Pressure Gauge	1	*
C.29878	Water Temperature Gauge	1	*
C.16895	Element, in Manifold for Water Gauge	1	*
C.2296/1	Copper Washer, on Element	1	

PART NO.	Description.	NO. PER UNIT.	REMARKS

Electrical Equipment (Continued).

PART NO.	Description.	NO. PER UNIT.	REMARKS	
C.28497	Time Clock	1		*
11594	Strap securing Clock	1		
C.27103	Battery for Time Clock	1		*
C.15485	Voltage Control Unit at Back of Instrument Panel	1		*
C.28575	Resistor, on Instrument Panel	1		
C.15789	Lucar Blade Earthing Instrument Panel	1		
C.30913	Speedometer (miles)	1)	For us with 3.31:1 Rear	*
C.29543	Speedometer (Kilos)	1)	Axle Ratio and S.P. Tyres	*
C.29165	Speedometer (Miles)	1)	For use with 3.54:1 Rear	
C.29544	Speedometer (Kilos)	1)	Axle Ratio and S.P. Tyres	
C.30914	Speedometer (Miles)	1)	For us with 2.88:1 Rear Axle Ratio and	
C.29545	Speedometer (Kilos)	1)	S.P.Tyres	
C.30915	Speedometer (Miles)	1)	For use with 3.07:1 Rear Axle	
C.29546	Speedometer (Kilos)	1)	Ratio and S.P.Tyres	
C.26162	Remote Control for Speedometer Trip Mileage Recorder	1		
C.24878	Speedometer Cable Complete	1	R.H.Drive) For	**
11078	Inner Cable only	1	) Open	*
11079	Outer Cable only	1	) and	*
			) F.H.Coupe	
C.24870	Speedometer Cable complete	1	L.H.Drive) Models	**
8241	Inner Cable only	1	) only	*
1119	Outer Cable only	1	)	*
C.25566	Speedometer Cable Complete	1	R.H.Drive)	**
11309	Inner Cable only	1	) For	
11310	Outer Cable only	1	) 2+2	*
			) Models	
C.25567	Speedometer Cable Complete	1	L.H.Drive) only	**
11311	Inner Cable only	1	)	*
11312	Outer Cable only	1	)	*
C.25547	Right-Angle Gearbox for Speedometer Cable Drive	1		**
C.30916	Revolution Counter	1		*
C.28500	Cigar Lighter Assembly	1		*
C.18638/2	Element Assembly	1		**
C.16367	Switch in Door Hinge Pillar operating Map Lamp above instrument panel	2)	For Open and F.H.Coupe Models	*
C.9653	Switch in Door Hinge Pillar operating Map Lamp above Instrument Panel	2)	For 2+2 Models	*

PART NO.	Description.	NO. PER UNIT.	REMARKS

Electrical Equipment (Continued).

PART NO.	Description.	NO. PER UNIT.	REMARKS
C.17337	Headlamp Dipper Switch on Facia Panel	1	*
C.20305	Escutcheon for Headlamp Dipper Switch	1	
C.16927	Warning Light, for Direction Indicator	1	
8641	Window	1	
8642	Body	1	
987	Bulb	2	
11135	Bulb Holder	2	
C.16661	Warning Light, for Handbrake and Brake Fluid Level	1	
8096	Cover and Window	1	
8638	Lucar Blade for Cable	1	
8639	Insulator for Blade	1	
8640	Lucar Blade	1	
987	Bulb	1	
C.2607	Rubber Sleeve over Warning Light Terminals	1	
C.19637	Escutcheon, for Handbrake and Brake Fluid Warning Light	1	
C.16660	Switch operating Handbrake and Brake Fluid Warning Light	1	*
UFN.225/L	Nut, securing Switch to Bracket	2	
C.29109	Warning Light, for Choke Control	1	
C.16660	Switch, operating Choke Warning Light	1	*
UFN.225/L	Nut, securing Switch	2	
C.30549	Choke Control Arm	1	
BD.33473	Knob Assembly, for Control Arm	1	
BD.33347/1	Rivet, securing Knob to Arm	2	
C.17908	Quadrant Plate, for Control Arm	1	
UFS.125/4R	Setscrew, securing Quadrant Plate	1	
UFN.125/L	Nut, on Setscrew	1	
C.724	Shakeproof Washer, under Nut	1	
BD.11489	Ball Bearing, between Arm and Quadrant Plate	1	
C.17910	Leaf Spring, tensioning Ball Bearing	1	
C.17911	Pivot Bolt, for Control Arm	1	
C.8737/2	Nut, on Pivot Bolt	1	
FW.105/T	Plain Washer, under Nut	1	
UFB.131/9R	Bolt, securing Quadrant Plate to Facia	1	
BD.32743	Distance Piece, on Bolt	1	
UFN.131/L	Nut, on Bolt	1	
FG.105/X	Spring Washer, under Nut	1	
C.30660	Inner Cable for Choke Control	1)	*
BD.11721	Pin, securing Cable to Control Arm	1)	
UCS.113/2R	Setscrew, Clamping Cable in Pin	1)	Not required
C.8667/20	Nut, securing Pin to Control Arm	1)	for U.S.A.,
AW.104/T	Plain Washer, under Nut	1)	Canada,
		)	Newfoundland or
C.30661	Outer Cable, for Choke Control	1)	Hawaii
C.26508	Insulating Sleeve, on Outer Cable	1)	

PART NO.	Description.	NO. PER UNIT.	REMARKS

Electrical Equipment (Continued).

PART NO.	Description.	NO. PER UNIT.	REMARKS
C.15998	Pivot for Outer Cable	1)	
UFS.119/4R	Setscrew, securing Pivot	1)	NOT required for
C.5203/1	Washer, on Setscrew	1)	U.S.A., Canada
BD.1708/2	Double Coil Spring Washer on Setscrew	1)	Newfoundland or
		)	Hawaii
BD.11524	Grommet, for Outer Cable in Dash	1)	
C.29043	Choke Cable Assembly	1)	Open and) *
		)	F.H.Coupe)
		)	only)
C.31397	Choke Cable Assembly	1	2+2 only) *
			)
C.29044	Inner Cable Holder	1	)
UCS.113/2R	Setscrew, Clamping Inner Cable in Holder	2	) For) U.S.A.
C.8667/20	Nut, securing Holder to Control Arm	1	) Canada
AW.104/T	Plain Washer, under Nut	1	) Newfoundland) and
C.29045	Pivot, for Outer Cable	1	) Hawaii
UFS.119/4R	Setscrew, securing Pivot	1	)
C.5203/1	Washer, on Setscrew	1	)
BD.1708/2	Double Coil Spring Washer on Setscrew	1	)
FW.106/T	Plain Washer	1	)
			)
C.16393	Grommet, for Choke Cable	2	)
BD.32487	Choke operation Plate	1)	Fitted from 1R7748
BD.33017/1	Hammed Drive Screw, securing Plate	2)	1R25431 1R40434
C.25653	Headlamp Complete	2)	*
11551	Outer Rim	2)	
11576	Clip retaining Outer Rim	2)	
9266	Plate, retaining Sealed Beam Unit	2)	For
5221	Screw, securing Plate	6)	All
9271	Rim, seating Sealed Beam Unit	2)	R.H.Drive
10763	Sealed Beam Unit (75W/45W)	2)	Cars **
7764	Adaptor	2)	
11577	Gasket, for Headlamp Body	2)	
9404	Spring, retaining Seating Rim	2)	
9405	Trimmer Screw, for Beam Adjustment	4)	
11453	Retainer, for Trimmer Screws	4)	
C.25654	Headlamp Complete	2)	L.H.Drive Cars *
10465	Sealed Beam Unit (50W/40W)	2)	**
	All other items as for Headlamp C.25653		

PLEASE NOTE :- The above Headlamps are fitted to Cars Exported
to the following Countries.
Brazil, Canada, Chile, Colombia, Cuba, Dominican
Republic, Egypt,El Salvador,Greece,Guatamala,Haiti,
Hawaii,Jordan,Lebanon,Madeira,Mexico,Newfoundland,
Nicaragua,Panama,Persian Gulf, Peru,Phillippines,
Puerto Rico,Saudi Arabia,Syria,Uruguay,U.S.A.,
Venezuela,Viet-Nam(Sud) Israel up to 31/7/69

PART NO.	Description.	NO. PER UNIT.	REMARKS

Electrical Equipment (Continued).

PART NO.	Description.	NO. PER UNIT.	REMARKS
C.25655	Headlamp Complete	2)	*
7762	Light Unit	2) L.H.Drive Cars	**
7763	Bulb (45W/40W)	2)	**
7765	Spring Retaining Bulb	2)	

All other items as for Headlamp C.25653.

PLEASE NOTE :- The above Headlamps are fitted to cars exported
to the following countries.
Austria, Belgium,Belgian Congo,Canary Isles,Curaccao
Cyrenaica,Denmark,Finland,Germany,Holland,Iceland,
Italy,Libya,Luxembourg,Norway,Portugal,Spain,
Sweden,Switzerland. Israel from 1/8/69

PART NO.	Description.	NO. PER UNIT.	REMARKS
C.25656	Headlamp complete	2)	*
7762	Light Unit	2) L.H.Drive Cars	**
8612	Bulb (Yellow)(45W/40W)	2)	**
7765	Spring retaining Bulb	2)	

All other items as for Headlamp C.25653.

PLEASE NOTE :- The above headlamps are fitted to Cars exported
to the following Countries.
Algeria,France,Morocco,Tangiers and Tunisia.

PART NO.	Description.	NO. PER UNIT.	REMARKS
DAZ.408/10C	Screw, securing Headlamp	8	
BD.8536/1	Spire Nut, on Screw	8	
C.30875	R.H.Front Side/Flasher Lamp with White/Amber Lens	1	*
12282	Lens	1	*
12344	Gasket, seating Lens	1	*
3455	Interior,Bulbholder, Side Lamp	1	
989	Bulb,Side Lamp	1	**
5311	Interior,Bulbholder.Flasher	1	
C.9126	Bulb, Flasher.	1	**
11719	Gasket, seating Lamp	1	
C.30876	L.H.Front Side/Flasher Lamp with White/Amber Lens	1	*
12283	Lens	1	*
11722	Gasket, seating Lamp	1	

All other items as for Lamp C.30875

PLEASE NOTE :- The above Lamps are fitted to Cars used
in the United Kingdom.

PART NO.	Description.	NO. PER UNIT.	REMARKS
C.30877	R.H.Front Side/Flasher Lamp with Amber Lens	1	*
11723	Lens	1	*
11718	Gasket, seating Lens	1	*
3455	Interior.Bulbholder.Side Lamp	1	
989	Bulb.Side Lamp	1	**
5311	Interior Bulbholder.Flasher	1	
C.9126	Bulb.Flasher	1	**
11719	Gasket Seating Lamp	1	

PART NO.	Description.	NO. PER UNIT.	REMARKS

Electrical Equipment (Continued).

PART NO.	Description.	NO. PER UNIT	REMARKS
C.30878	L.H.Front Side/Flasher Lamp with Amber Lens	1	*
11724	Lens	1	*
11721	Gasket, seating Lens	1	*
11722	Gasket, seating Lamp	1	

All other items as for Lamp C.30877

PLEASE NOTE :- The above lamps are fitted to cars exported to Canada, Hawaii,Newfoundland and U.S.A.

PART NO.	Description.	NO. PER UNIT	REMARKS
C.31148	R.H.Front Side/Flasher Lamp with White Lens	1	*
11725	Lens	1	*
12344	Gasket, seating Lens	1	*
5311	Interior.Bulbholder	1	
C.9125	Bulb	1	**
11719	Gasket, seating Lamp	1	
C.31149	L.H.Front Side/Flasher Lamp with White Lens	1	*
11726	Lens	1	*
11722	Gasket, seating Lamp	1	

All other items as for Lamp C.31148

PLEASE NOTE :- The above lamps are fitted to Cars exported to Greece, Italy and Japan.

PART NO.	Description.	NO. PER UNIT	REMARKS
C.31150	R.H.Front Side/Flasher Lamp with White/Amber Lens	1	*
11717	Lens	1	*
11718	Gasket, seating Lens	1	*
3455	Interior,Bulbholder.Side Lamp	1	
989	Bulb.Side Lamp	1	**
5311	Interior.Bulbholder.Flasher	1	
C.9126	Bulb.Flasher	1	**
11719	Gasket, seating Lamp	1	
C.31151	L.H.Front Side/Flasher Lamp with White/Amber Lens	1	*
11720	Lens	1	*
11721	Gasket, seating Lens	1	*
11722	Gasket, seating Lamp	1	

All other items as for Lamp C.31150

PLEASE NOTE :- The above lamps are fitted to cars for All countries other than those noted above

PART NO.	Description.	NO. PER UNIT	REMARKS
C.30883	Front Side Marker Reflex R.H.	1	*
12323	Lens	1	**
11728	Gasket, for Lens	1	**
C.30884	Front Side Marker Reflex L.H.	1	*
12322	Lens	1	**
11728	Gasket, for Lens	1	**
BD.35732	Gasket, seating Front Side Marker	2	*

PART NO.	Description.	NO. PER UNIT.	REMARKS

Electrical Equipment (Continued).

PART NO.	Description.	NO. PER UNIT.	REMARKS
DAZ.808/12C	Screw, securing Front Side Marker	2	
BD.8536/6	Spire Nut, on Screw	2	
UCS.416/6H	Setscrew, securing Front Side Marker	2	
UCN.116/L	Nut, on Setscrew	2	
C.722	Shakeproof Washer, under Nut	2	
C.30879	R.H.Stop/Tail/Flasher Lamp with Red/Amber Lens	1	*
12284	Lens	1	**
C.30880	L.H.Stop/Tail/Flasher Lamp with Red/Amber Lens	1	*
12285	Lens	1	**

PLEASE NOTE :- The above Lamps are <u>NOT</u> required for cars
exported to Canada, Hawaii, Greece, Newfoundland
Portugal and U.S.A.

PART NO.	Description.	NO. PER UNIT.	REMARKS
C.30881	R.H.Stop/Tail/Flasher Lamp with Red Lens	1	*
12286	Lens	1	**
C.30882	L.H.Stop/TAil/Flasher Lamp with Red Lens	1	*
12321	Lens	1	**

PLEASE NOTE :- The above lamps are fitted to cars exported to
Canada, Greece, Hawaii, Newfoundland, Portugal
and U.S.A.

PART NO.	Description.	NO. PER UNIT.	REMARKS
C.31308	Rear Side Marker Reflex R.H.	1	*
11731	Lens	1	**
11728	Gasket, seating Lens	1	**
C.31309	Rear Side Marker Reflex L.H.	1	*
11732	Lens	1	**
11728	Gasket, seating Lens	1	**
BD.35733	Gasket, seating, Rear Side Marker	2	*
C.31304/6	Screw, securing Rear Side Marker	4	
C.16063	Flasher Unit	1	*
UCS.313/8H	Setscrew, securing Flasher Adaptor to Body	1	
C.30885	Reverse Lamp	2	*

PLEASE NOTE :- The above lamp is NOT required for cars exported
to Algeria,France, Morocco,Tangier or Tunisia.

PART NO.	Description.	NO. PER UNIT.	REMARKS
C.30886	Reverse Lamp	2	*

PLEASE NOTE :- The above lamp is fitted to cars exported to
Algeria, France, Morocco, Tangiers and Tunisia.

PART NO.	Description.	NO. PER UNIT.	REMARKS
C.1083	Switch, on Gearbox for Reverse Lamp	1	*
C.30887	Number Plate and Boot Illumination Lamp	1	
12338	Rim for Number Plate Light	1	
12339	Gasket, seating Rim and Lamp	1	
12340	Lens for Number Plate Light	1	

PART NO.	Description.	NO. PER UNIT.	REMARKS	
	Electrical Equipment (Continued).			
12341	Lens for Boot Light	2		
3455	Interior. Bulbholder	2		
989	Bulb	2		
BD.36159/4	Screw, securing Number Plate Lamp	2		
C.22254	Horn (High Note)	1		*
10209	Bracket on Horn	1		
C.22255	Horn (Low Note)	1		*
10209	Bracket on Horn	1		
C.25115	Bracket, on Crossmember Mounting Horns	2		
C.8667/1	Nut, securing Horns to Bracket	4		
C.17338	Horn Relay	1		*
UFS.419/3H	Setscrew, securing Horn Relay	2		
UFN.119/L	Nut, on Setscrew	2		
C.723/A	Shakeproof Washer, under Nut	2		
AW.102/T	Plain Washer, under Shakeproof Washer	2		
C.26654	Horn Mute fitted in Horn Trumpet	2	For Holland only	
C.28489	Direction Indicator/Horn/Headlamp Flasher Switch	1		*
C.28490	Cover, for Switch	1		
C.28573	Motif Assembly, in Centre of Steering Wheel	1		
C.30601	Steering Column Lock and Ignition Switch Assembly	1)	Fitted to Cars) exported to) countries where steering) lock is compulsory.	
C.28133	Electric Motor Driving Radiator Fan	2		*
C.18110	Grommet Mounting Fan Motor	8		
C.8667/17	Nut, securing Fan Motor to Brackets	8		
C.18111	Plain Washer, under Nut	8		
C.26573	Thermostatic Switch in Radiator Controlling Fan Motor	1		**
C.2475	Gasket, under Switch	1		
UFS.119/4R	Setscrew, securing Switch	3		
C.723/A	Shakeproof Washer, on Setscrew	3		
C.28357	Extension Cable for Thermo., Switch	1		
C.28065	Harness for Fan Motors	1		
C.18122	Relay (Thermo,Switch Protection)	1		*
C.28171	Harness for Relay	1		

PART NO.	Description.	NO. PER UNIT.	REMARKS

Electrical Equipment (Continued).

PART NO.	Description.	NO. PER UNIT.	REMARKS	
C.28134	Bracket Mounting Relay	1		
UFN.119/L	Nut, securing Relay to Bracket	2		
C.723/A	Shakeproof Washer, under Nut	2		
UFS.137/3R	Setscrew, securing Bracket	1		
C.726	Shakeproof Washer, on Setscrew	1		
C.16062	Stop Light Switch	1		
C.30892	Screen Wiper Motor and Primary Link	1)	) Open	*
C.30874	Backplate and Wheel Boxes Assembly	1) R.H.Drive	) and	*
12312	Screen Wiper Arm	3)	) F.H.	**
11589	Blade, for Wiper Arm	3)	) Coupe	**
			) Models	
C.30893	Screen Wiper Motor and Primary Link	1)	) only	*
C.28485	Backplate and Wheelboxes Assembly	1) L.H.Drive	)	*
11586	Screen Wiper Arm	3)	)	**
11589	Blade for Wiper Arm	3)	)	**
C.31003	Screen Wiper Motor and Primary Link	1)	)	*
C.31005	Backplate and Wheelboxes Assembly	1)	)	*
12310	Screen Wiper Arm.R.H.(Driver)	1) R.H.Drive	)	**
12308	Screen Wiper Arm.L.H.(Passenger)	1)	)	**
12311	Blade, for Wiper Arm	2)	)	**
			) 2+2	
C.31004	Screen Wiper Motor and Primary Link	1)	) only	*
C.31005	Backplate and Wheelboxes Assembly	1)	)	*
12310	Screen Wiper Arm L.H. (Driver)	1) L.H.Drive	)	**
12309	Screen Wiper Arm R.H.(Passenger)	1)	)	**
12311	Blade, for Wiper Arm	2)	)	**
C.16718	Gasket at Wiper Motor Mounting	1	Open and F.H.Coupe only	
BD.35897	Gasket at Wiper Motor Mounting	1	2+2 only	
UFS.125/4R	Setscrew, securing Wiper Motor	4		
C.724	Shakeproof Washer, on Setscrew	4		
C.15486	Map Lamp	1		
989	Bulb, for Map Lamp	1		**
C.17436	Insulator for Map Lamp	1		
BD.1814/1	Pop Rivet, securing Map Lamp	2		
C.16498	Interior Lamp	1)		
8602	Lens	1)		
8601	Gasket, seating Lens	1)		
8603	Base	1) Open Models only		
C.9126	Bulb	1)		**
		)		
DZZ.406/6C	Screw, securing Interior Lamp	2)		
C.1094	Spacing Washer, on Screw	2)		
C.18347	Interior Lamp	1)		
BD.14049/1	Lens	1)		
8703	Backplate and Bulbholder	1) F.H.Coupe and		
989	Bulb	2) 2+2 Models		**
		)		
DA.506/12C	Screw, securing Interior Lamp	2)		
BD.8633/4	Spire Nut, for Screw	2)		

PART NO.	Description.	NO. PER UNIT.	REMARKS	

Electrical Equipment (Continued).

PART NO.	Description.	NO. PER UNIT.	REMARKS	
C.28516	Interior Mirror	1	Not for U.S.A.	**
C.33151	Interior Mirror	1	For U.S.A.	**
BD.32397	Boss, on Windscreen for Mirrors	1		*
C.28475	Plastic Screw, securing Mirror to Boss	1		**
C.30827	Door Mirror R.H.	1		
11611	Plastic Gasket seating Mirror	1		
11618	Screw, securing Mirror	2		
C.28517	Door Mirror L.H.	1		
11611	Plastic Gasket seating Mirror	1		
11618	Screw, securing Mirror	2		
C.19909	Wing Mirror	2		

PLEASE NOTE :- Door and Wing Mirrors are fitted as required.

PART NO.	Description.	NO. PER UNIT.	REMARKS	
C.28520	Hazard Flasher Unit	1		**
UCS.313/8H	Setscrew, securing Flasher Unit	1		
UCN.113/L	Nut, on Setscrew	1		
C.721	Shakeproof Washer, under Nut	1		
C.29087	Bracket for Flasher Unit	1)		
DJZ.408/6C	Screw, securing Bracket	2)	Open and F.H.Coupe	
BD.8633/7	Spire Nut, for Screw	2)	only	
UCS.313/8H	Setscrew, Flasher Socket Mounting	1		
UCN.113/L	Nut, on Setscrew	1		
C.28521	Hazard Warning Light Lens	1		
C.29131	Locknut	1		
C.28900	Spacing Nut	1		
C.28518	Escutcheon-Hazard Warning	1		
C.24158	Relay for Hazard Warning	1		*
C.27537	Battery	1		
C.16473	Battery Tray	1		
C.10640/2	Drain Tube (Rubber) for Tray 5" long	1		
C.16474	Battery Clamp	1		
C.16475	Rod through Clamp securing Battery	2		
C.17084	Wing Nut on Rod	2		
FG.204/X	Double Coil Spring Washer under Wing Nut	2		
C.24495	Battery Cable (Negative to Earth)	1		
UFS.137/5R	Setscrew, securing Cable to Scuttle	1		
C.726	Shakeproof Washer, on Setscrew	1		
FW.106/T	Plain Washer, under Shakeproof Washer	1		
C.24496	Battery Cable (Positive)	1		
C.2609	Screw, securing Cables to Battery Posts	2		

PART NO.	Description.	NO. PER UNIT.	REMARKS

Electrical Equipment (Continued).

PART NO.	Description.	NO. PER UNIT.	REMARKS
C.22257	Terminal Post. Assembly	1	
C.24497	Cable.Terminal Post to Starter Motor	1	
C.30897	Forward Harness	1	R.H.Drive
C.28510	Forward Harness	1	L.H.Drive
C.24498	R.H.Body Harness	1)	Open and F.H.Coupe
C.24499	L.H.Body Harness	1)	) Models
C.24653	R.H.Body Harness	1)	
C.24654	L.H.Body Harness	1)	) 2+2
C.30895	Instrument Panel Harness	1	R.H.Drive
C.30896	Instrument Panel Harness	1	L.H.Drive
C.31031	Alternator Harness.R.H.Drive	1	Fitted up to 1R1012. Open. 1R20006. F.H.C. 1R35010. 2+2
C.31156	Alternator Harness. R.H.Drive	1	Fitted from 1R1013. Open 1R20007. F.H.C. 1R35011. 2+2
C.28514	Alternator Harness. L.H.Drive	1	Fitted up to 1R7442. Open 1R25283.F.H.C. 1R40207.2+2
C.31155	Alternator Harness. L.H.Drive	1	Fitted from 1R7443. Open 1R25284. F.H.C. 1R40208. 2+2
C.25164	Front Lamp Harness	1	
C.16921	Connector (8 Pin Male) for Front Lamp Harness	1	
C.16997	Fixing Plate, for Male Connector	1	
UFS.125/3R	Setscrew, securing Connector to Bonnet Diaphragm	3	
C.724	Shakeproof Washer, on Setscrew	3	
C.17003	Washer (Sorbo) at Connector Mounting	1	
C.18175	Washer (Hard Rubber) at Connector Mounting	1	
C.16922	Cable, Instrument Link	1	
C.16917	Cable, Instrument Illumination	1	
C.17356	Cable, R.H.Side Lamp Connector	1	
C.17357	Cable, L.H.Side Lamp Connector	1	

PART NO.	Description.	NO. PER UNIT.	REMARKS

Electrical Equipment (Continued).

PART NO.	Description.	NO. PER UNIT.	REMARKS
C.24655	Cable, Brake Fluid Level Warning Lamp Connector	1	R.H.Drive only
C.17474	Cable, Interior Lamp Connector	1	Open Cars only
C.17475	Cable, Interior Lamp Connector	1	F.H.Coupe and 2+2 only
C.17376	Cable, Heater Motor Connector	1	
C.31405	Cable Washer Bottle Jumper Lead	1	R.H.Drive only Open and F.H.Coupe
C.18728	Cable, Reverse Lamp Connector	1	Open and F.H.Coupe only
C.22140	Cable Headlamp Flasher	1	For Italy only
C.16919	Earth Cable (Engine to Body)	1	
C.25165	Earth Cable (Horns)	2	
C.18699	Earth Cable (Cigar Lighter)	1	
C.5204	Earth Terminal for Front Lamp Harness	2	
C.5204	Earth Terminal for Rear Lamp	2	
UFS.419/4H	Setscrew, securing Rear Lamp Earth	2	
UFN.119/L	Nut, on Setscrew	2	
C.723/A	Shakeproof Washer, under Nut	2	

PART NO.	Description.	NO. PER UNIT.	REMARKS

ELECTRICAL EQUIPMENT FOR AUTOMATIC TRANSMISSION. 2+2 ONLY.

PART NO.	Description.	NO. PER UNIT.	REMARKS
C.25463	Starter Cut-Out Switch on Selector Gate	1	**
UFN.125/L	Nut, locking Switch	1	
C.26831	Earth Lead, for Cut-Out Switch	1	
C.30898	Harness for Cut-Out Switch	1	
C.25777	Lamp.Illuminating Selector Lever Indicator	1	*
C.25274	Bulb	1	**
UCS.311/2H	Setscrew, securing Lamp	2	
C.720	Shakeproof Washer, on Setscrew	2	
C.26337	Light Filter, under Indicator Plate	1	
C.27133	Lucar Blade, earthing Indicator Lamp	1	
C.30915	Speedometer (Miles)	1)	For 2.88:1 Axle
		)	Ratio
C.29546	Speedometer (Kilos)	1)	and S.P.Tyres
C.30913	Speedometer (Miles)	1)	For 3.07:1 Axle
		)	Ratio
C.29543	Speedometer (Kilos)	1)	and S.P.Tyres
C.29165	Speedometer (Miles)	1)	For 3.31:1 Axle
		)	Ratio
C.29544	Speedometer (Kilos)	1)	and S.P.Tyres
C.24869	Flexible Speedometer Cable Complete	1)	
11322	Inner Cable only	1)	R.H.Drive only
11323	Outer Cable only	1)	
C.25403	Flexible Speedometer Cable Complete	1)	
11035	Inner Cable only	1)	L.H.Drive only
11036	Outer Cable only	1)	
C.26540	Clip, supporting Speedometer Cable	1)	

PART NO.	Description.	NO. PER UNIT.	REMARKS	

WINDSCREEN WASHERS.

PART NO.	Description.	NO. PER UNIT.	REMARKS	
C.25438	Windscreen Washer Unit Assembly	1)		*
11435	Motor with Coupling, Cover and Pump Assembly	1)		
11084	Reservoir	1)		
11085	Filler Cap, on Reservoir	1)		
11086	Bracket and Strap Assembly Holding Washer Unit	1)		
UFS.419/8H	Setscrew, securing Bracket and Strap Assembly	3)	Open and	
C.723/A	Shakeproof Washer, on Setscrew	6)	F.H.Coupe	
BD.18957/1	Distance Piece, on Setscrew	3)	only	
C.16663	Screen Washer Tubing (60"long)(R.H.Drive)	1)		
C.18393	Screen Washer Tubing (44" long)(L.H.Drive)	1)		
C.15644	"T" Piece, at Junction of Tubes	1)		
C.15645	Jet Assembly	2)		*
C.31049	Windscreen Washer Unit Assembly	1)		*
C.31237	Bracket Assembly, holding Washer Unit	1)		
C.31239	Gasket under Bracket	1)		
BD.32206/3	Taptite Screws, securing Bracket	4)	2+2 only	
C.28009/3	Screen Washer Tubing (15ft long)	1)		
BD.24519	Clip, securing Tubing	6)		
C.29780	Jet Assembly	1)		*
C.16145	Spacer, on Jet Assembly	1)		

PART NO.	Description.	NO. PER UNIT.	REMARKS

TOOL KIT.

PART NO.	Description.	NO. PER UNIT.	REMARKS
C.31164	Tool Roll	1	
C.996	Pliers	1	
C.11753	Tyre Pressure Gauge	1	
C.5444	Screwdriver for Distributor	1	
C.5587	Feeler Gauge	1	
C.993	Extractor for Tyre Valve	1	
C.20482	Screwdriver	1	
C.10155	Box Spanner for Spark Plugs and Cylinder Head Nuts	1	
C.2896	Tommy Bar, for Box Spanner	1	
C.4594	Open Ended Spanner ($\frac{3}{4}$ x $\frac{7}{8}$ A.F.)	1	
C.4595	Open Ended Spanner (9/16 x $\frac{5}{8}$ A.F.)	1	
C.4596	Open Ended Spanner (7/16 x $\frac{1}{2}$ A.F.)	1	
C.4638	Open Ended Spanner (11/32 x $\frac{3}{8}$ A.F.)	1	
C.20661	Jack complete with Handle	1)	Open and
C.27873	Handle only for Jack	1)	F.H.Coupe only
C.25183	Jack complete with Handle	1)	2+2 only
C.27873	Handle only for Jack	1)	
BD.23688	Container for Jack	1	
C.28637	Hub Nut Spanner	1)	For use with
C.27290	Mallet, for Hub Nut	1)	Wire Spoked Wheels
C.26864	Wheel Disc Wrench	1)	For use with
C.22401	Wheel Brace	1)	Pressed Spoke
		)	Wheels.

PART NO.	Description.	NO. PER UNIT.	REMARKS

OPTIONAL EXTRAS.

C.12816	Petrol Filler Cap. Locking	1	
9036	Key Fob (Leather)	1	
7205	Heating Element for Cylinder Block (240V)	1	Not for Canada.

ITEMS FOR HEATED BACKLIGHT.

BD.22740	Electrically Heated Back Door Glass (Clear Glass)	1)	
BD.22744	Electrically Heated Back Door Glass (Sundym Glass)	1)	
BD.27126	Rubber Seal around Back Door Glass	1)	
BD.20201	Rubber Insert, for Seal	1)	
C.20123	Backlight Connector	1)	
C.15639	Grommet	2)	
BD.18341	Grommet	3)	F.H.Coupe and
BD.22655	Clip, for Fuse Holder	1)	2+2
DAZ.404/4C	Screw, securing Clip	1)	
C.17001	Cable Strapping	1Ft.)	
C.17002	Stud, for Strapping	2)	
C.26471	Warning Light (Amber) for Backlight	1)	
C.28519	Escutcheon for Warning Light	1)	
C.26651	Relay complete with Resistance	1)	
DAZ.408/8C	Screw, securing Relay	2)	
C.31393	Harness, for Heated Backlight	1)	
C.31694	Link Lead	1)	

ITEMS FOR "PRESSED STEEL" WHEELS.

C.31210	Front Hub Assembly	2	
C.27779	Stud for Wheels	10	
C.3039	Hub sealing Cap	2	
C.3044/1	Grease Nipple on Hub (Straight)	2	
C.31251	Bolt, securing Brake Disc to Hub	10	
C.30949	Rear Hub Assembly	2	
C.13365	Stud for Wheels	10	
C.20813	Water Thrower on Hubs	2	
C.30951	Washer, on Half Shaft for Hub Location	2	
C.30073	"Pressed" Road Wheel	5	
C.3041	Nut, securing Road Wheels	20	
C.30283	Nave Plate, for Road Wheel	4	
C.31213	Medallion on Nave Plate	4	
C.22583	Spire Nut, securing Medallion	8	

SPARES DIVISION

SPARE PARTS CATALOGUE

for

JAGUAR 4·2 'E' TYPE

GRAND TOURING MODELS

Series 1

(Illustrations only)

PUBLICATION J.37

PUBLISHED NOVEMBER, 1965
Reprinted November, 1969

FIRST SUPPLEMENT

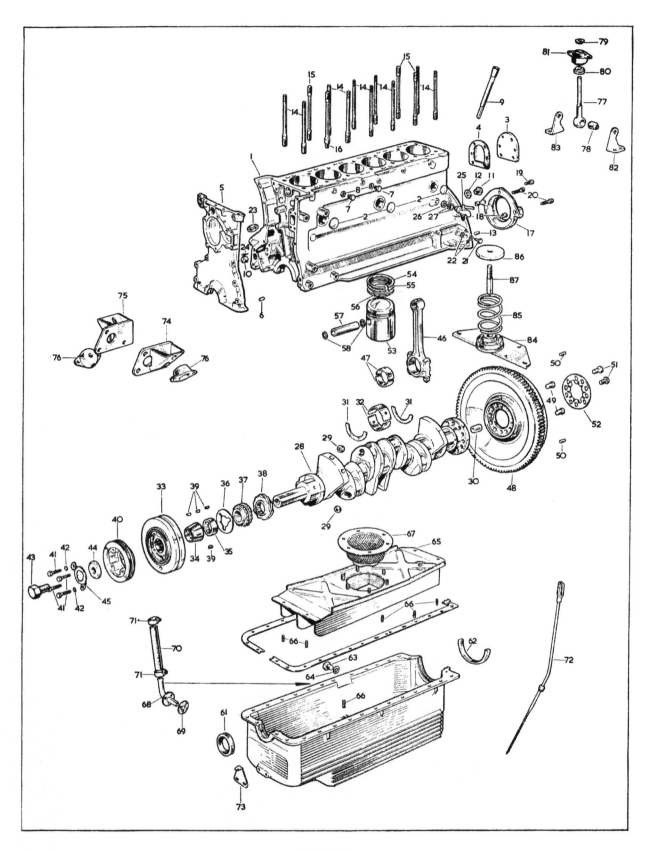

PLATE I

176

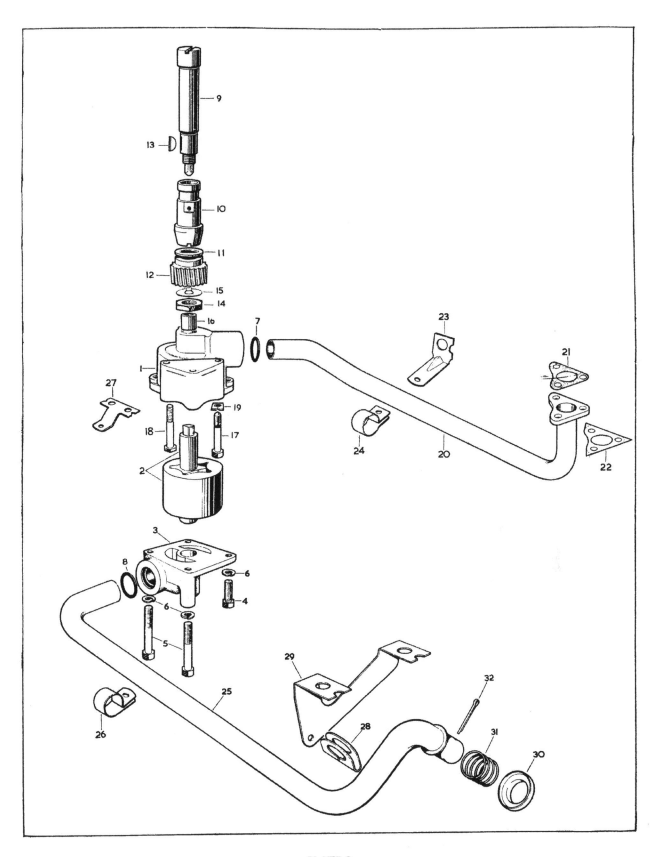

PLATE 2

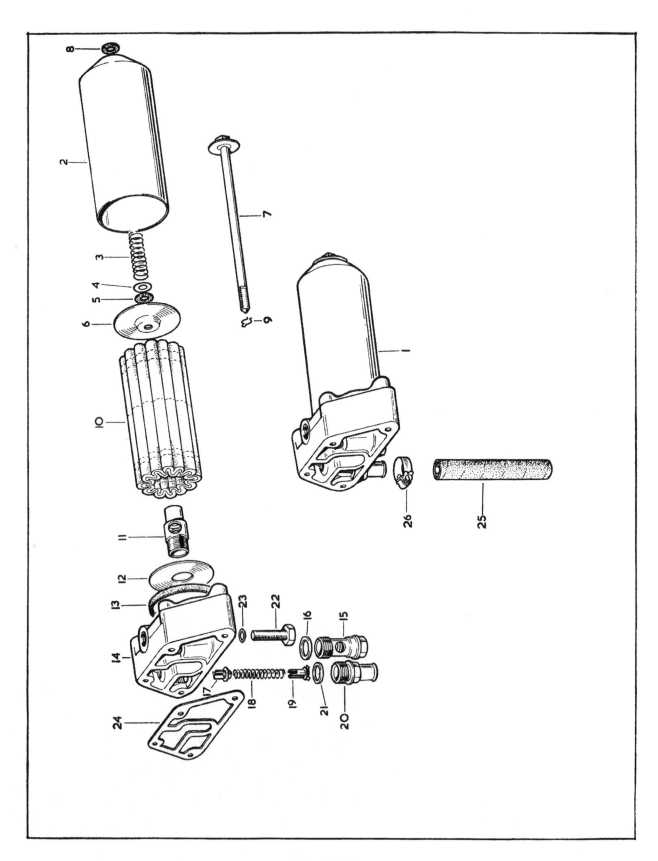

PLATE 3

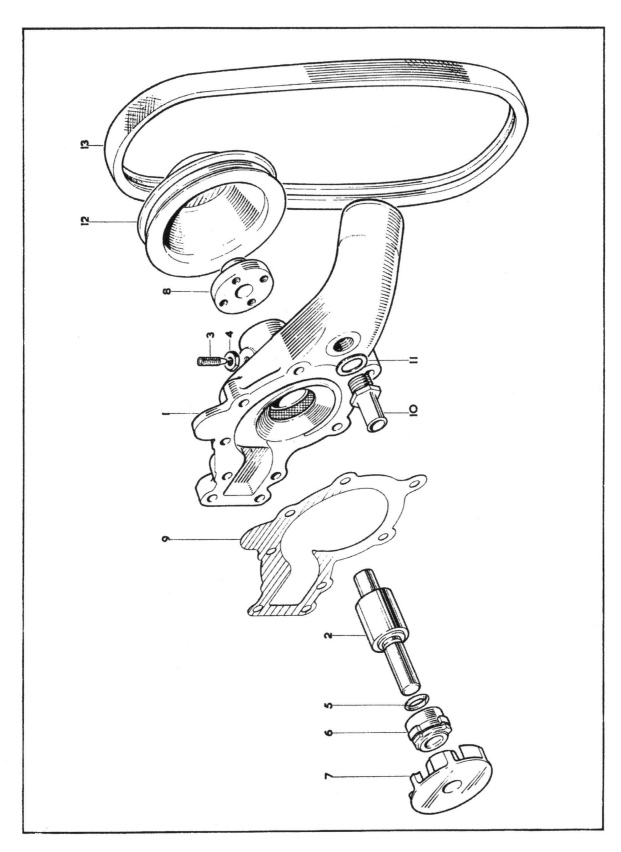

PLATE 4

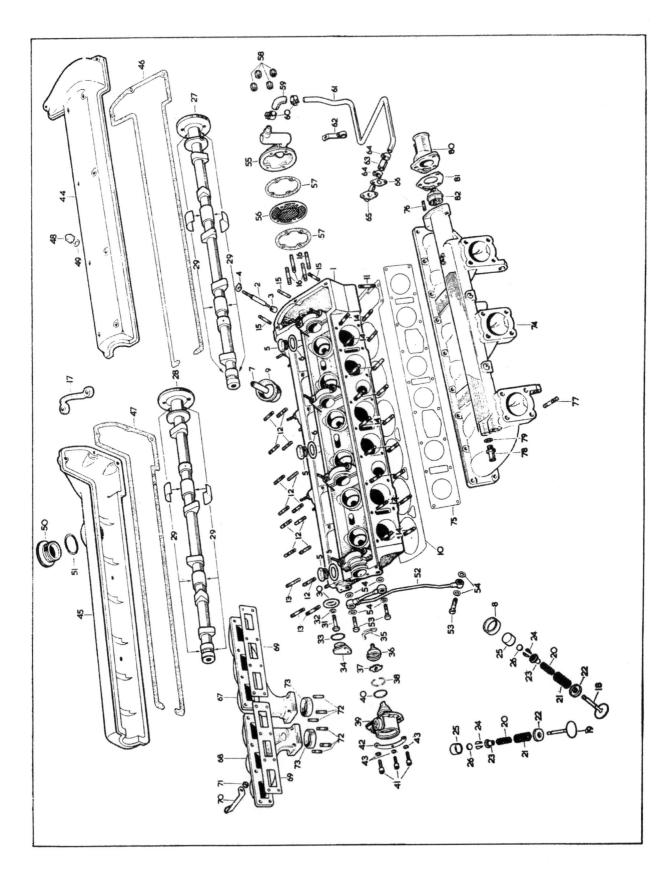

PLATE 5

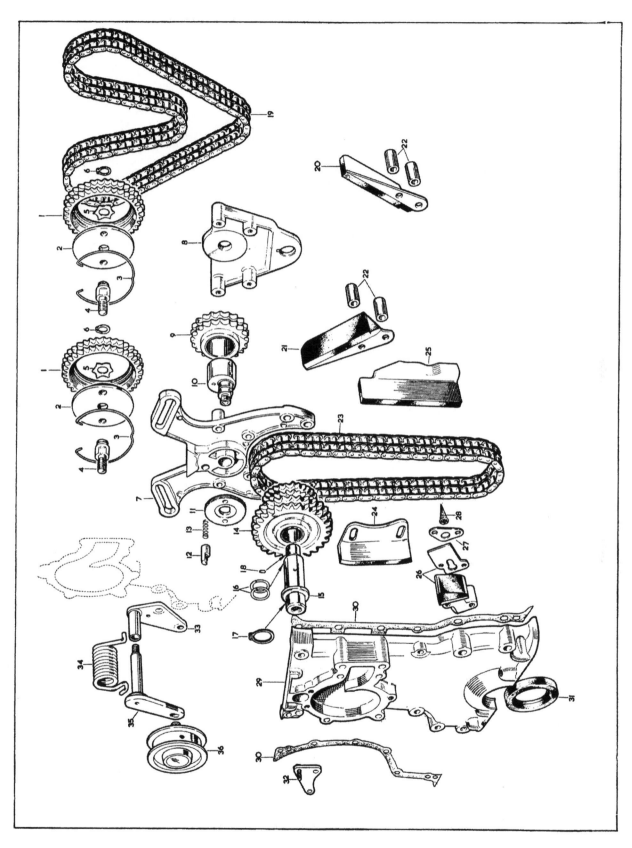

PLATE 6

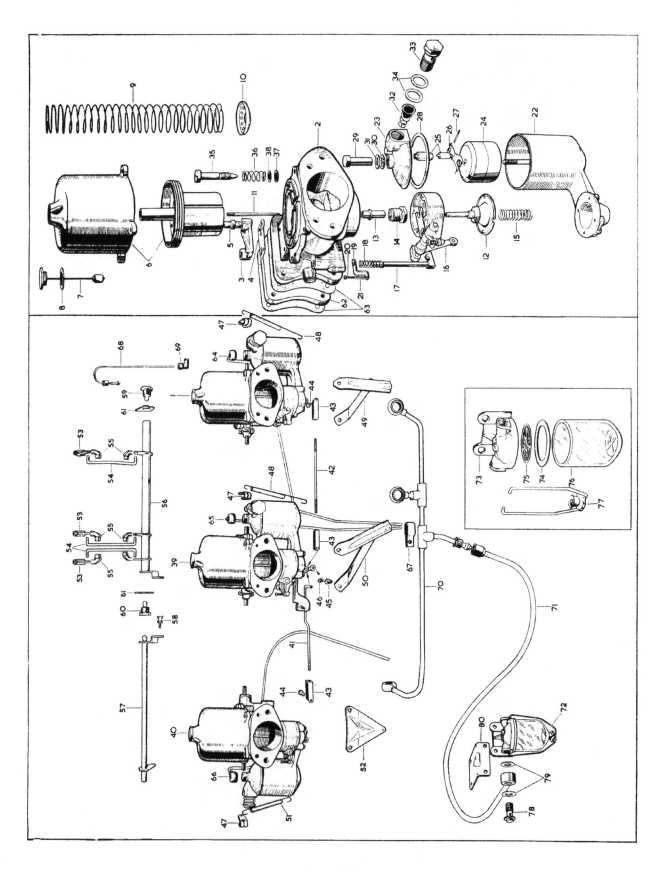

PLATE 7

182

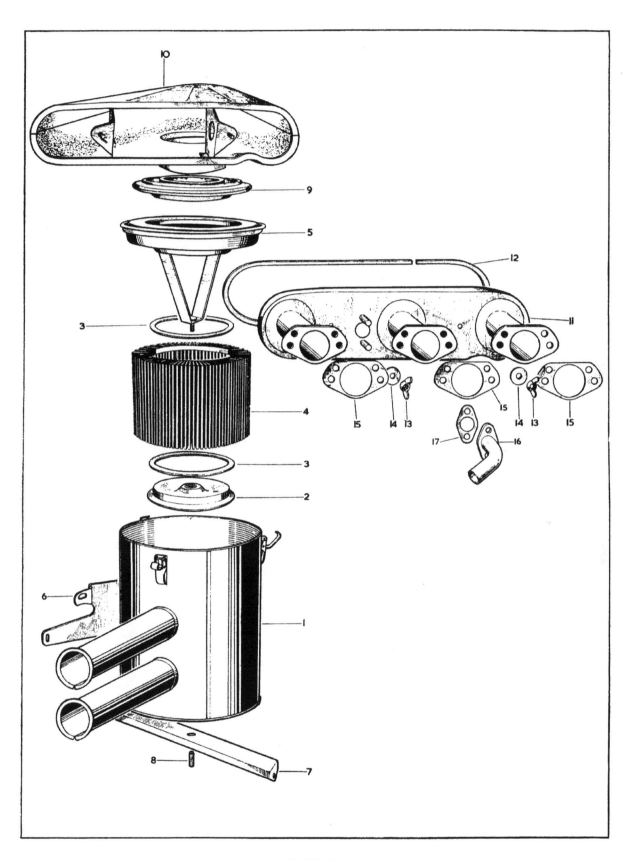

PLATE 8

183

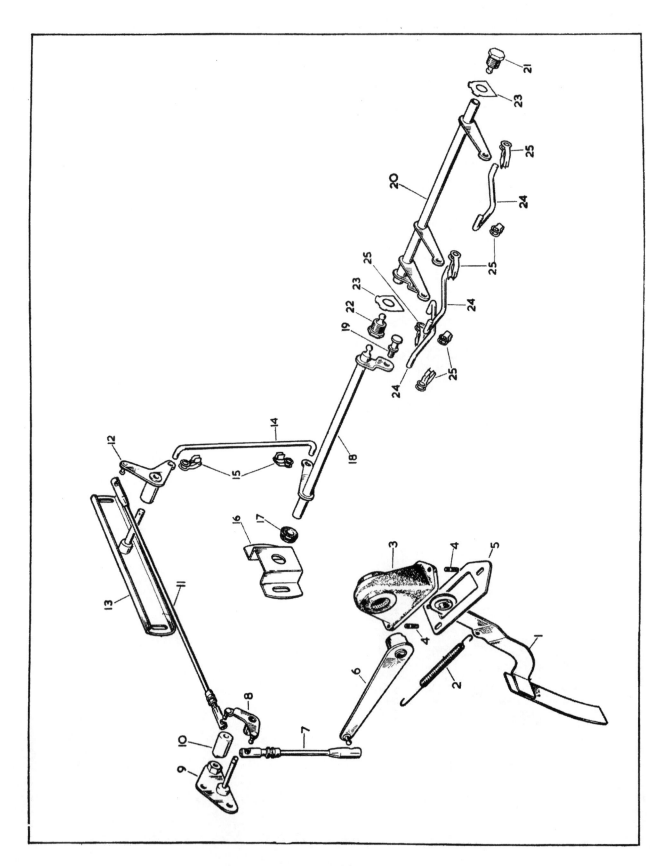

PLATE 9

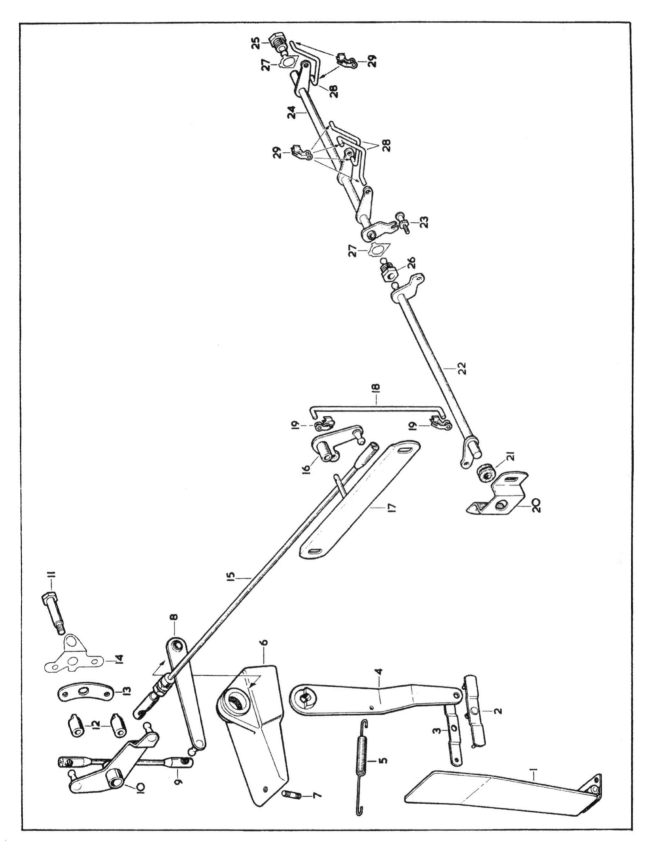

PLATE 10

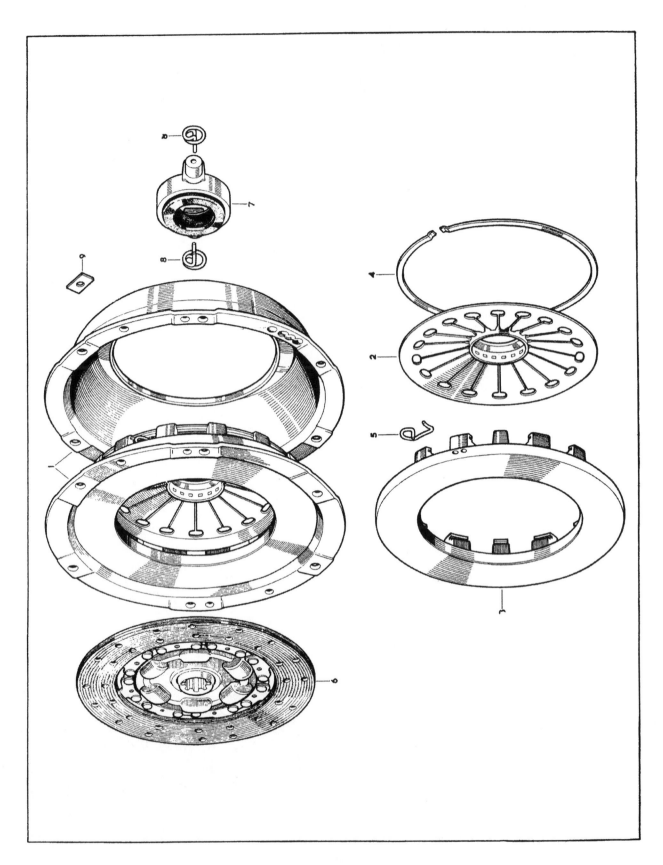

PLATE II

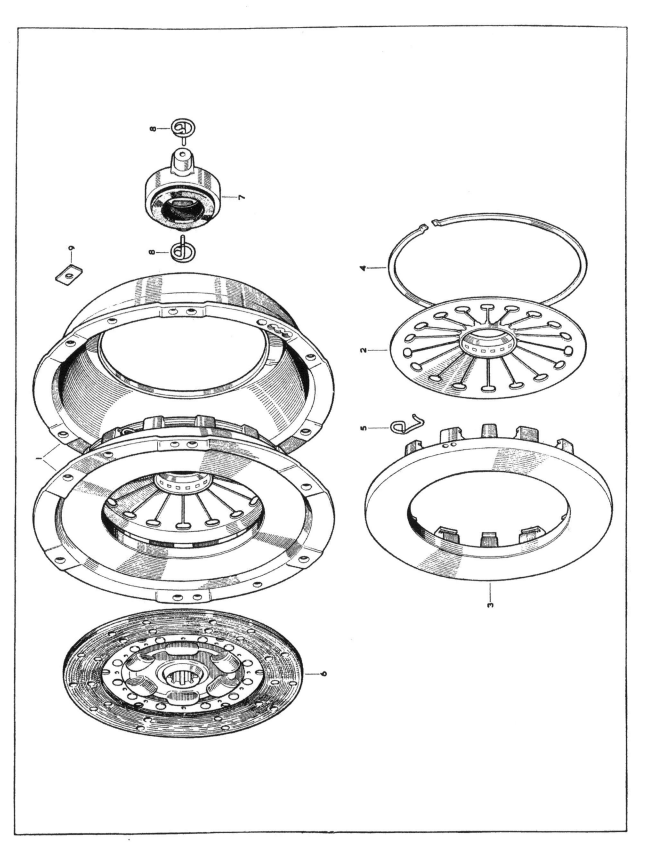

PLATE 12

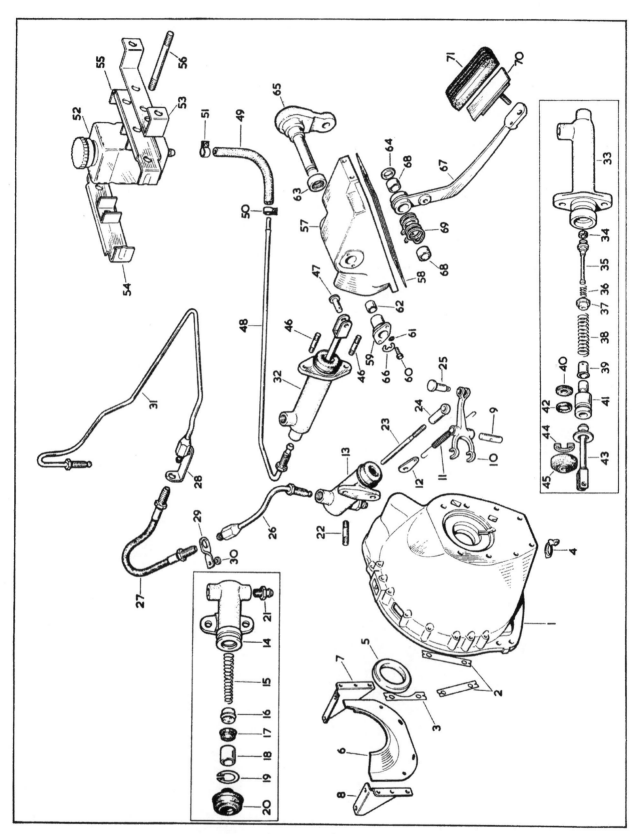

PLATE 13

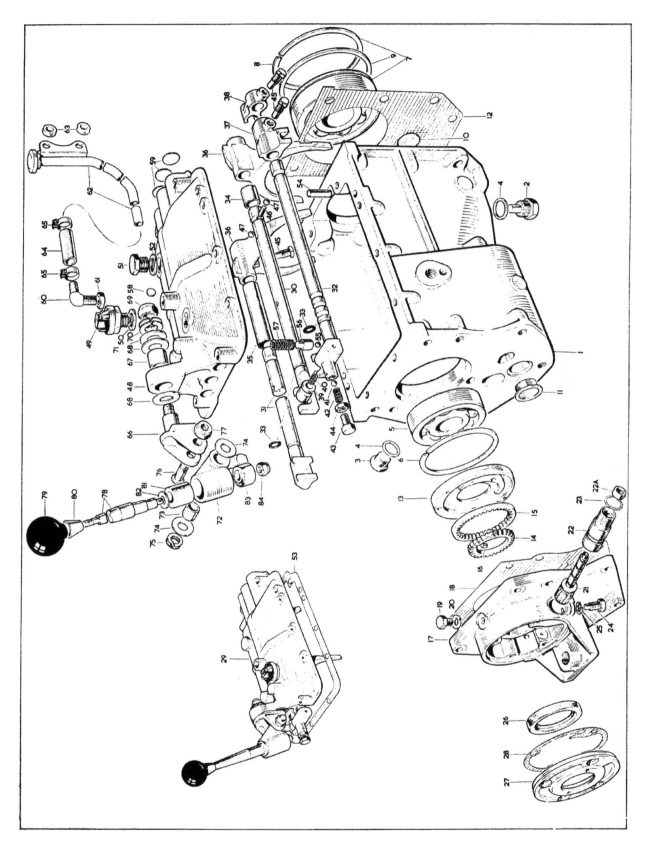

PLATE 14

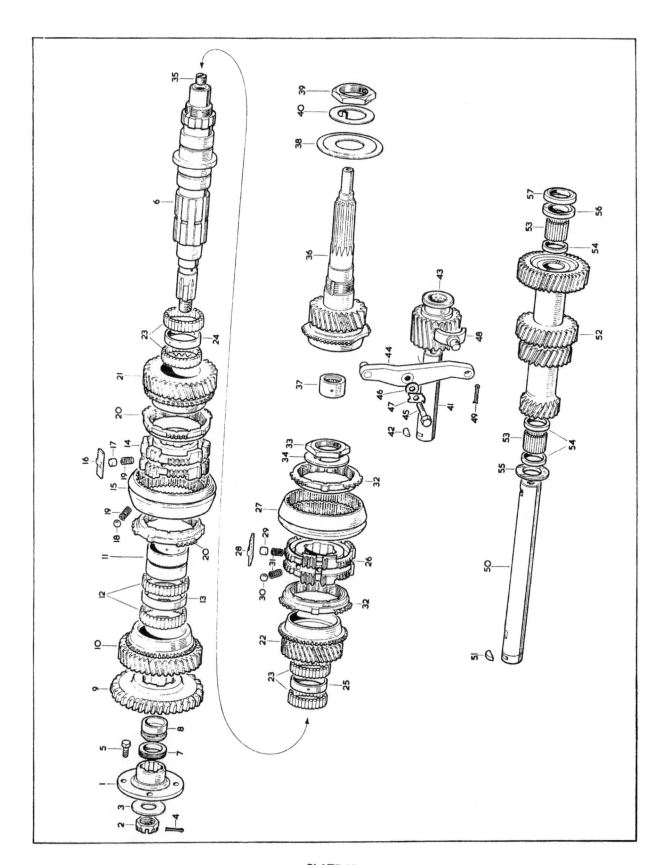

PLATE 15

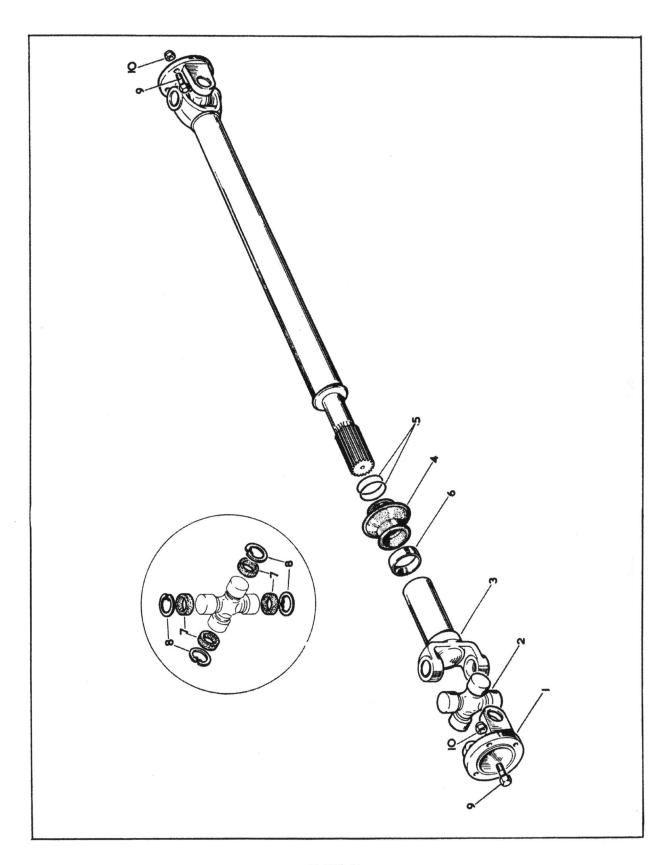

PLATE 16

191

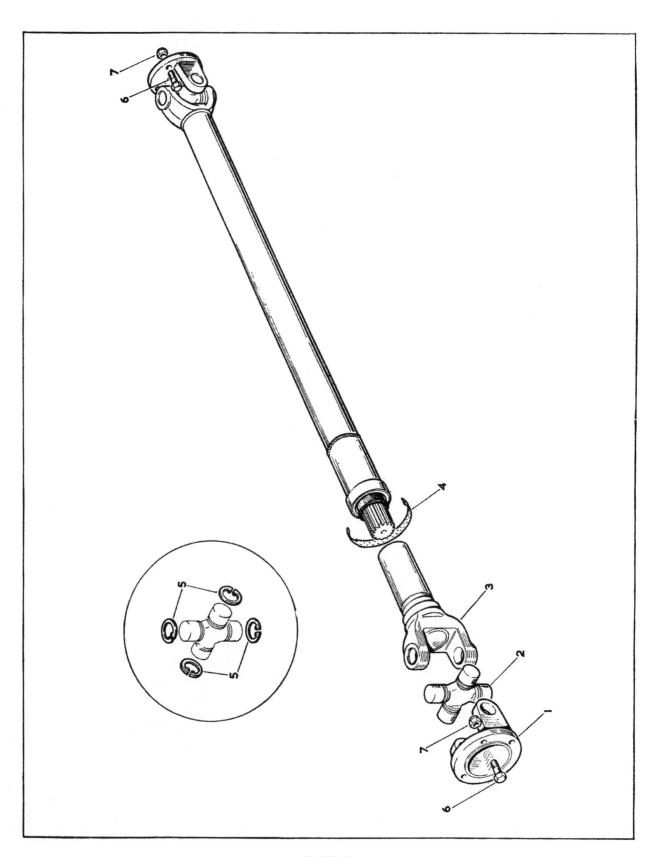

PLATE 17

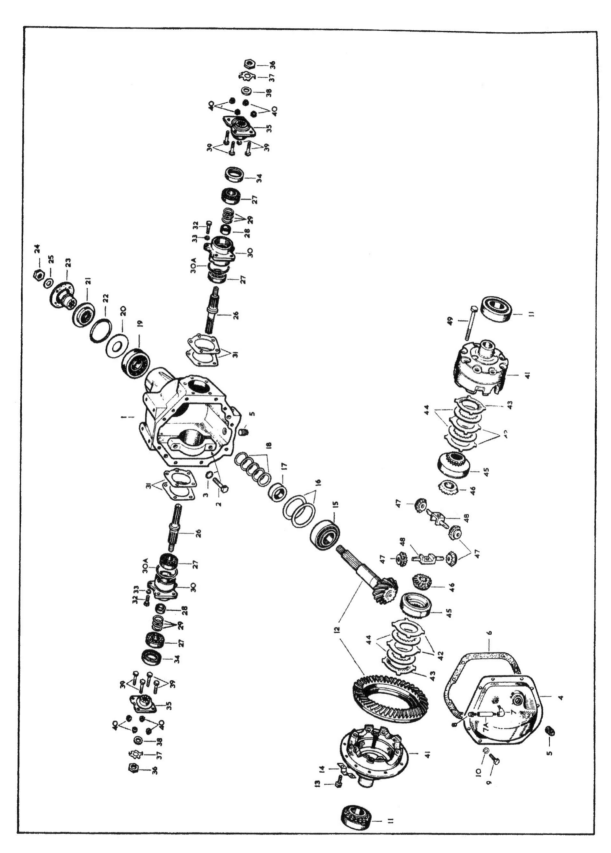

PLATE 18

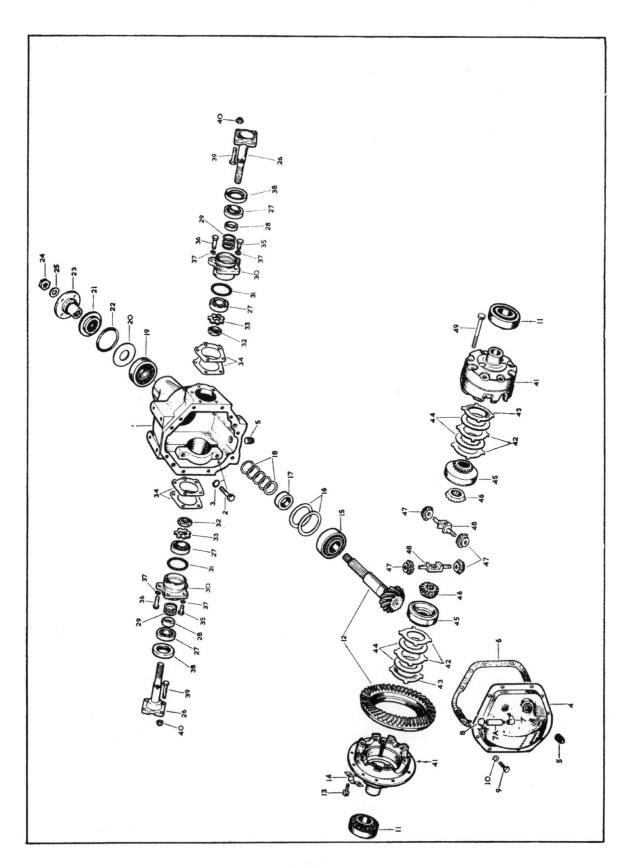

PLATE 19

194

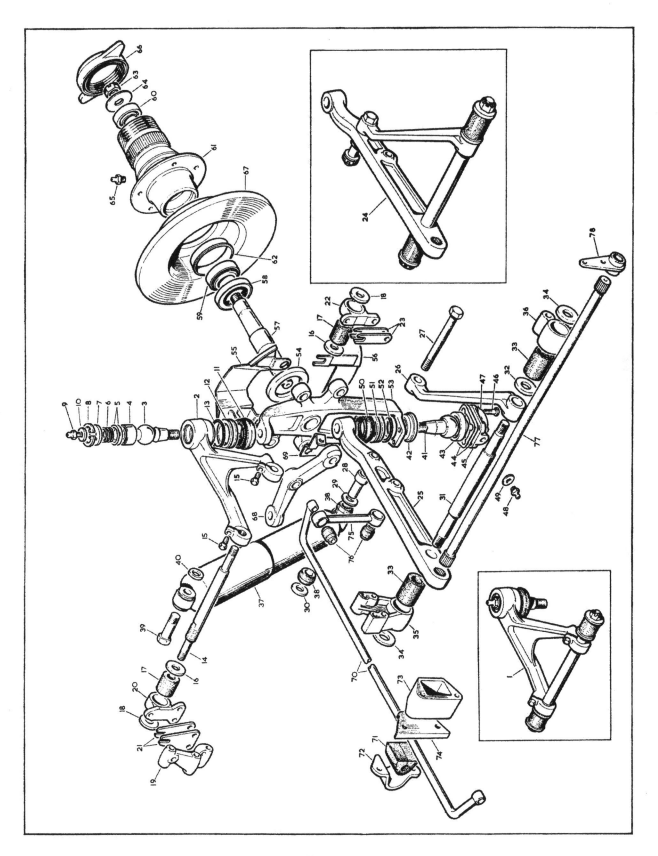

PLATE 20

195

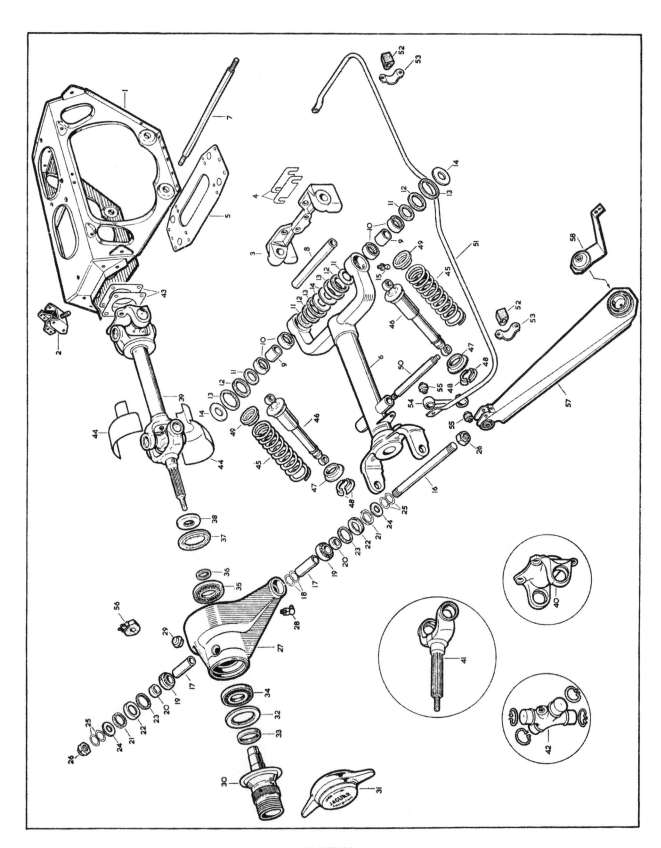

PLATE 21

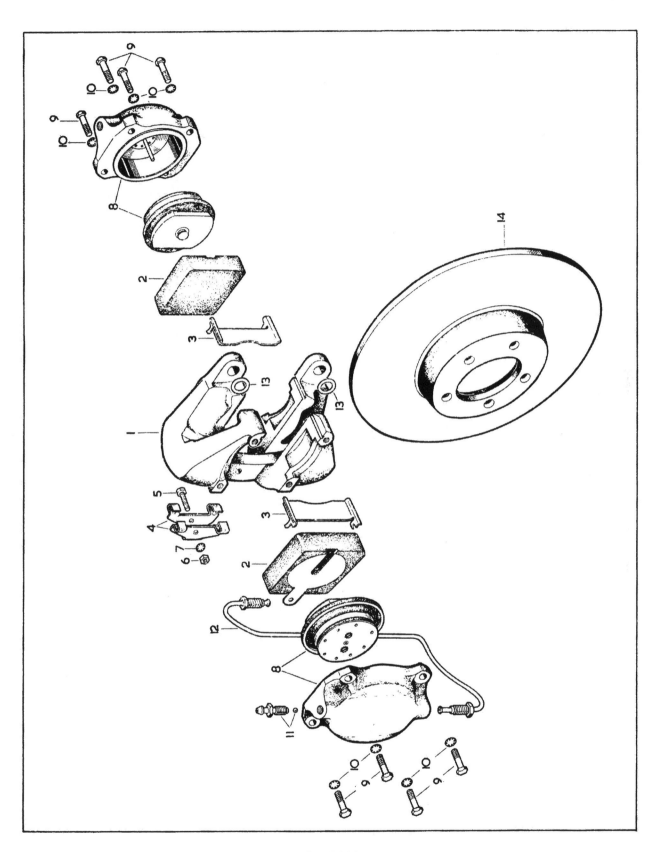

PLATE 22

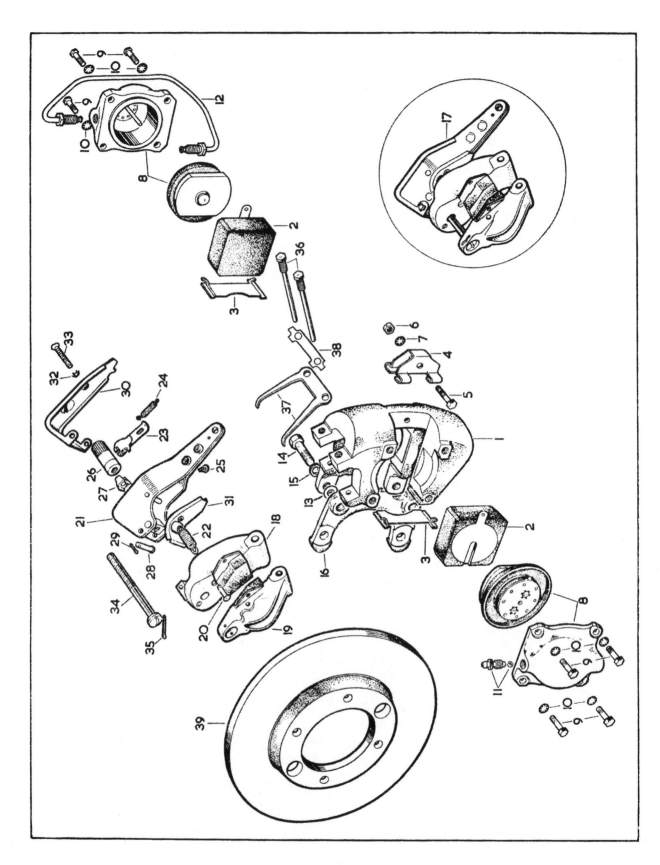

PLATE 23

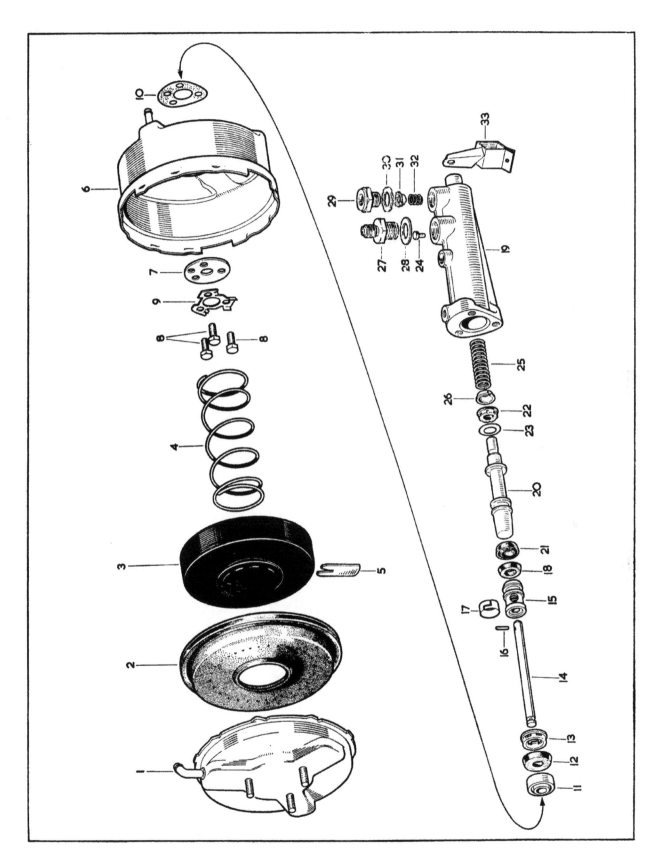

PLATE 24

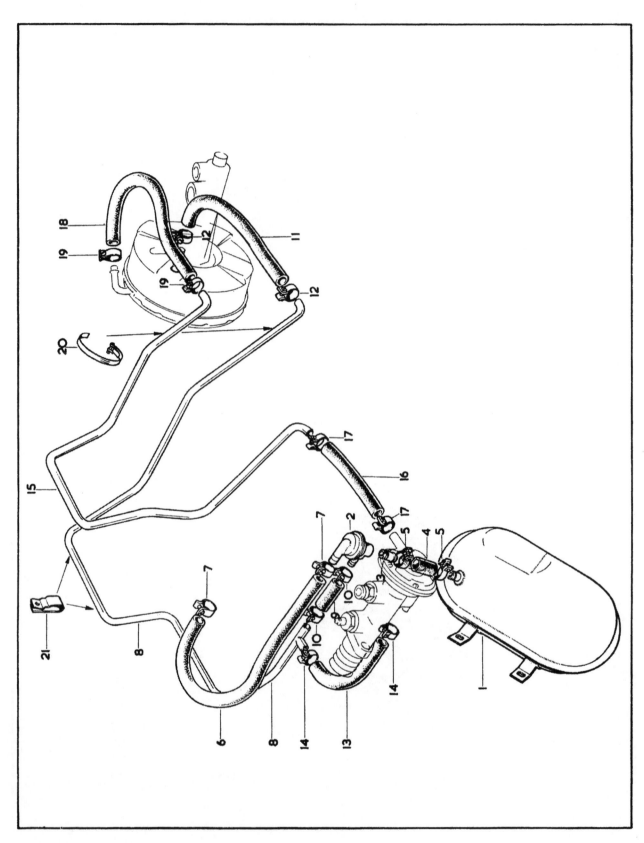

PLATE 25

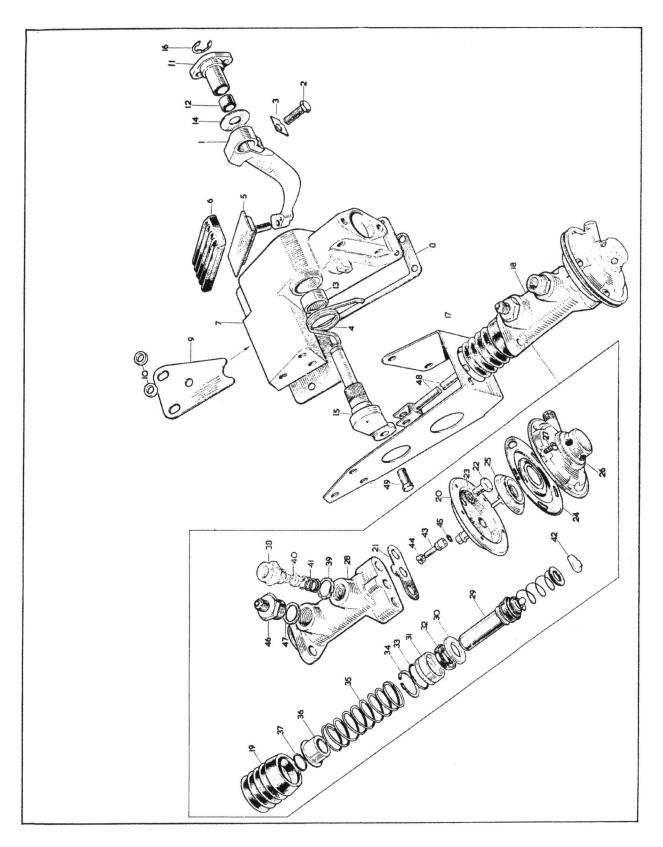

PLATE 26

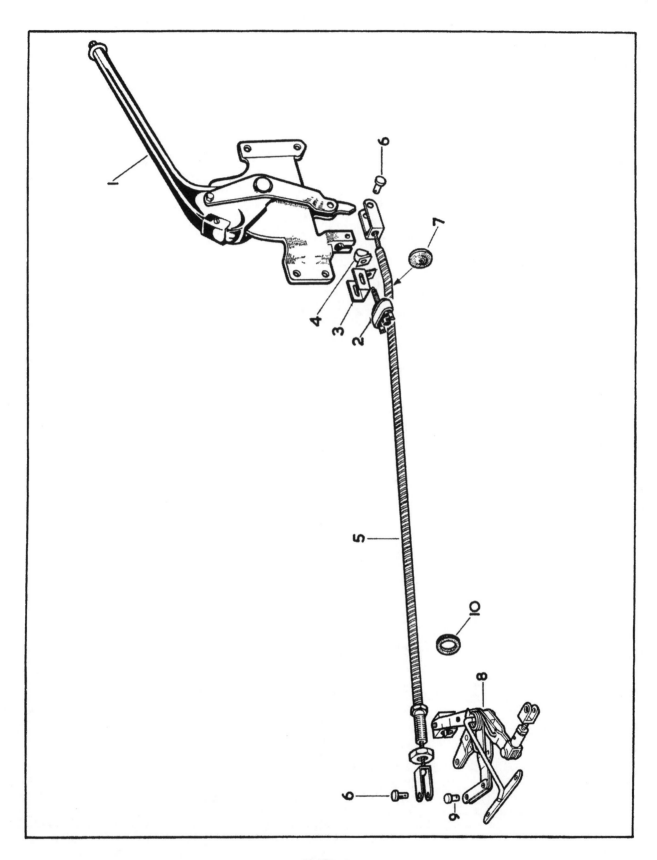

PLATE 27

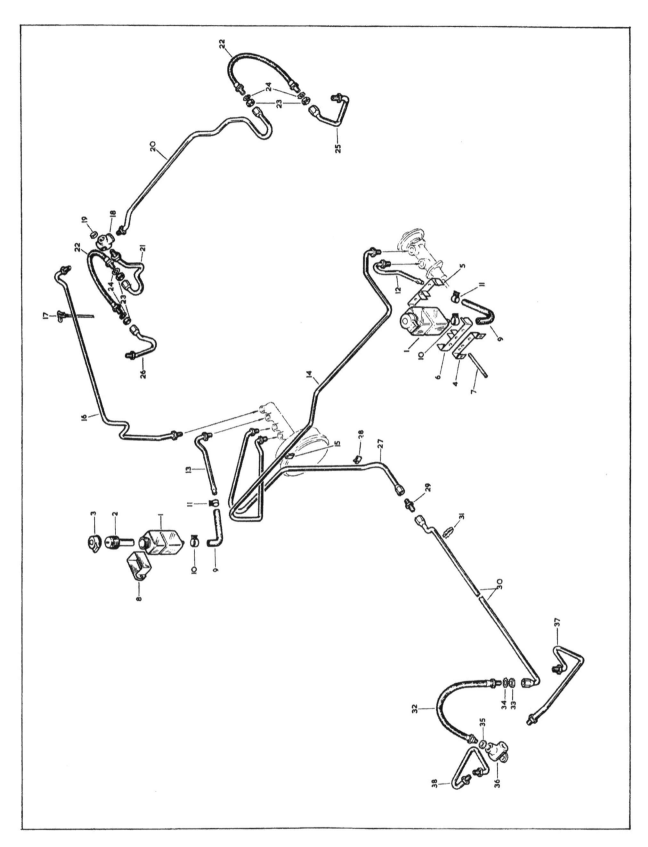

PLATE 28

203

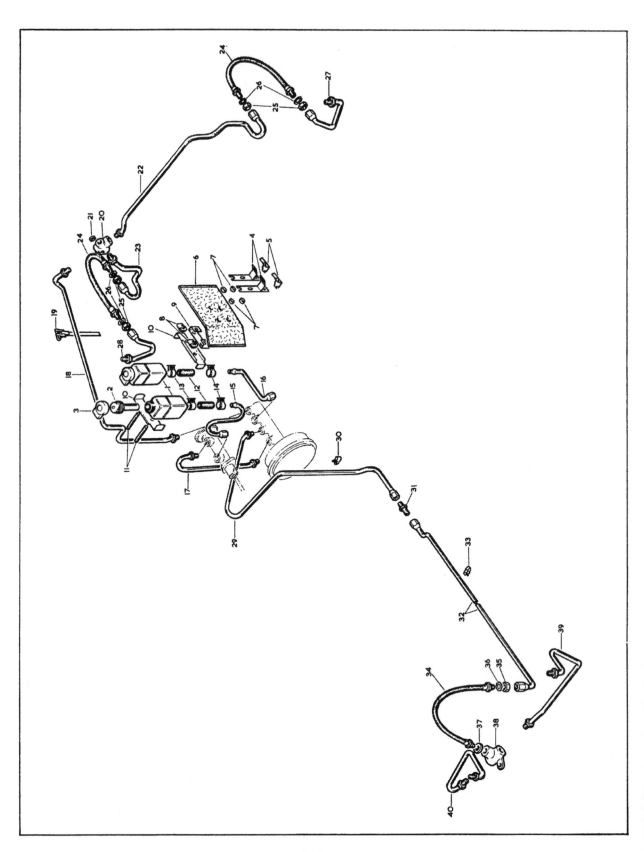

PLATE 29

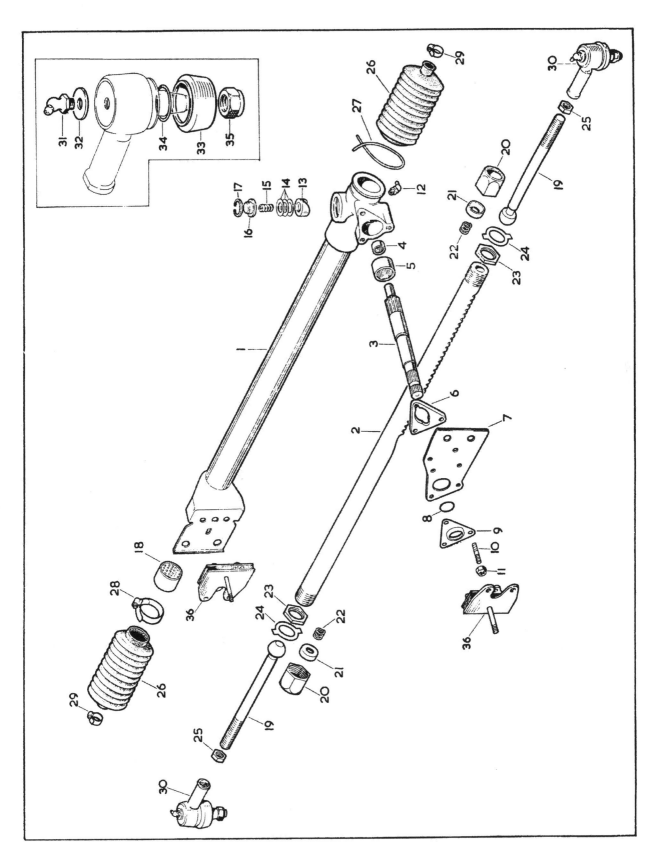

PLATE 30

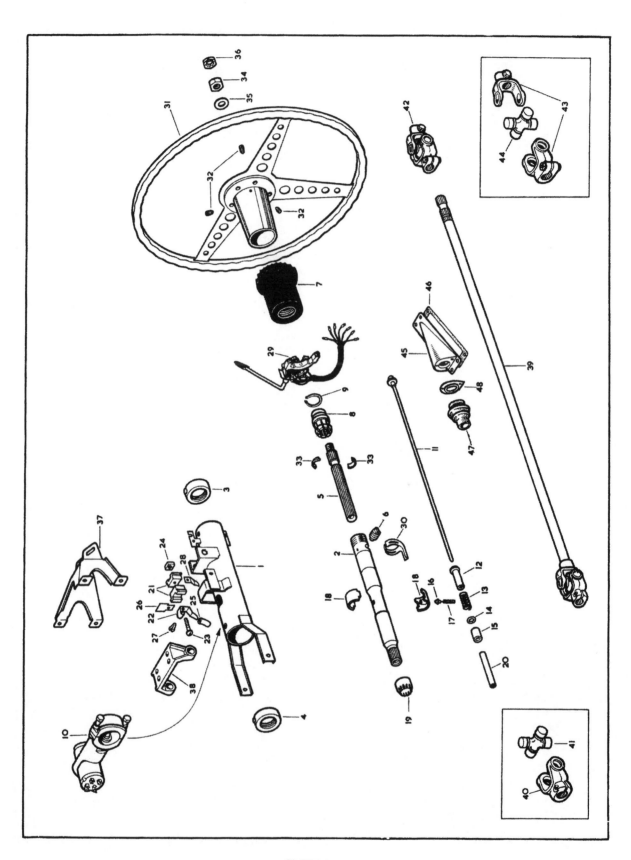

PLATE 31

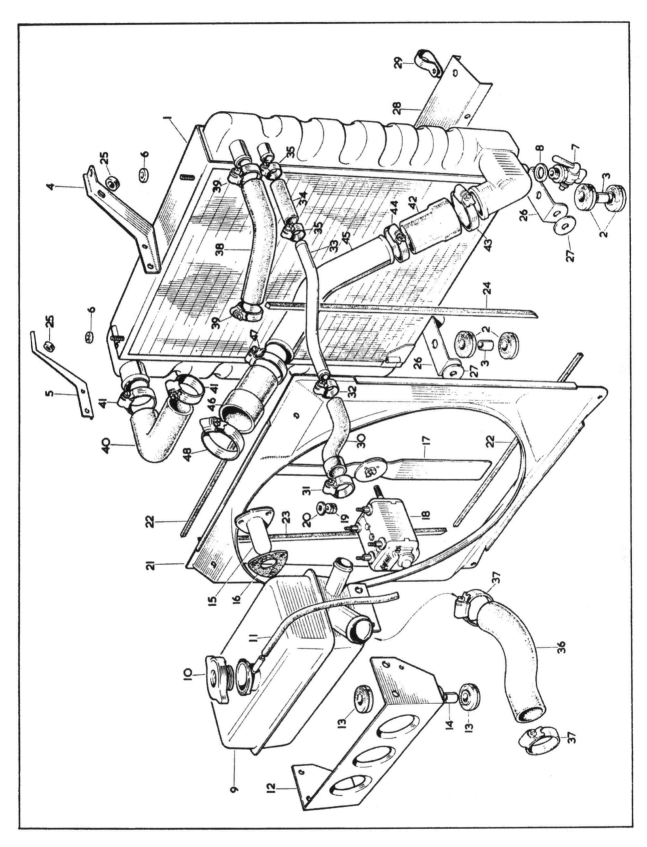

PLATE 32

207

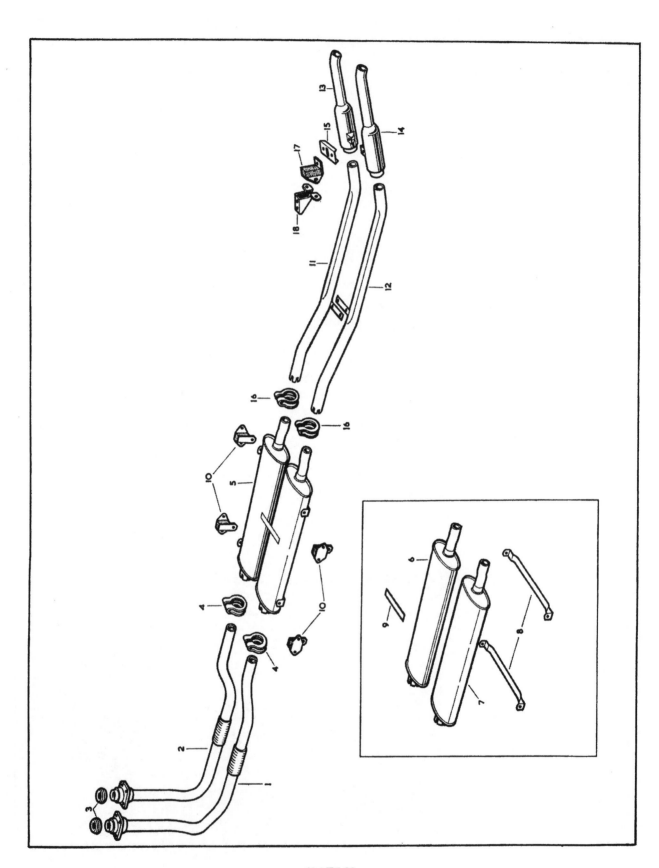

PLATE 33

208

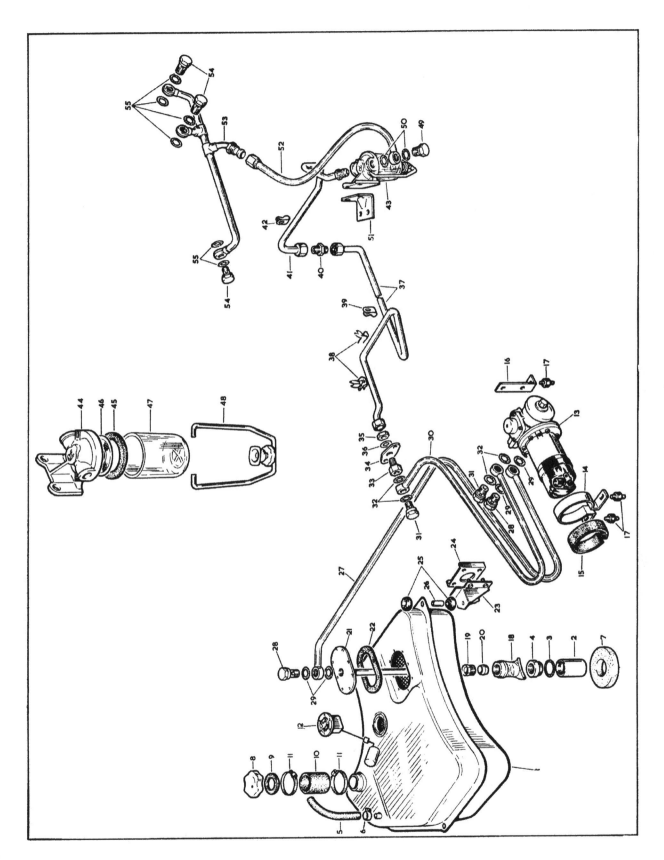

PLATE 34

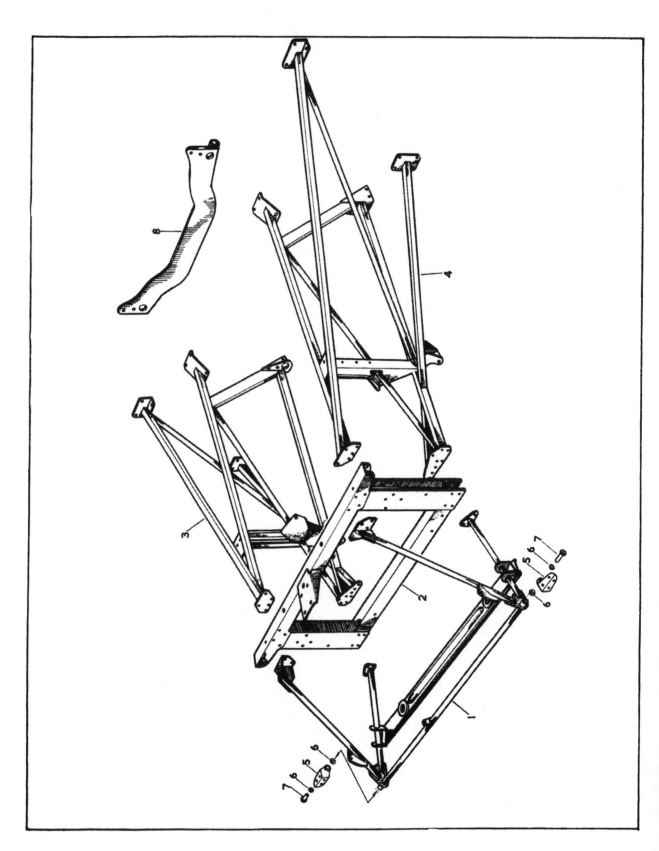

PLATE 35

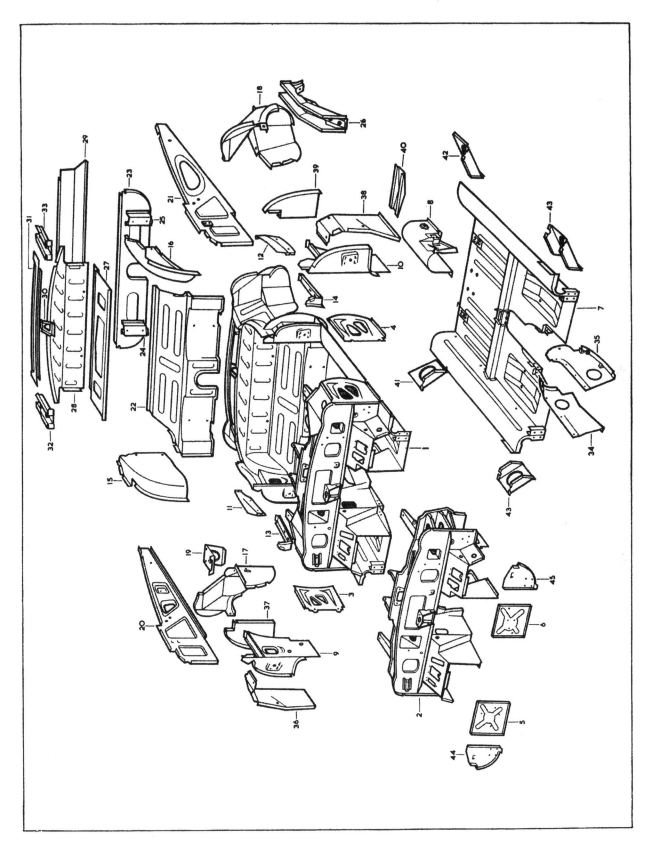

PLATE 36

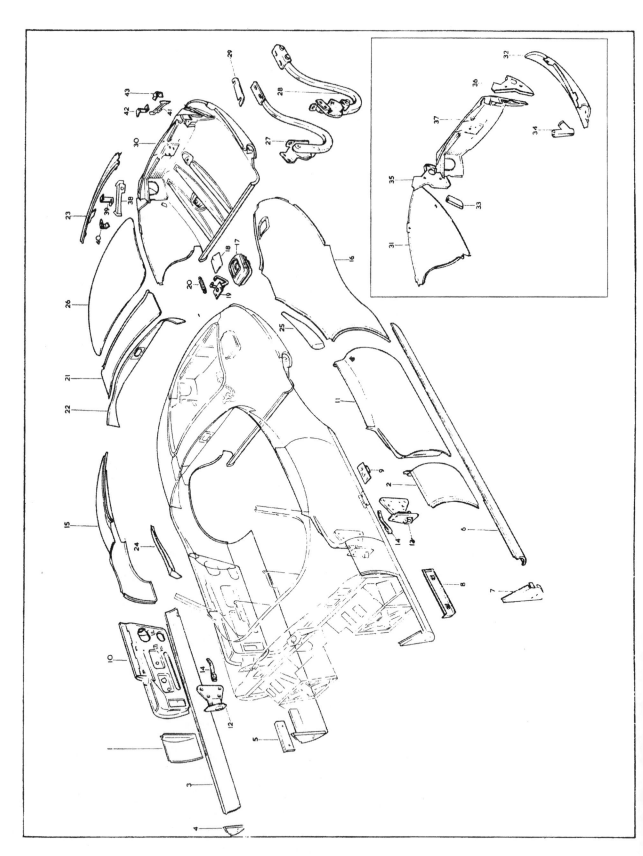

PLATE 37

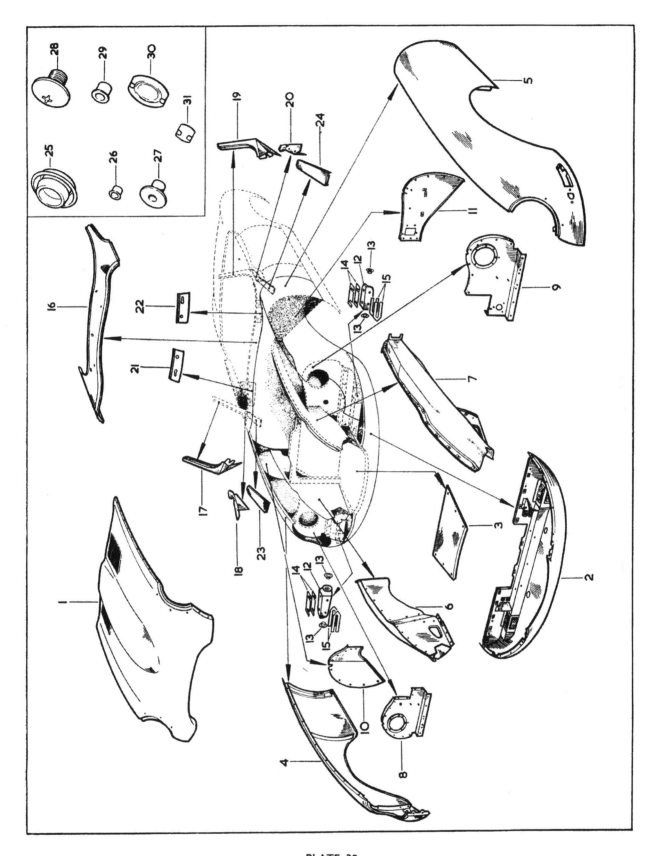

PLATE 38

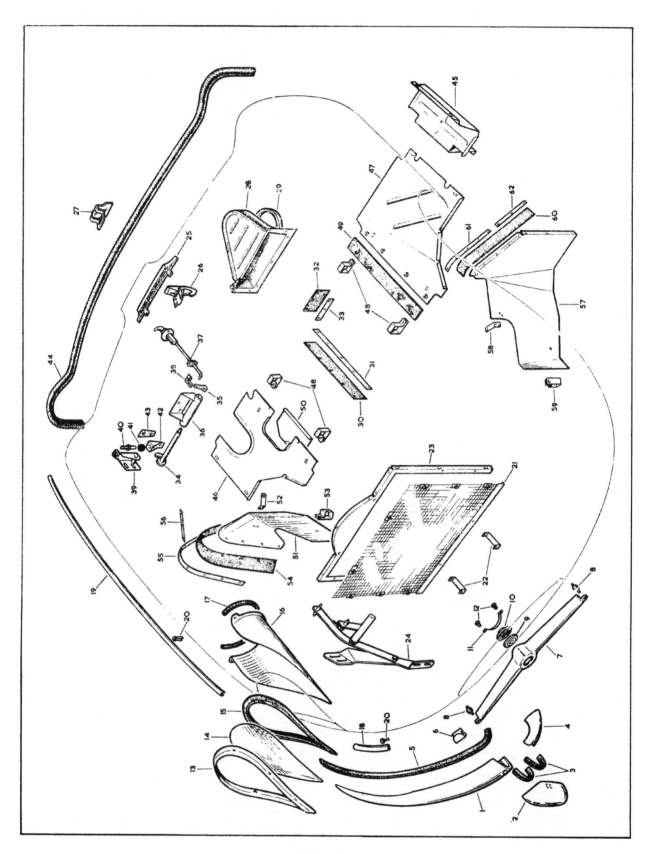

PLATE 39

214

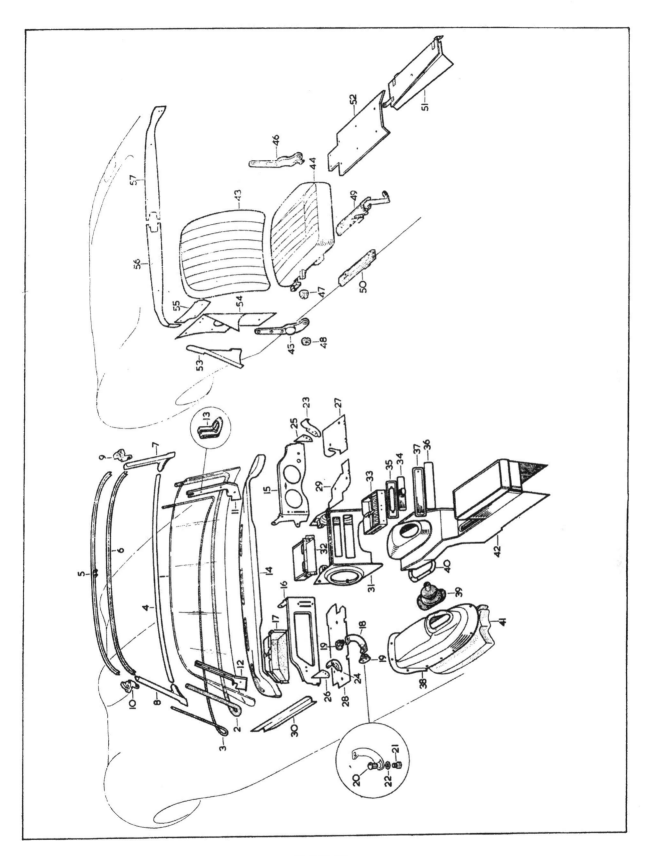

PLATE 40

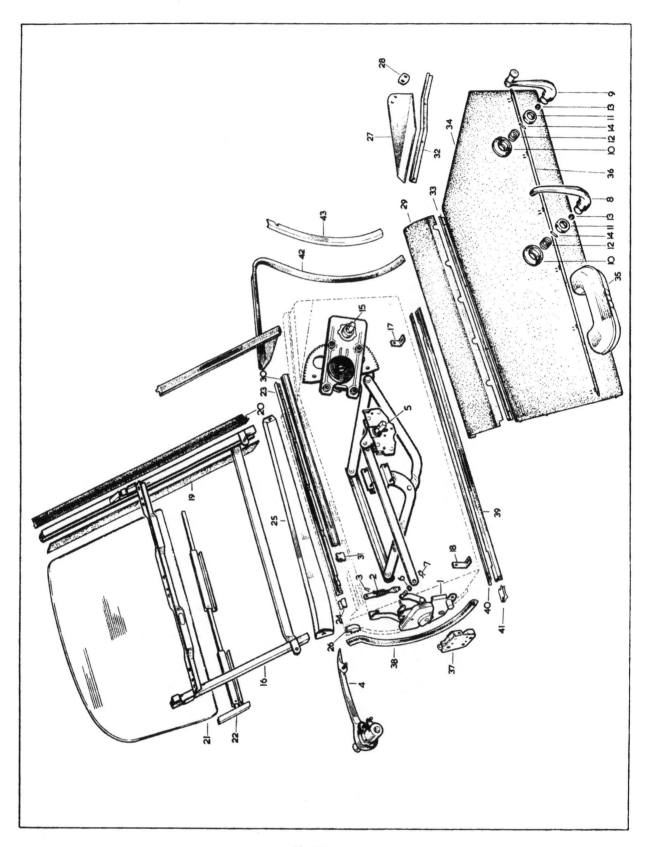

PLATE 41

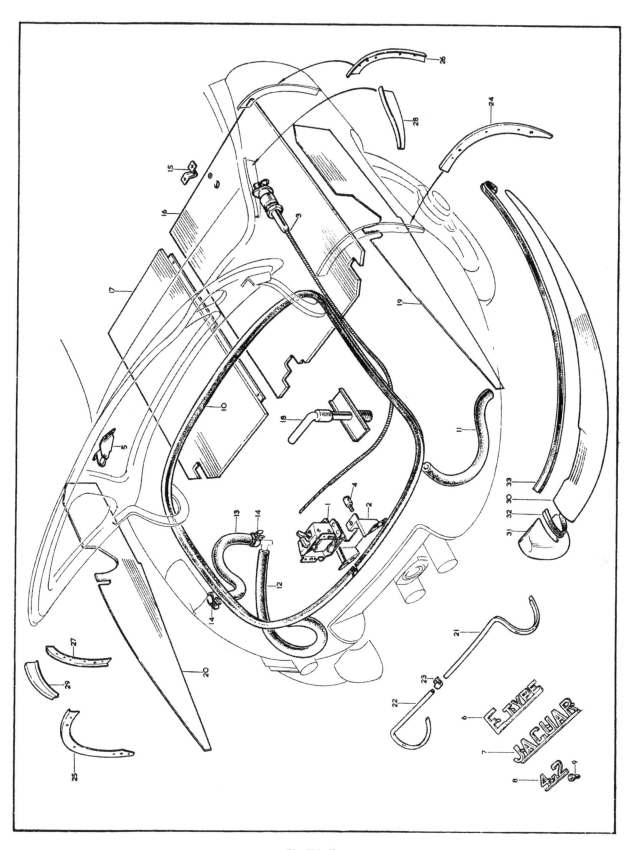

PLATE 42

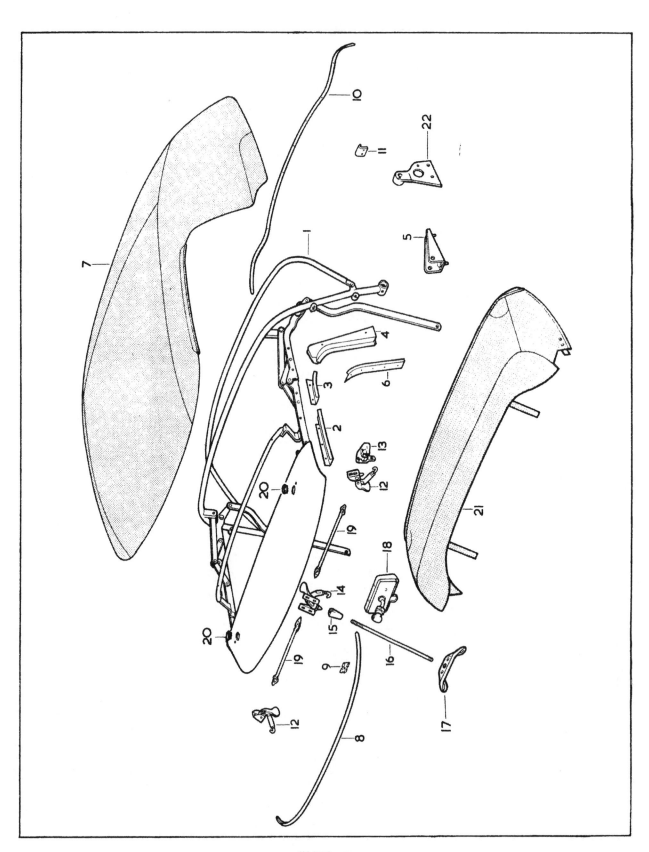

PLATE 43

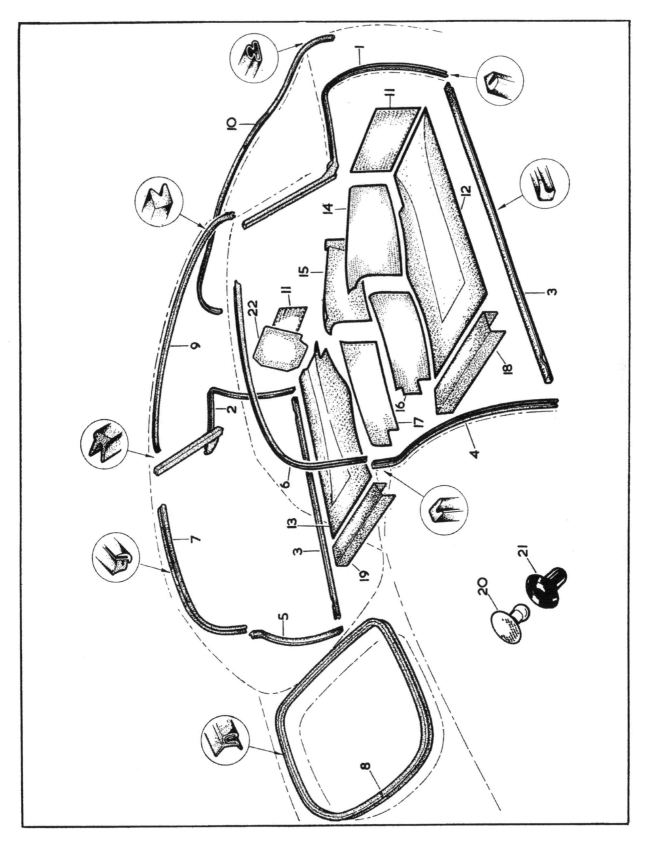

PLATE 44

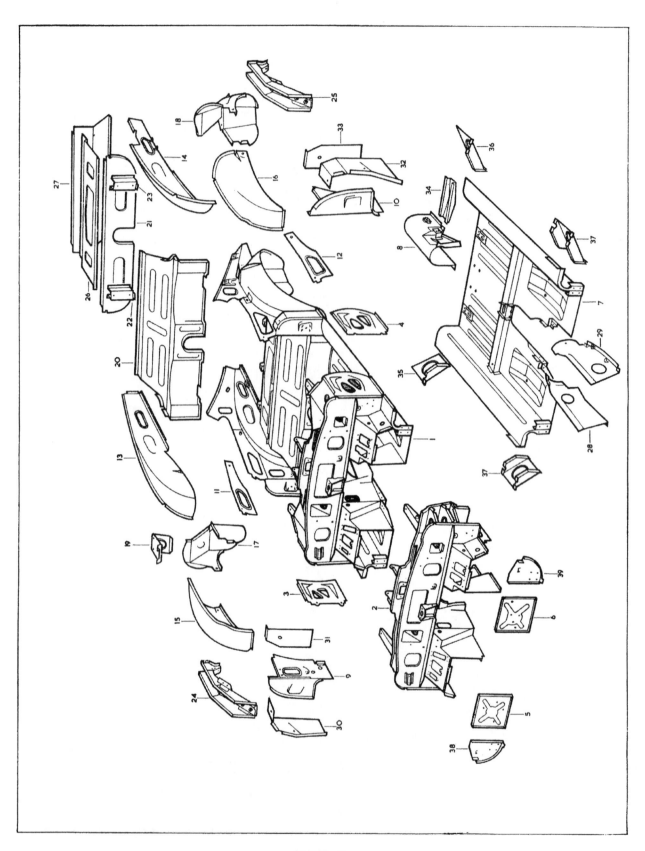

PLATE 45

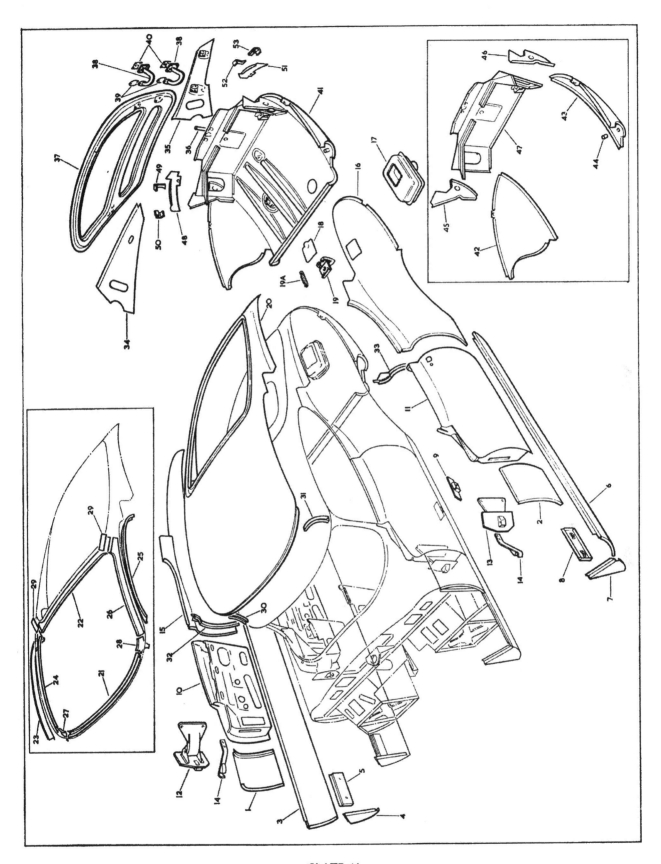

PLATE 46

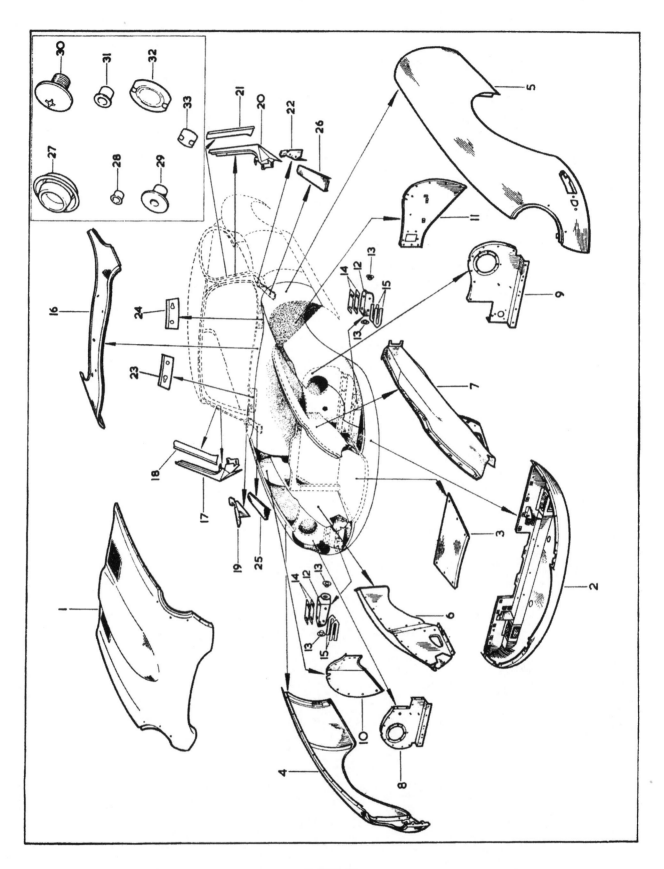

PLATE 47

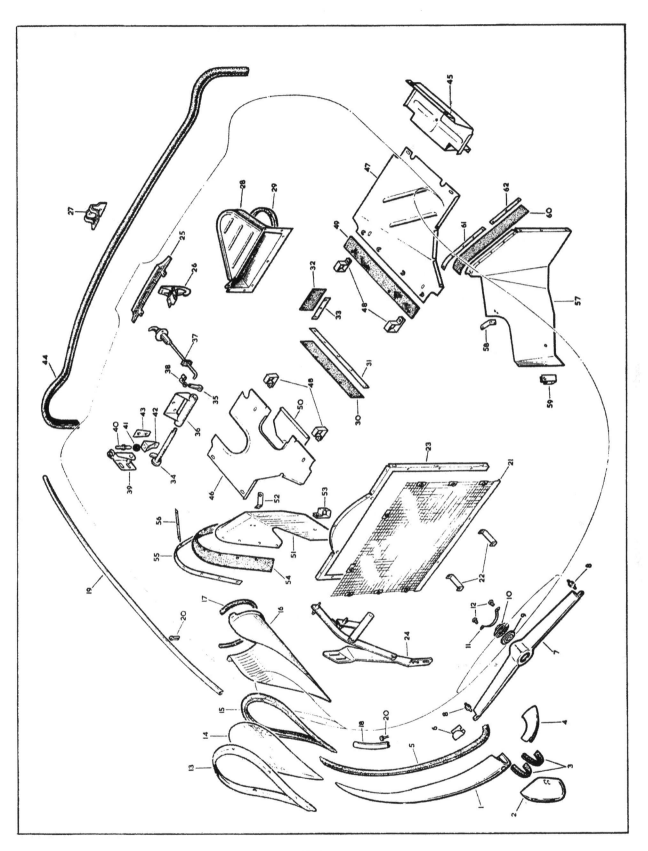

PLATE 48

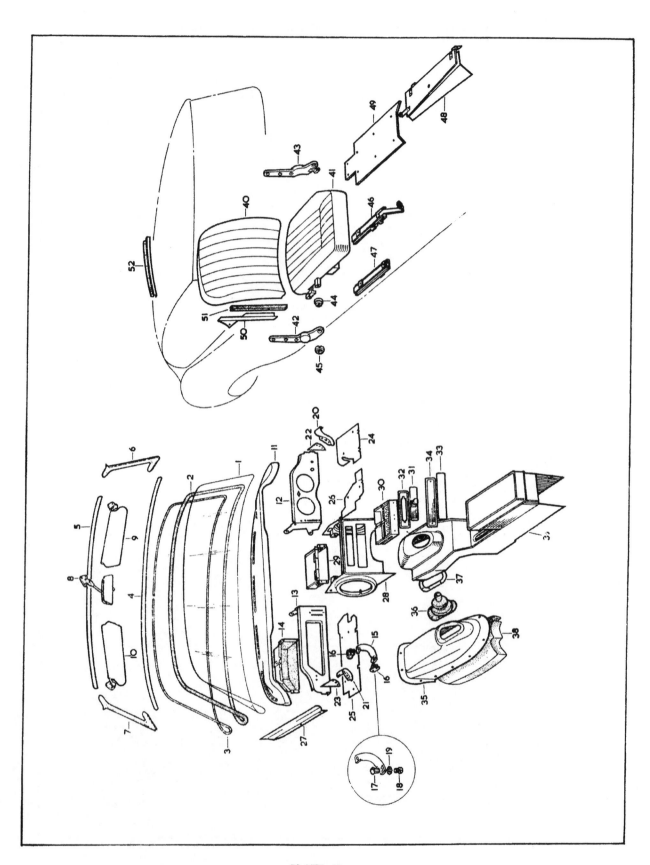

PLATE 49

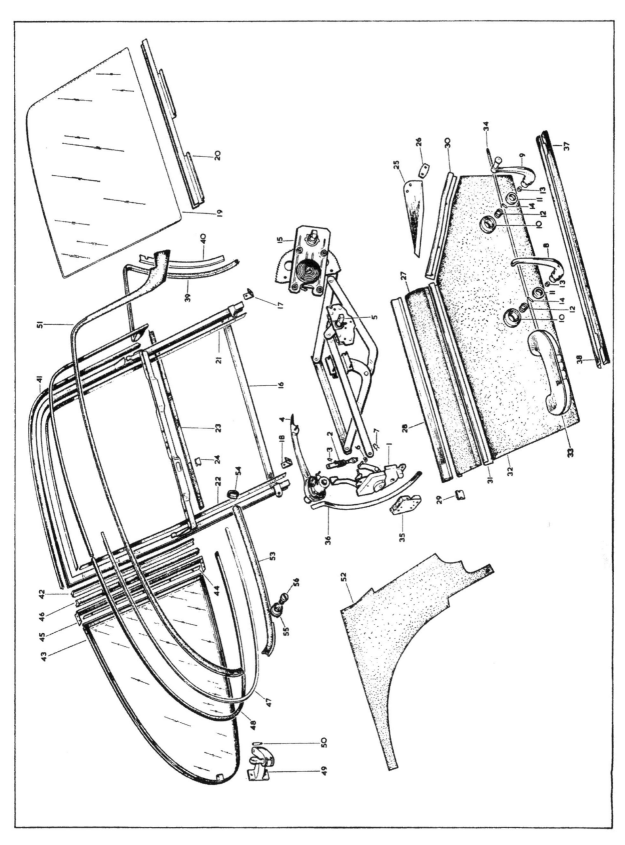

PLATE 50

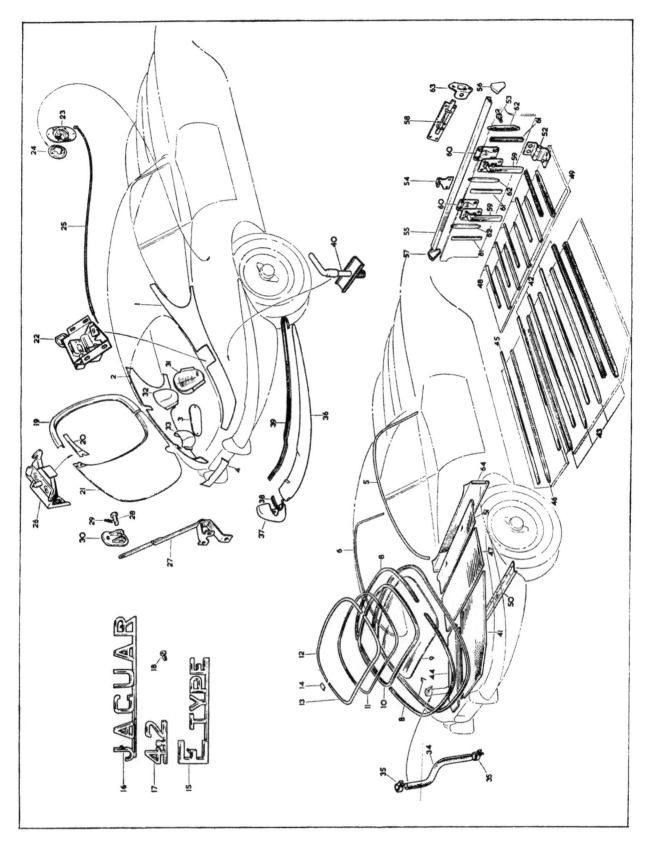

PLATE 51

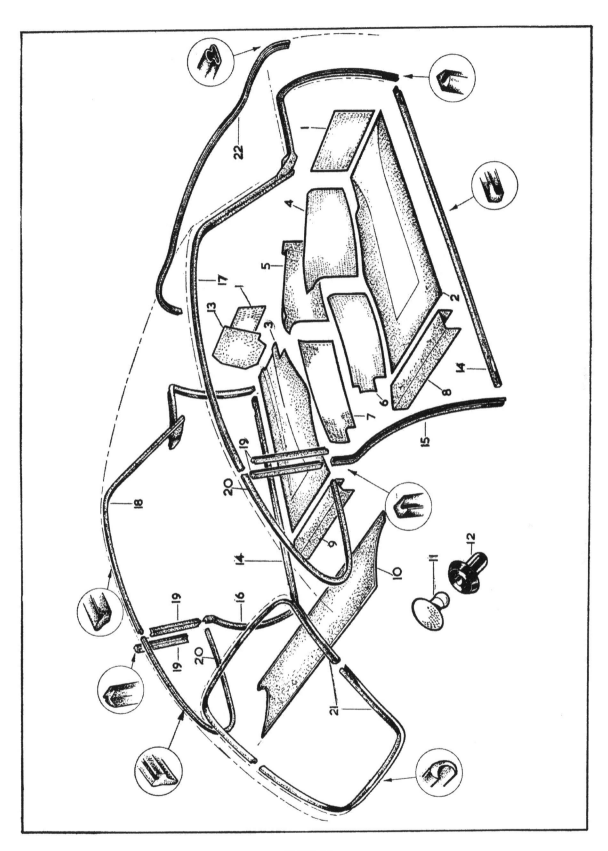

PLATE 52

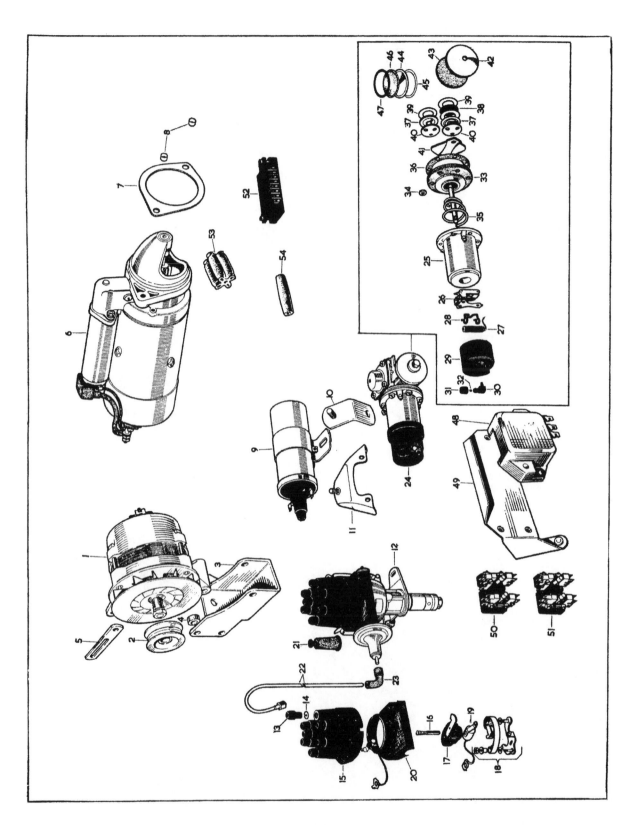

PLATE 53

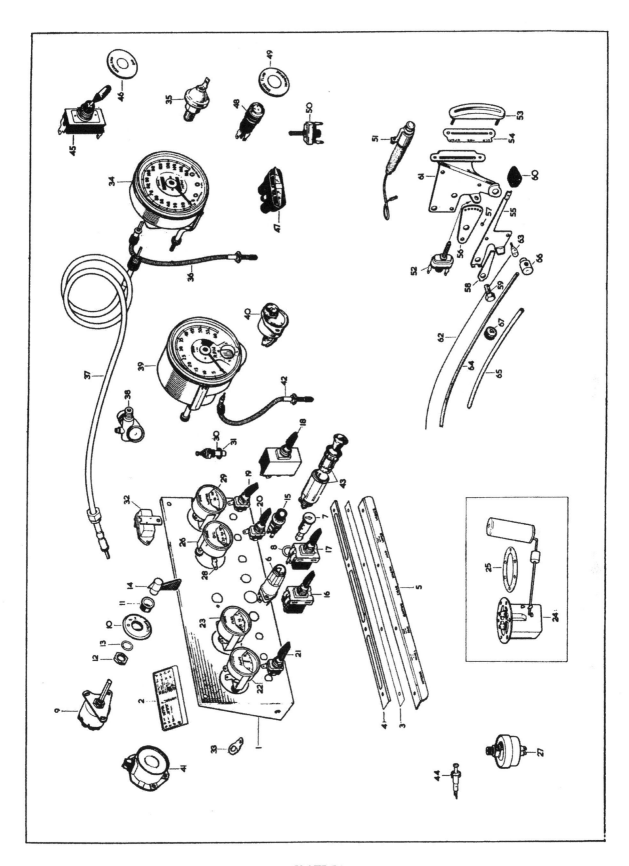

PLATE 54

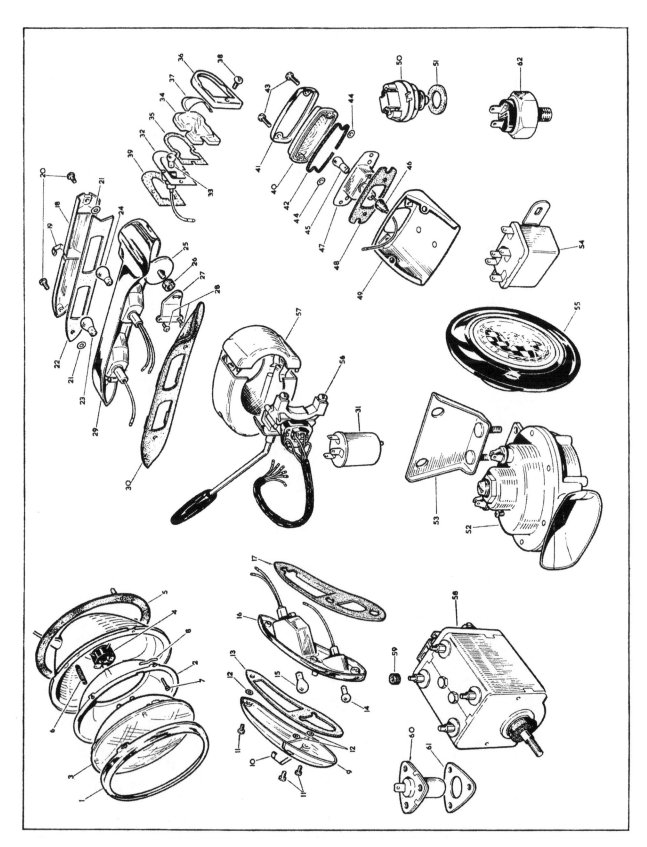

PLATE 55

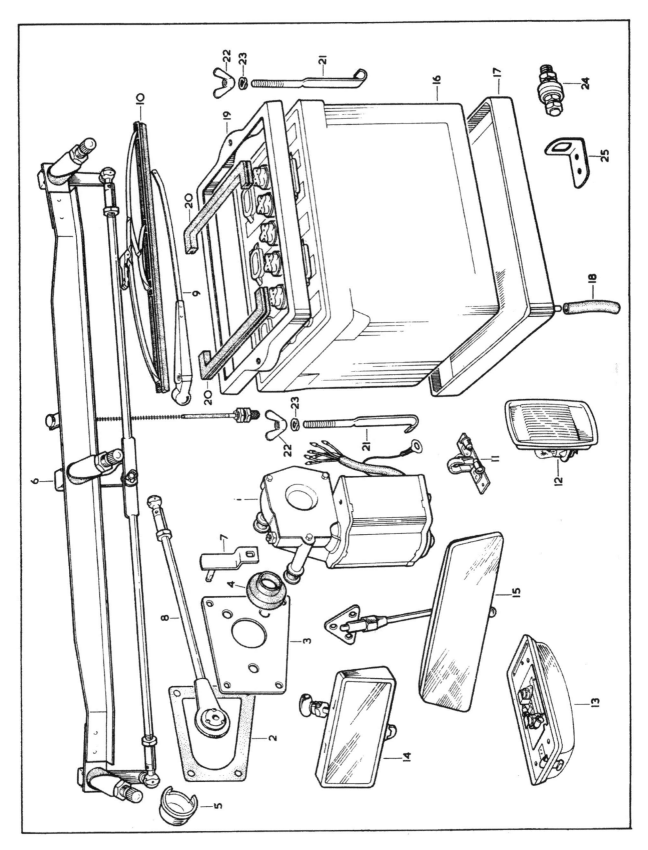

PLATE 56

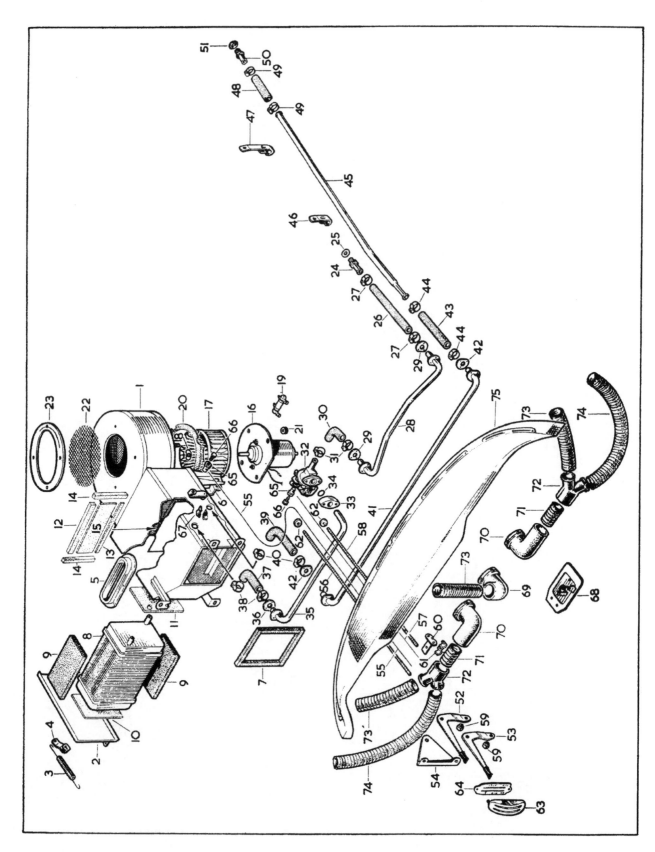

PLATE 57

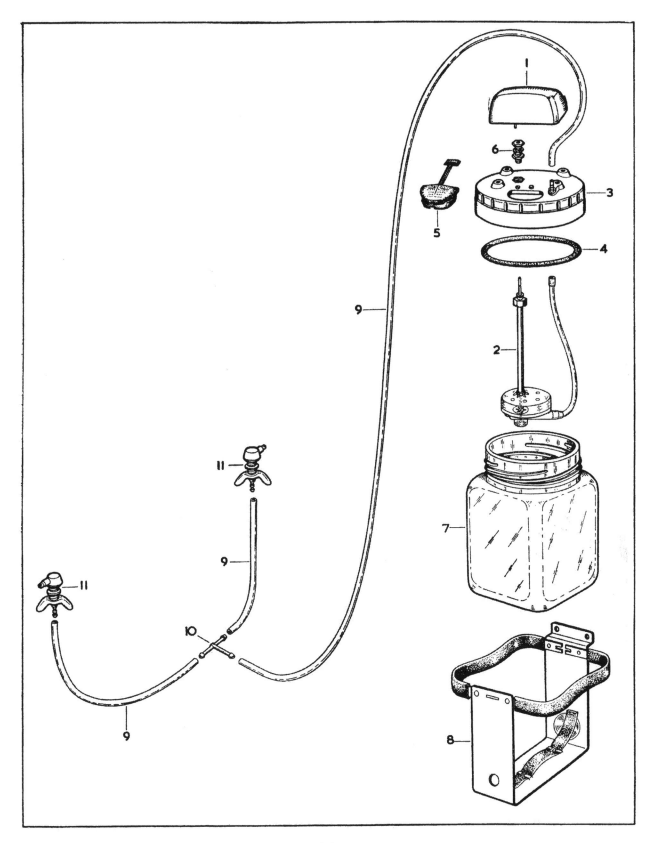

PLATE 58

233

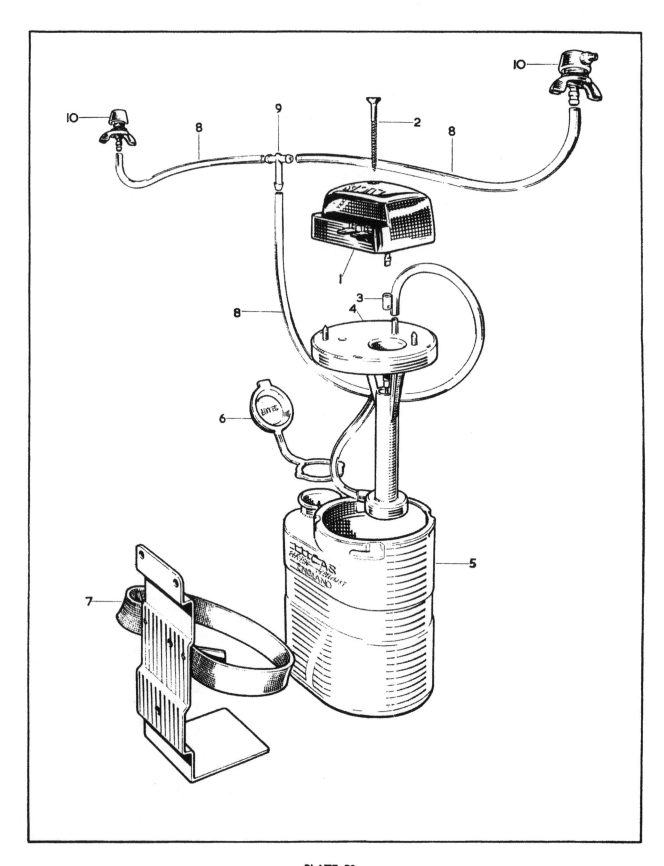

PLATE 59

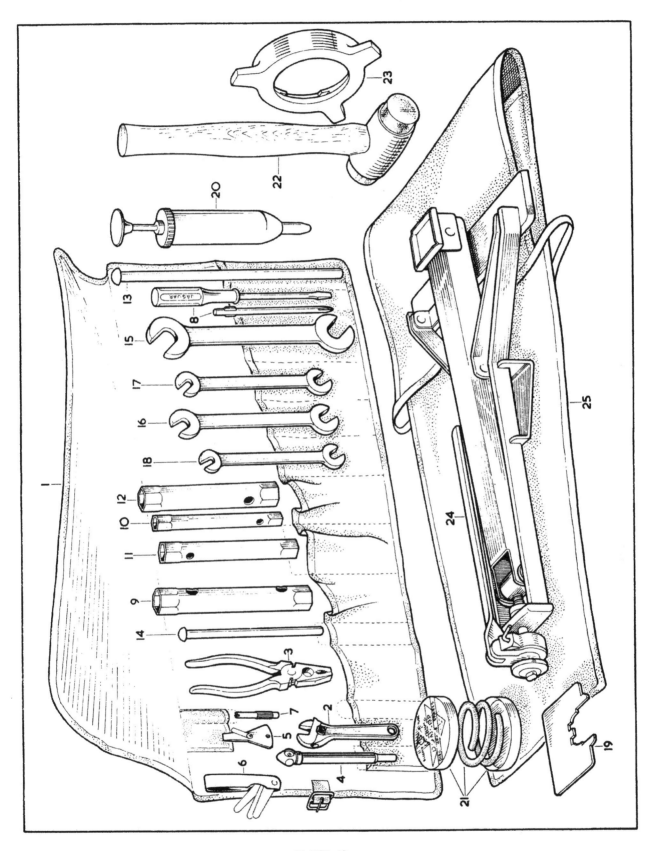

PLATE 60

SPARES DIVISION

SPARE PARTS CATALOGUE

for

JAGUAR 4·2 'E' TYPE '2+2'

GRAND TOURING MODEL

Series 1

(Illustrations only)

PUBLICATION J.38

PUBLISHED JANUARY, 1967
AMMENDED (A.L.1) AUGUST, 1967

SECOND SUPPLEMENT

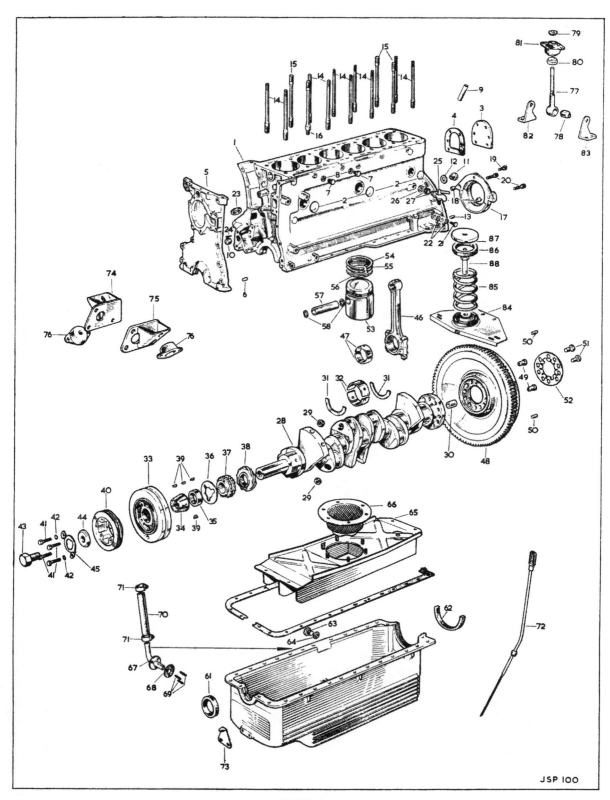

JSP 100

PLATE 1

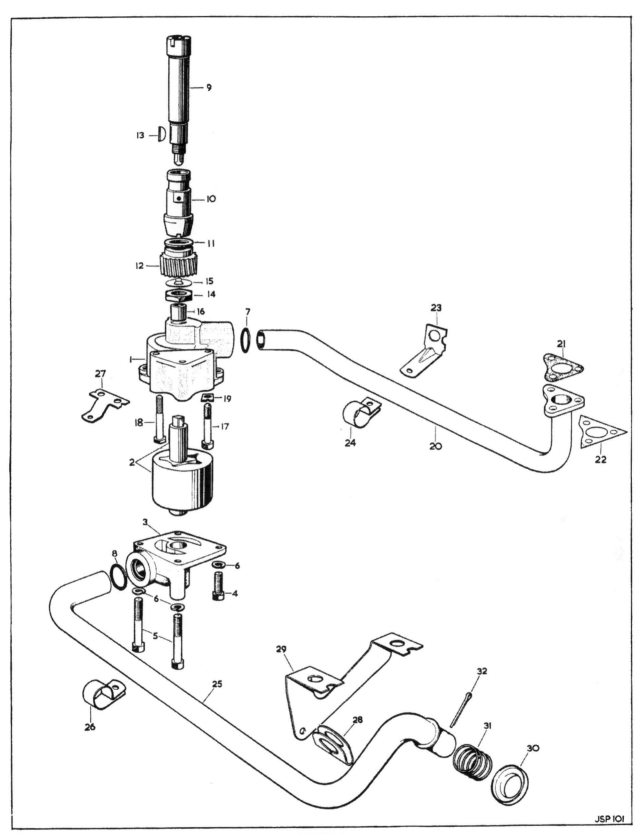

PLATE 2

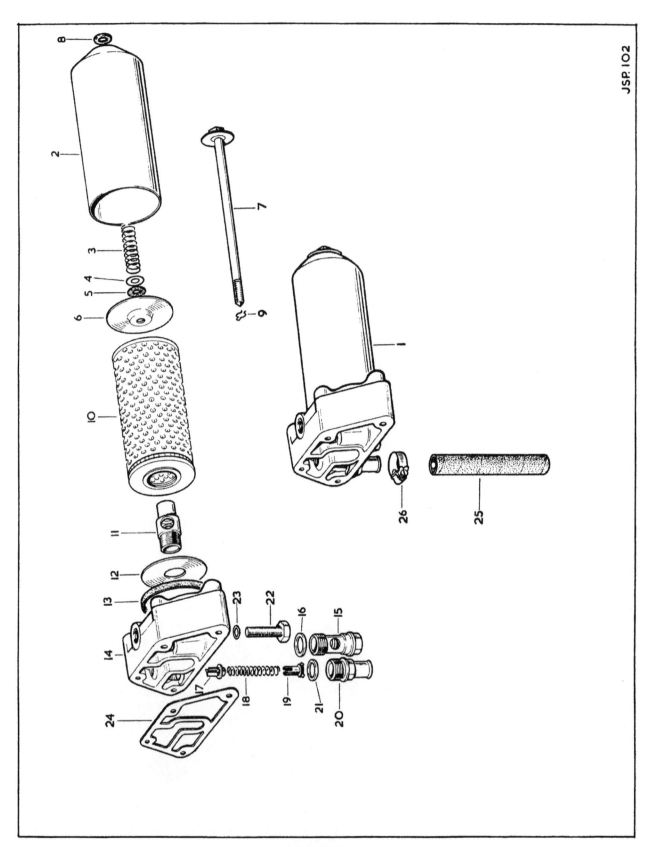

PLATE 3

240

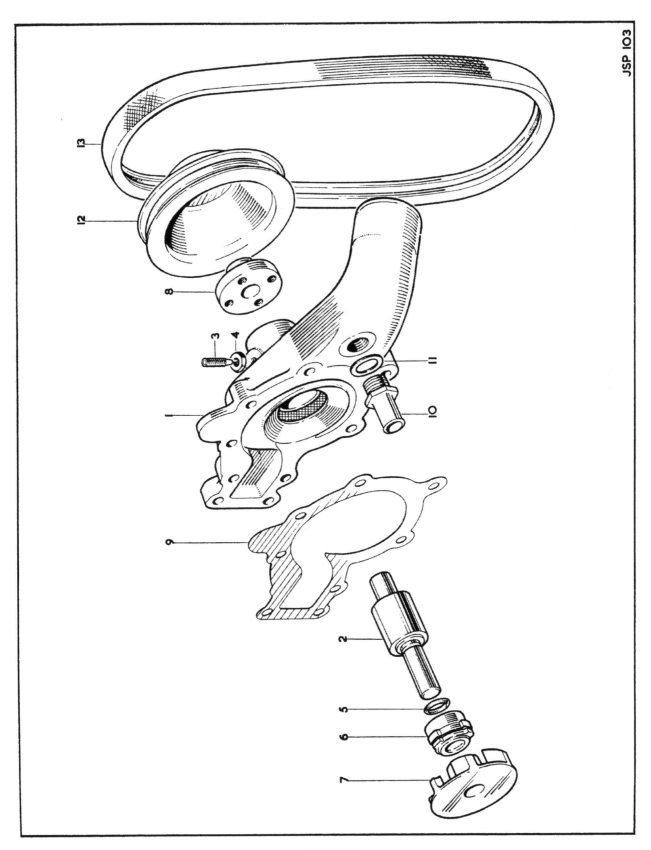

PLATE 4

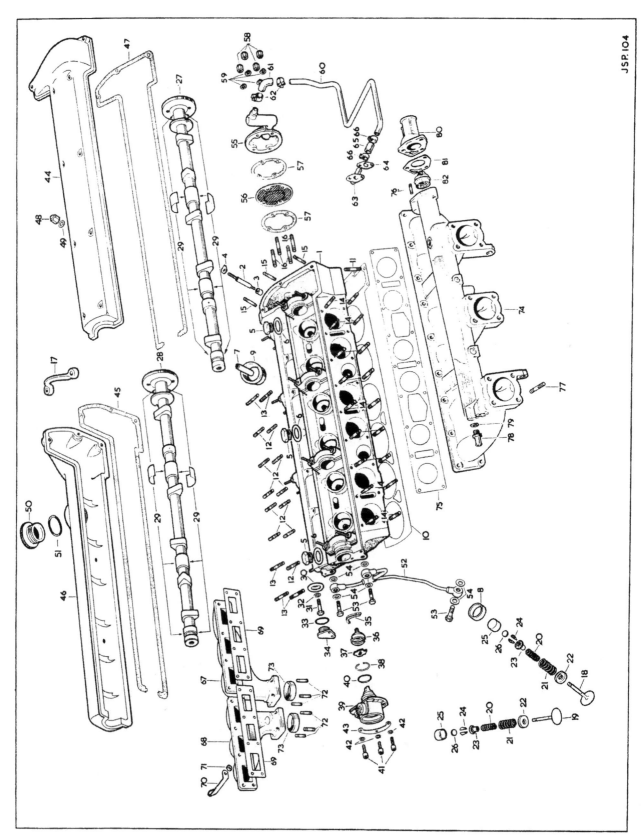

JSP.104

PLATE 5

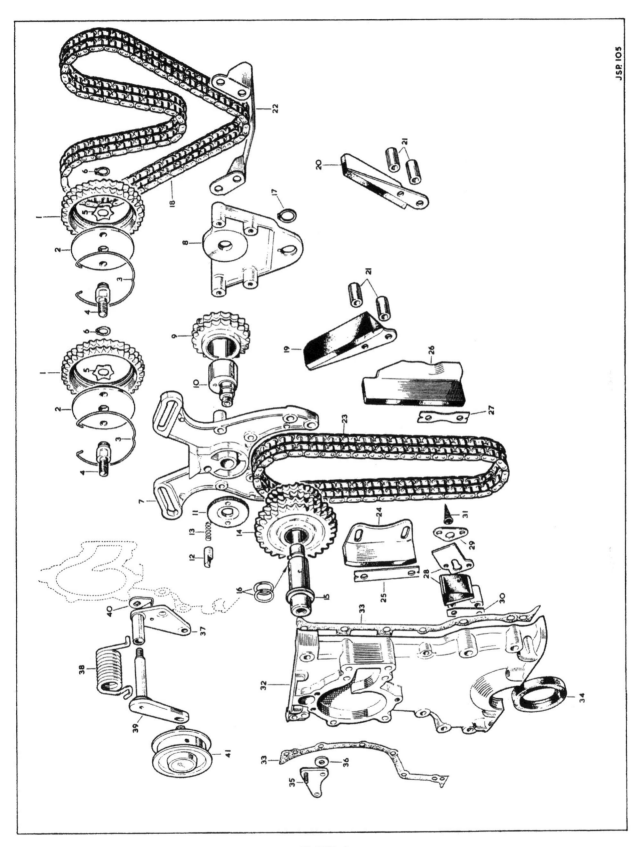

JSP 105

PLATE 6

243

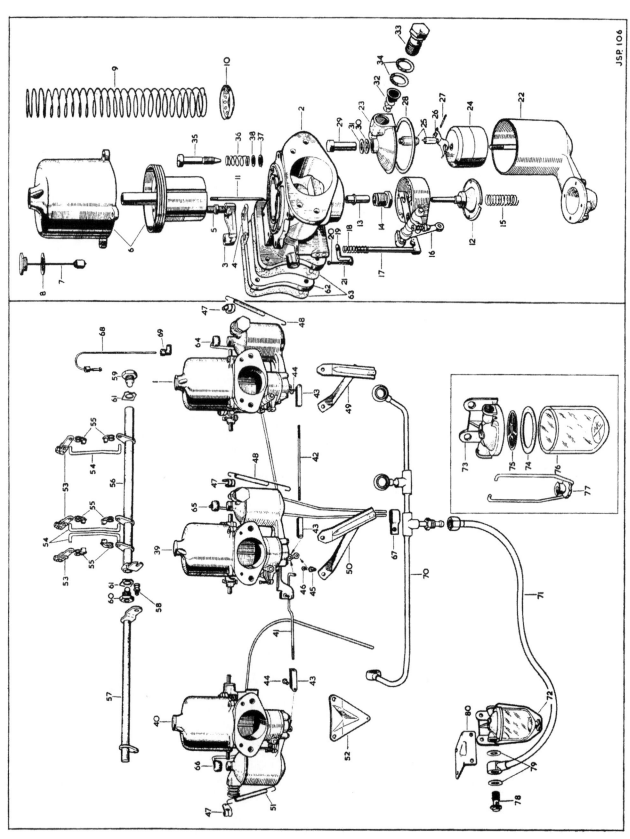

JSP. 106

PLATE 7

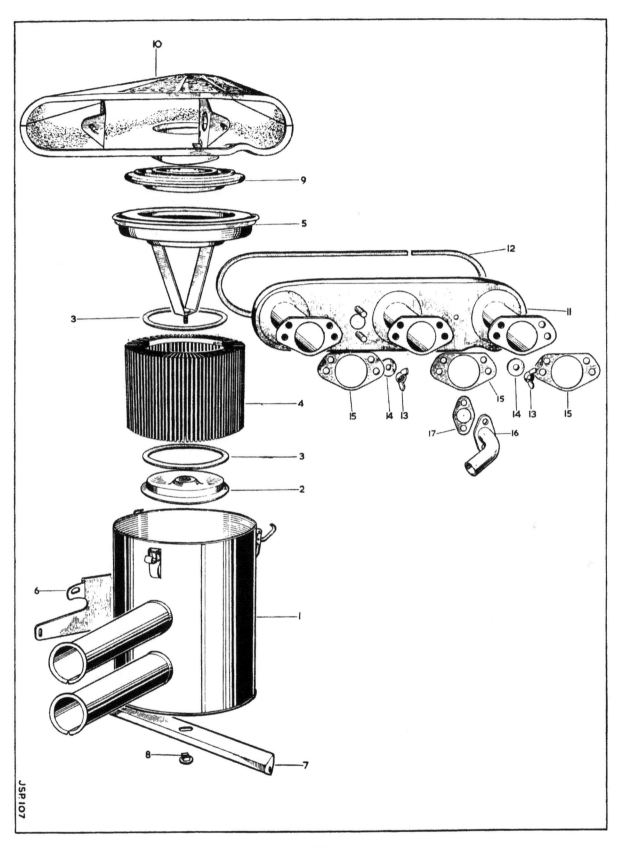

PLATE 8

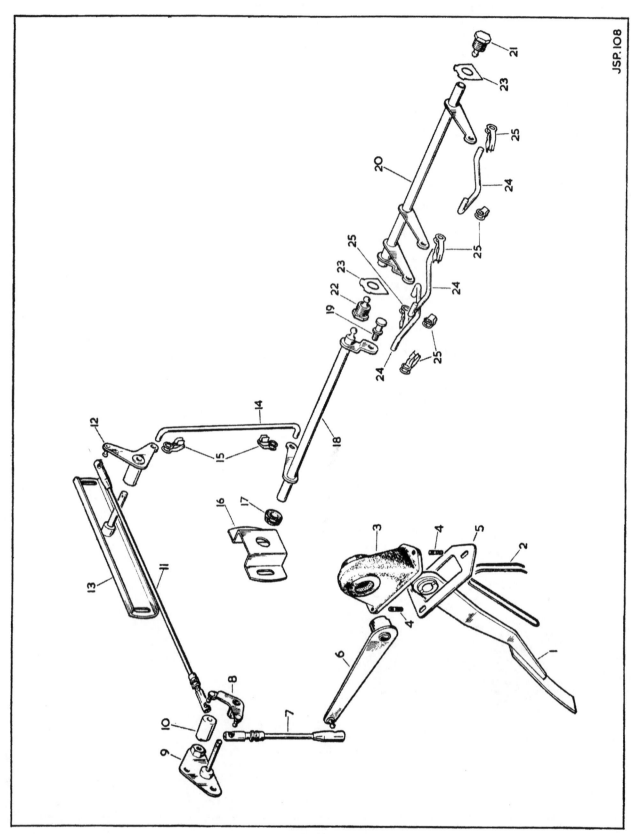

JSP.I08

PLATE 9

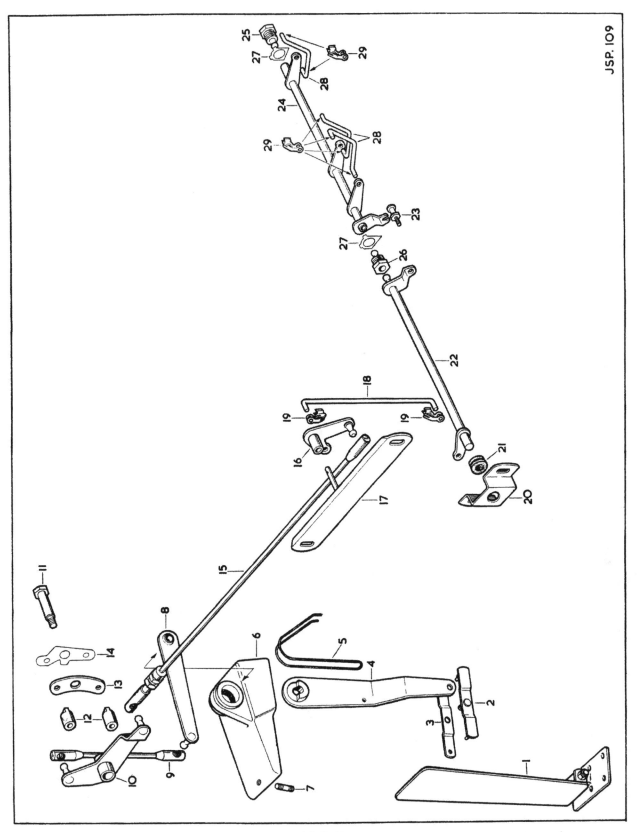

JSP. 109

PLATE 10

247

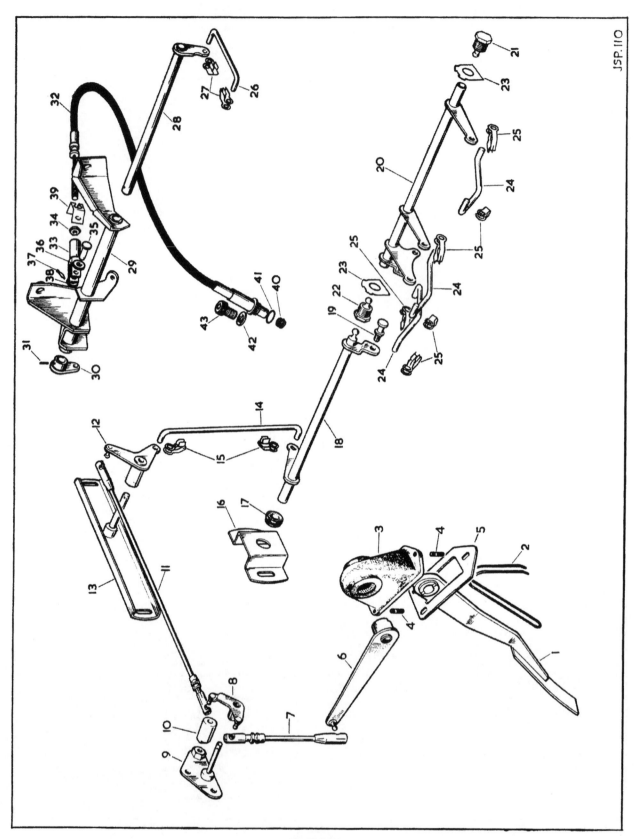

JSP.110

PLATE 11

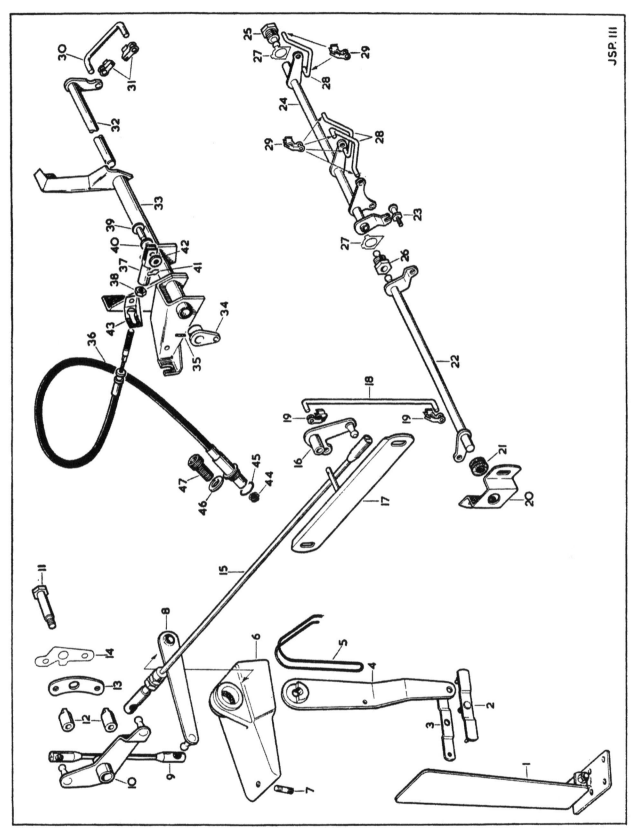

PLATE 12

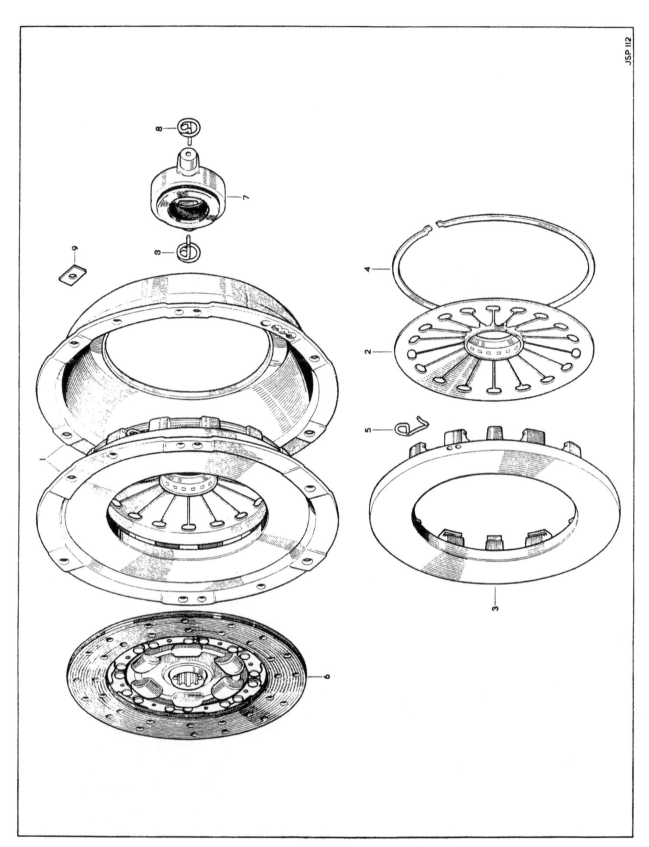

JSP 112

PLATE 13

250

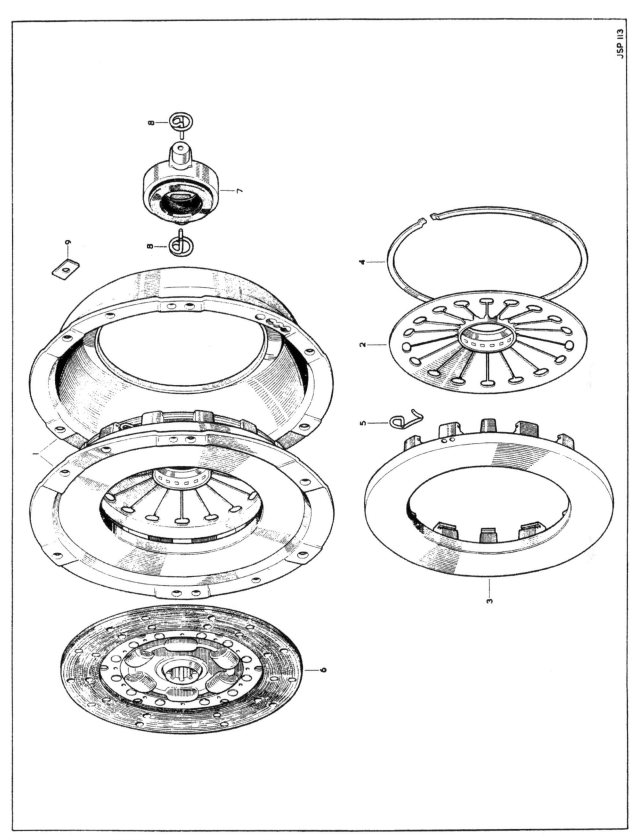

PLATE 14

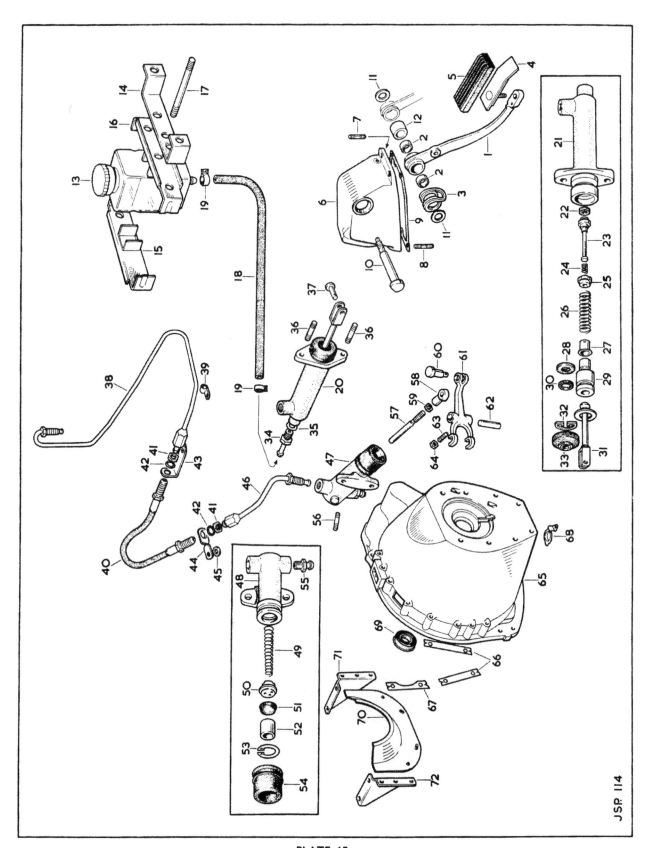

PLATE 15

JSP. 114

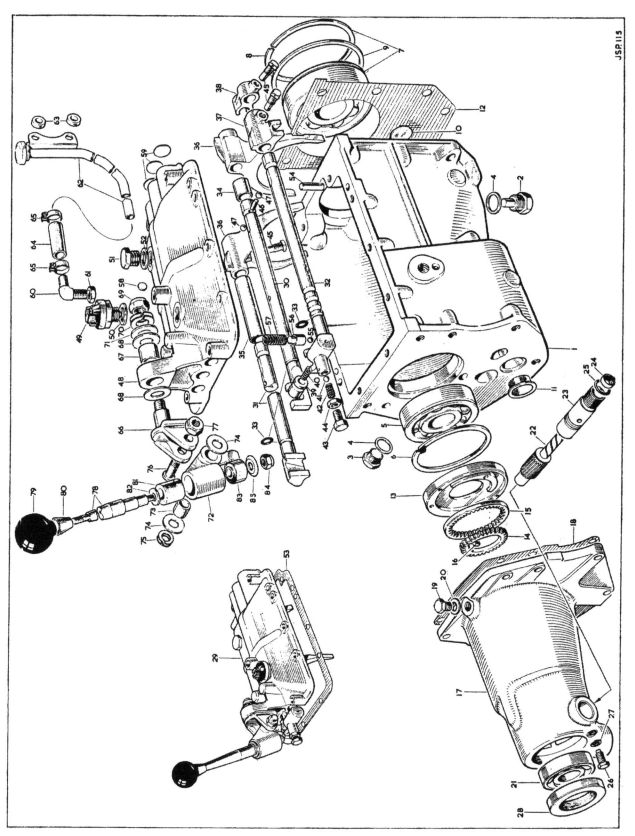

PLATE 16

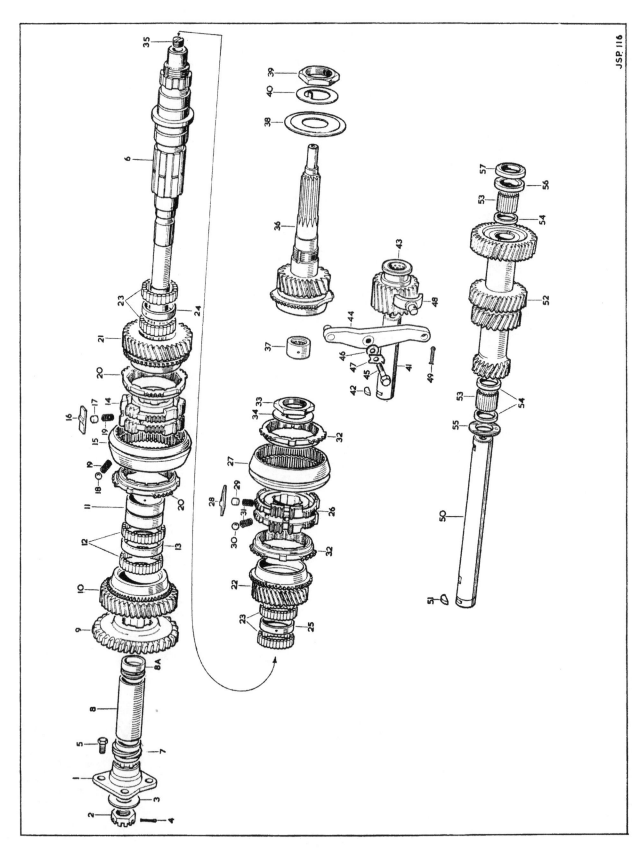

JSP 116

PLATE 17-20

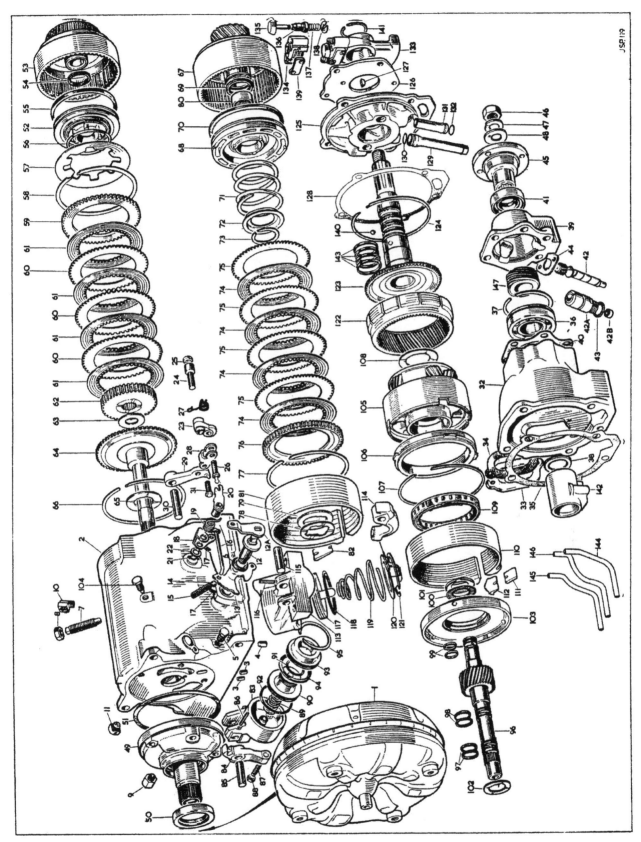

PLATE 21

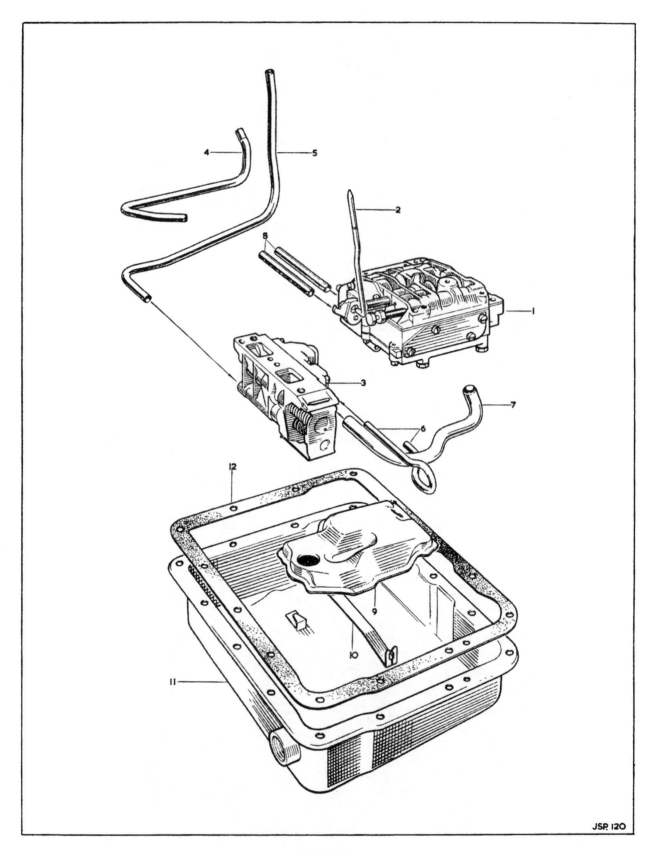

JSP. 120

PLATE 22

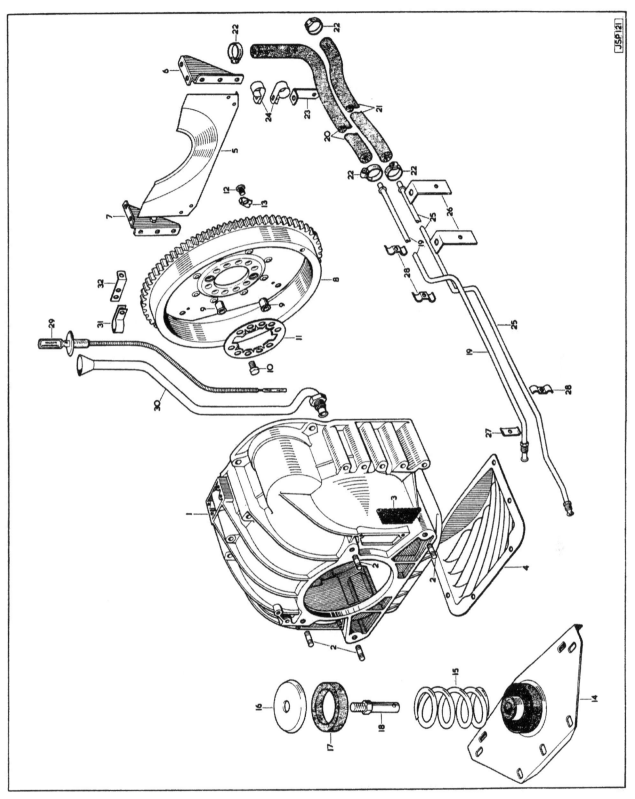

PLATE 23

257

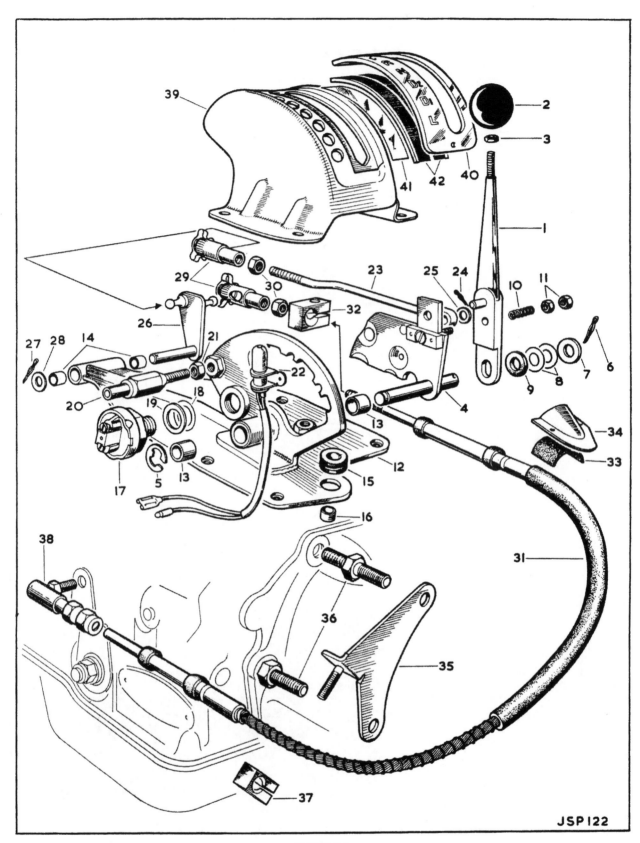

JSP122

PLATE 24

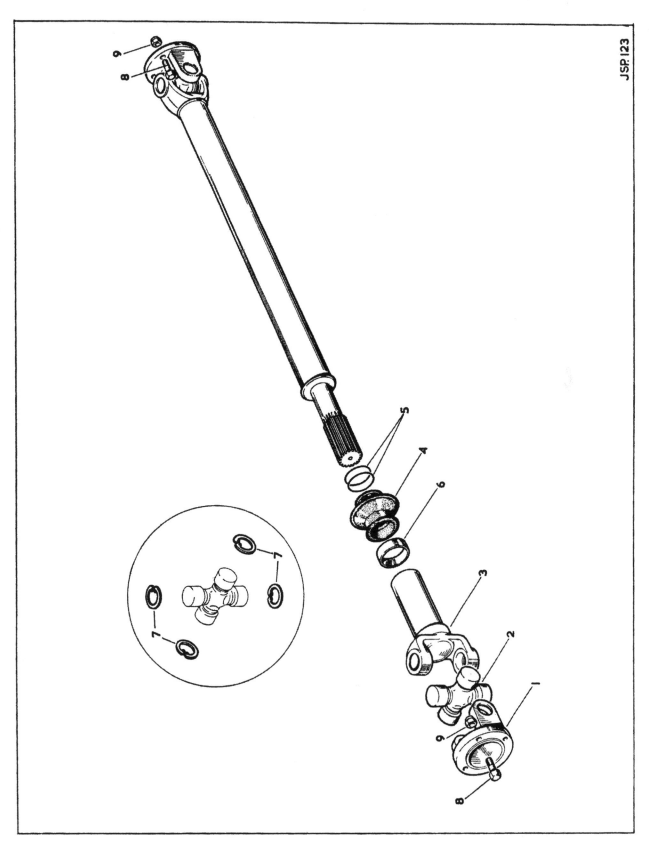

JSP 123

PLATE 25

259

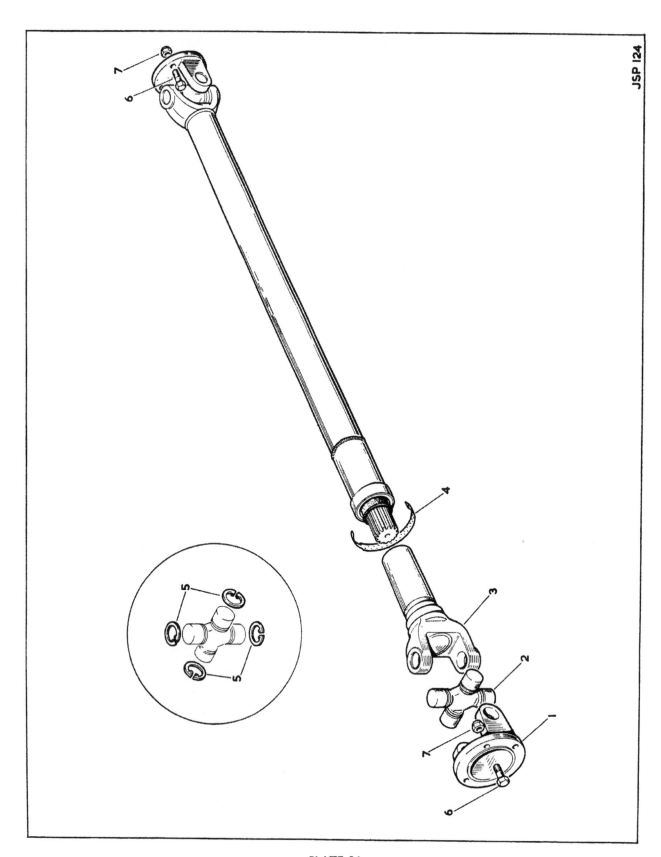

JSP 124

PLATE 26

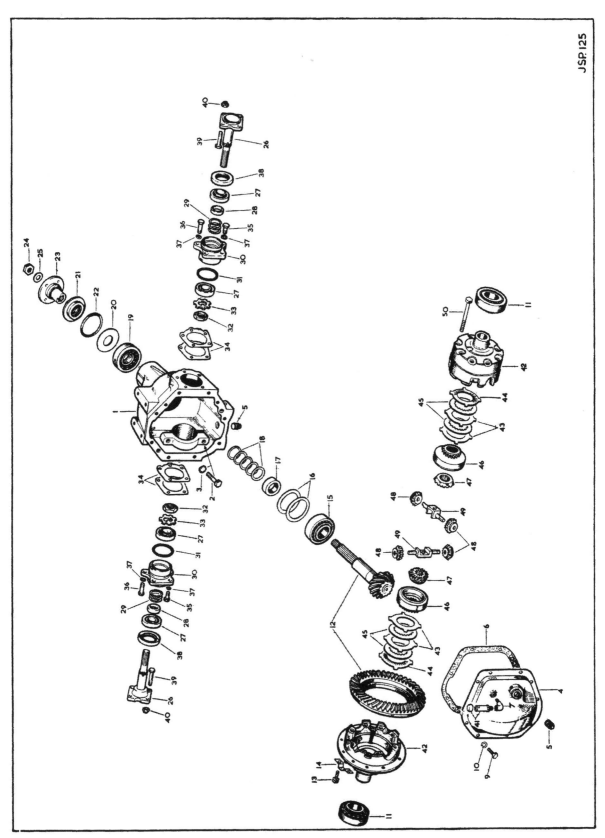

JSP. 125

PLATE 27

261

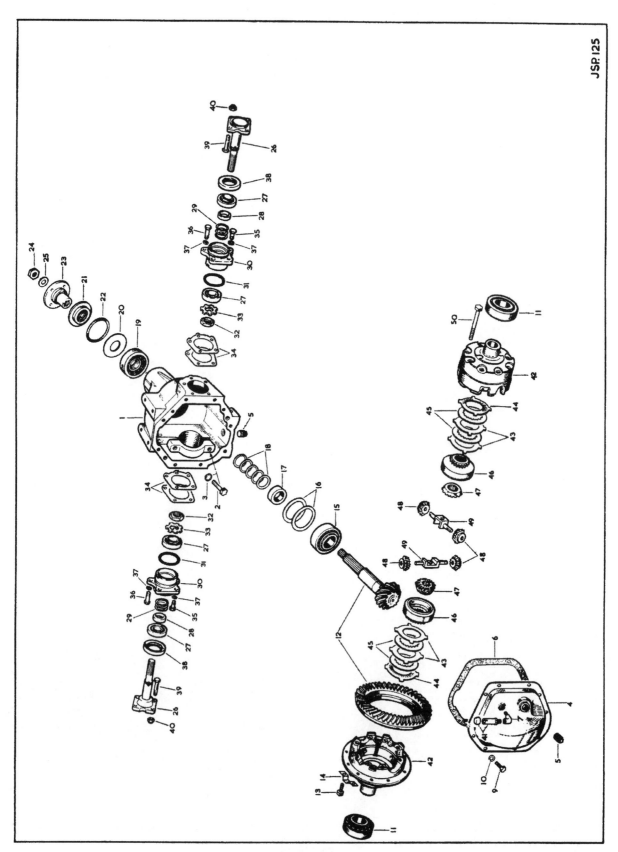

PLATE 28

262

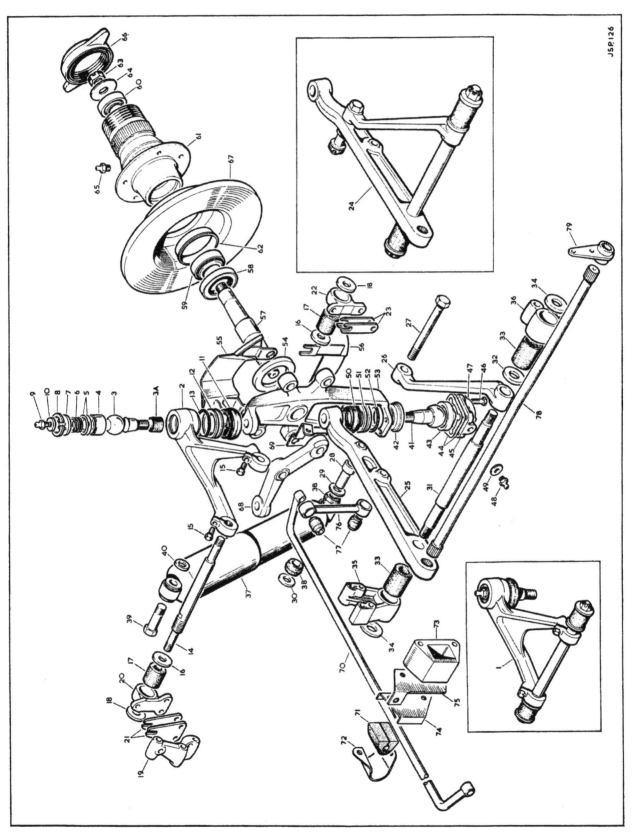

PLATE 29

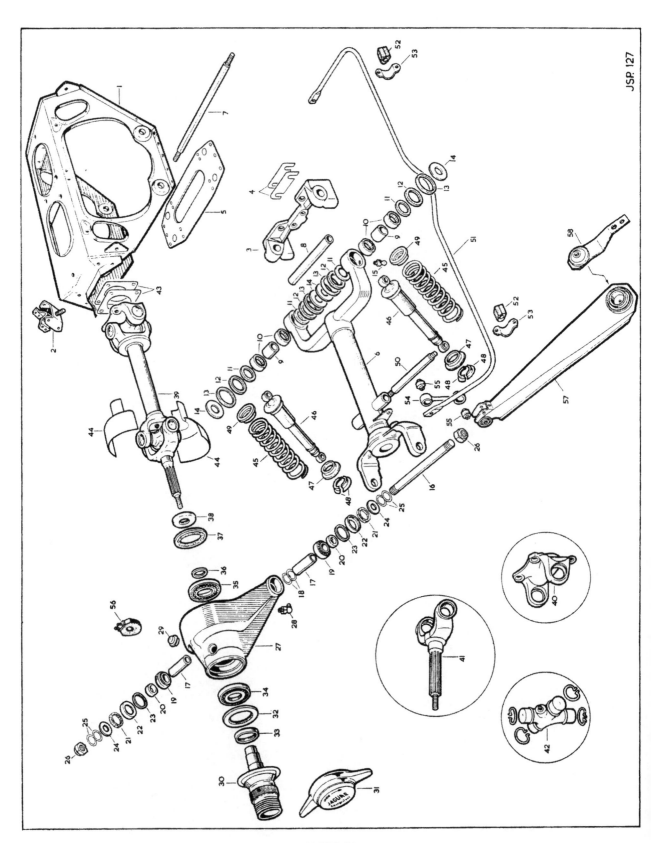

JSP. 127

PLATE 30

264

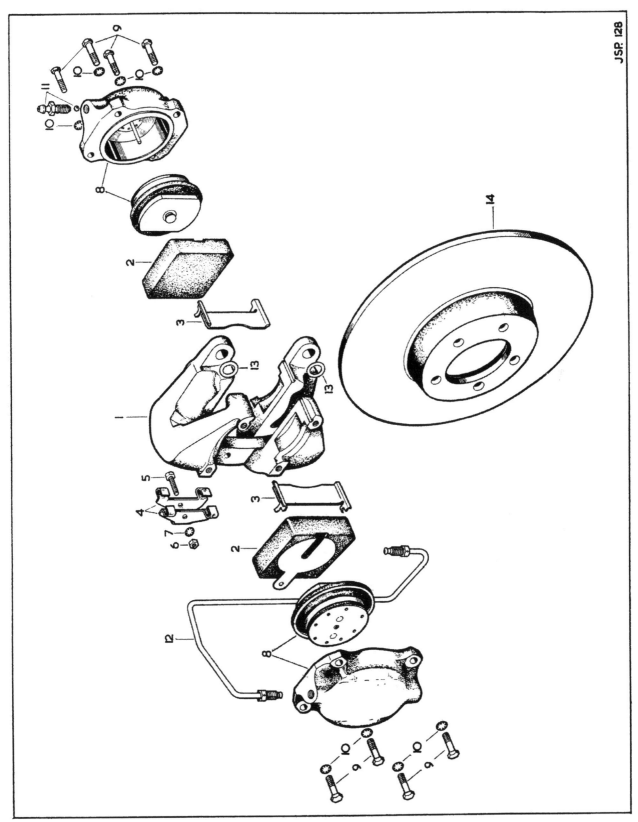

JSP. 128

PLATE 31

265

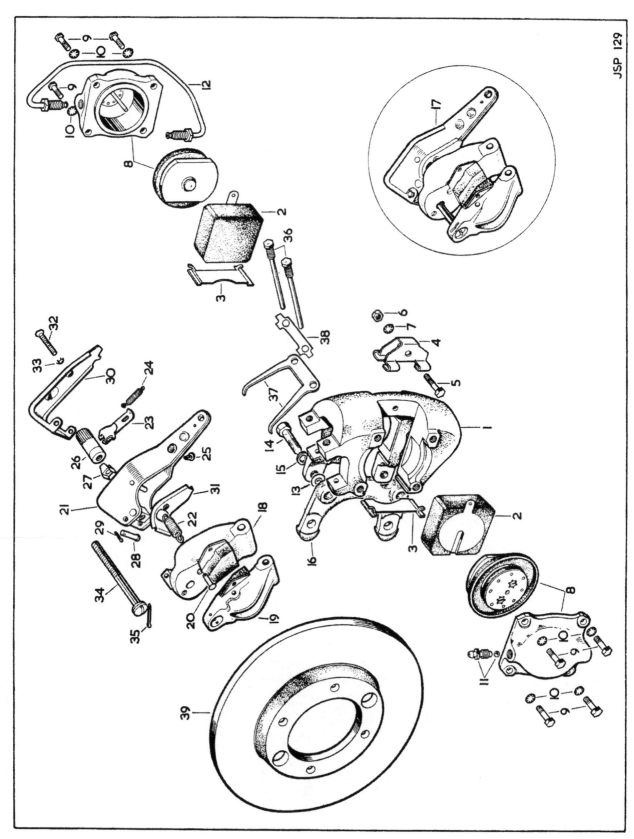

PLATE 32

266

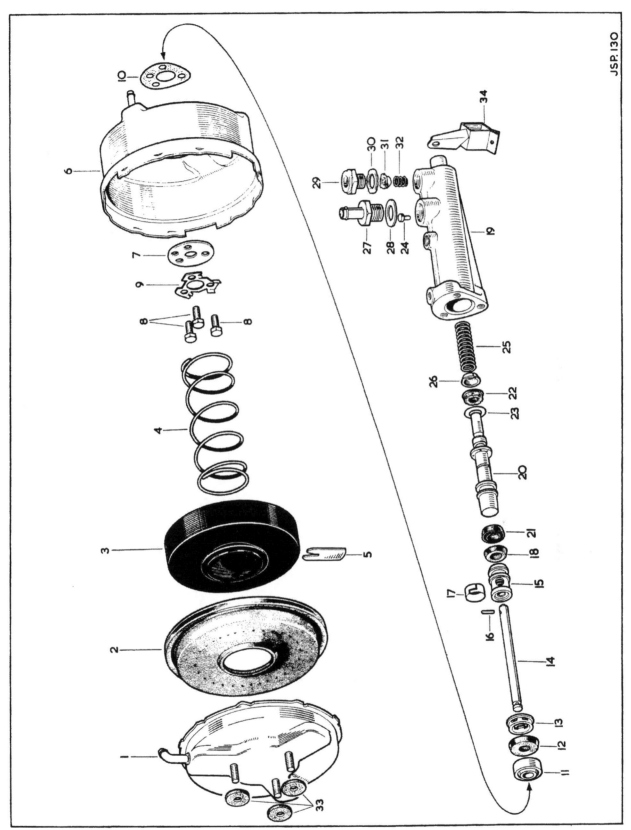

JSP.130

PLATE 33

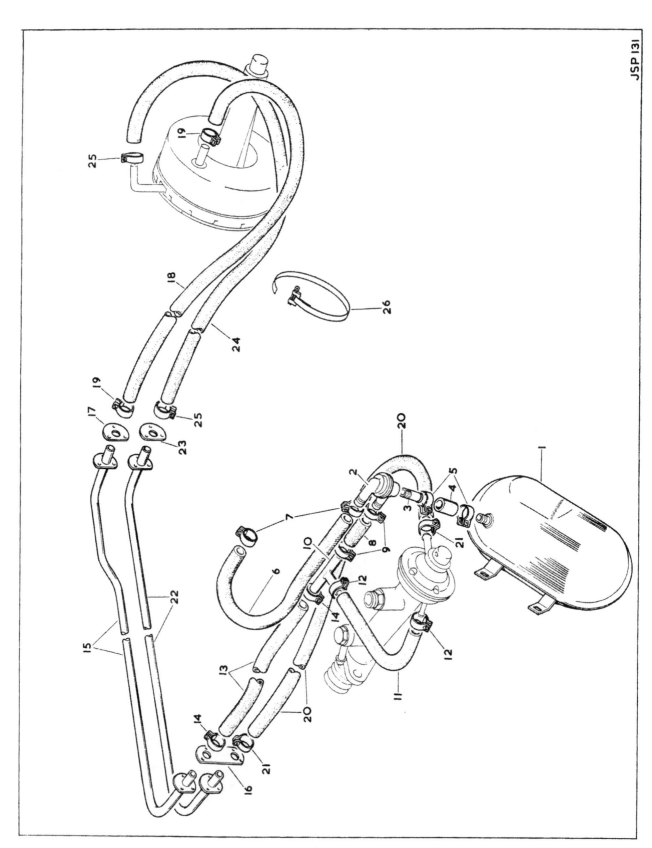

JSP 131

PLATE 34

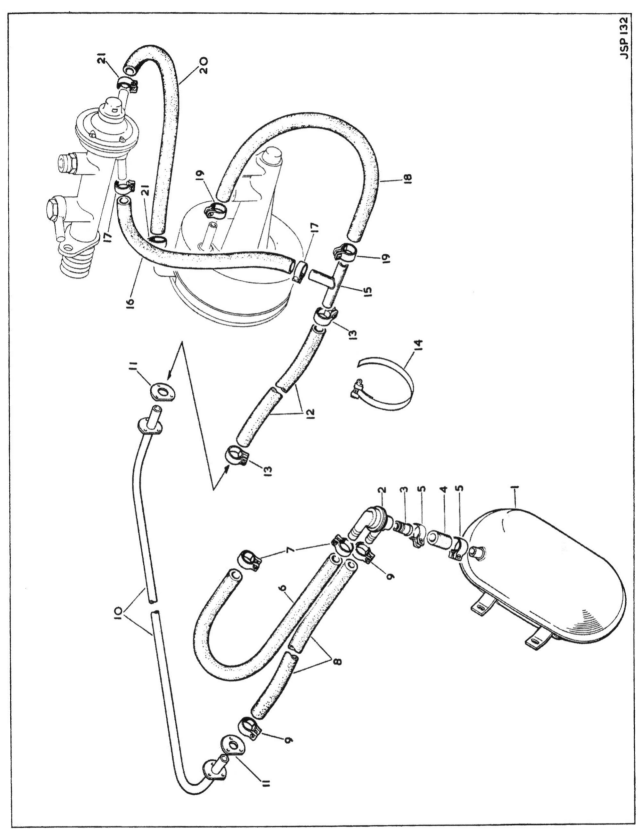

JSP 132

PLATE 35

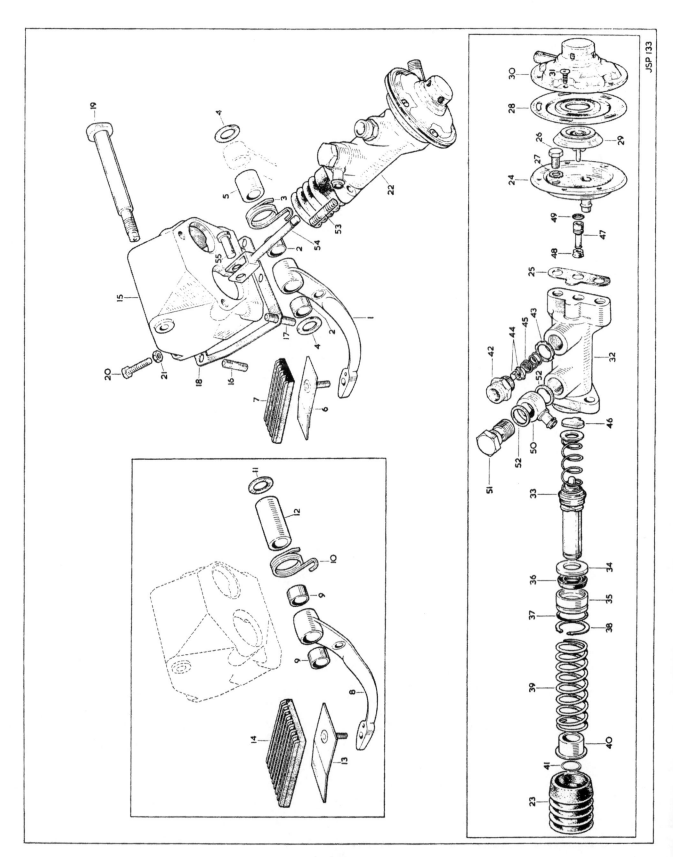

JSP 133

PLATE 36

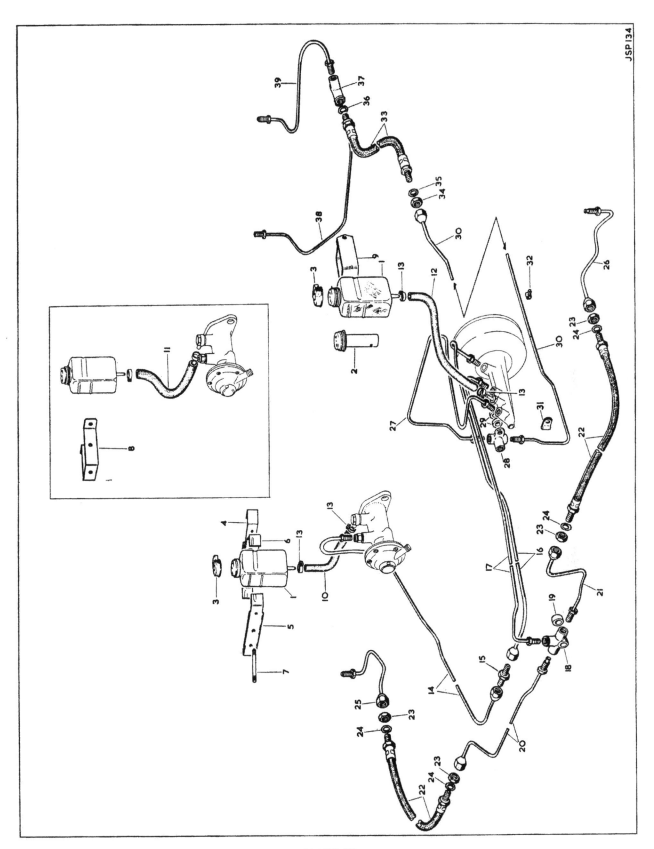

JSP 134

PLATE 37

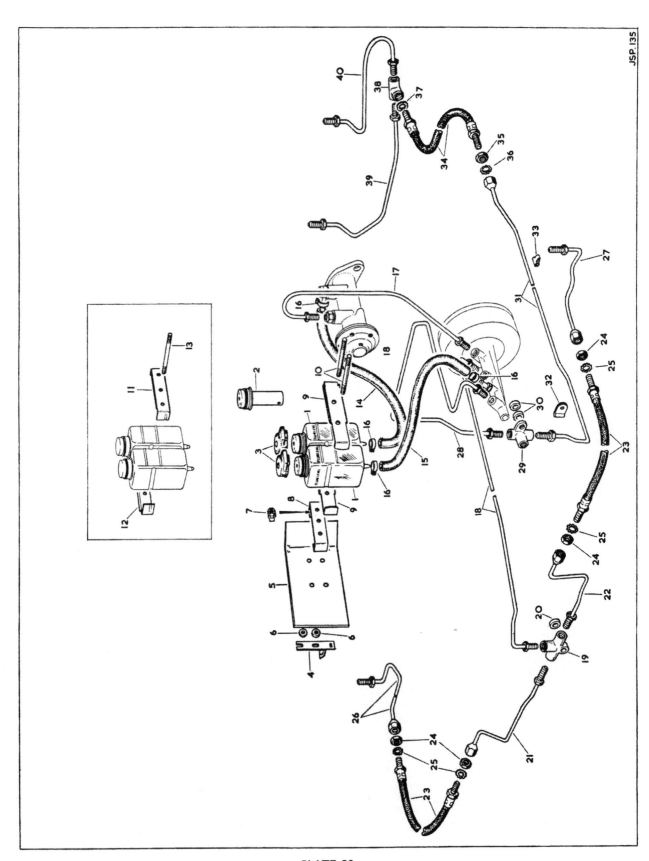

JSP.135

PLATE 38

272

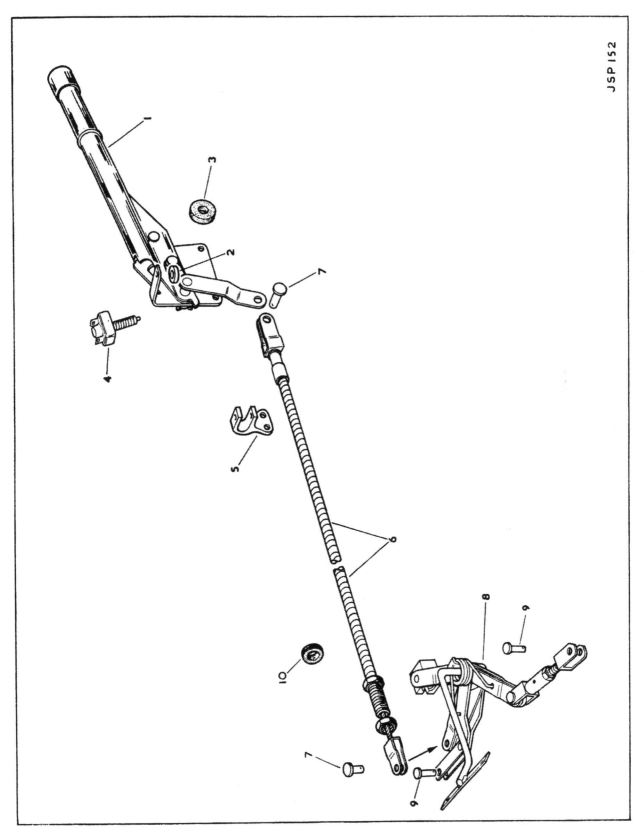

PLATE 39

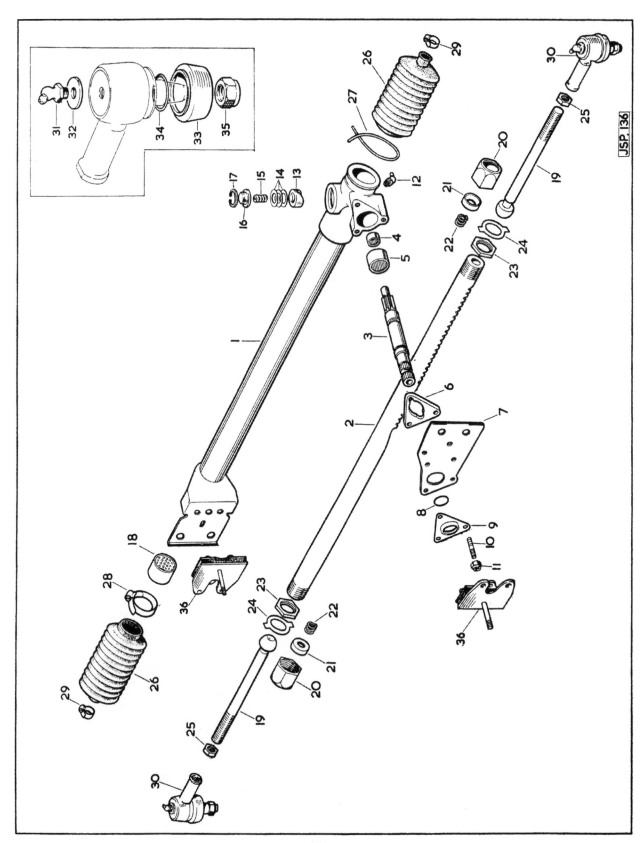

JSP. 136

PLATE 40

274

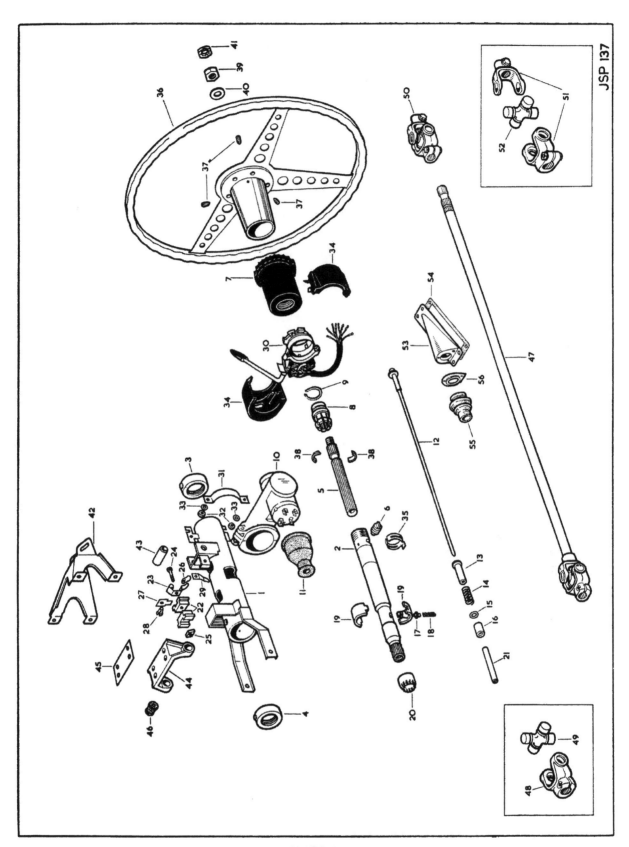

JSP 137

PLATE 41

275

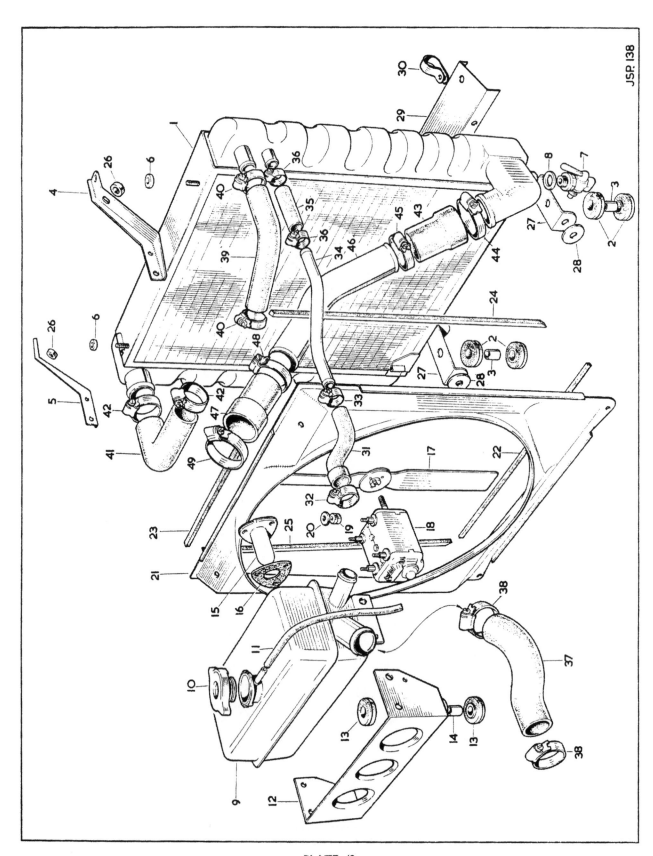

JSP. 138

PLATE 42

276

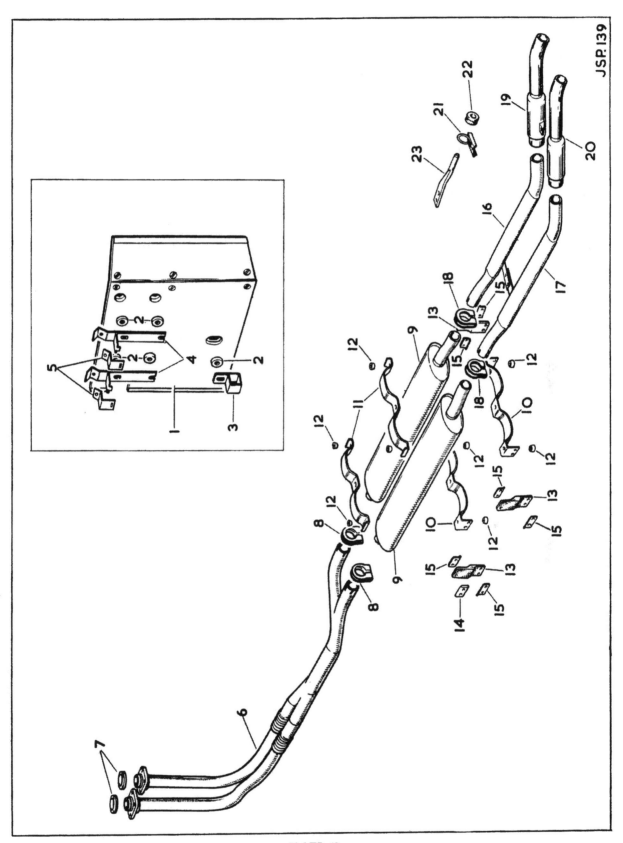

JSP.139

PLATE 43

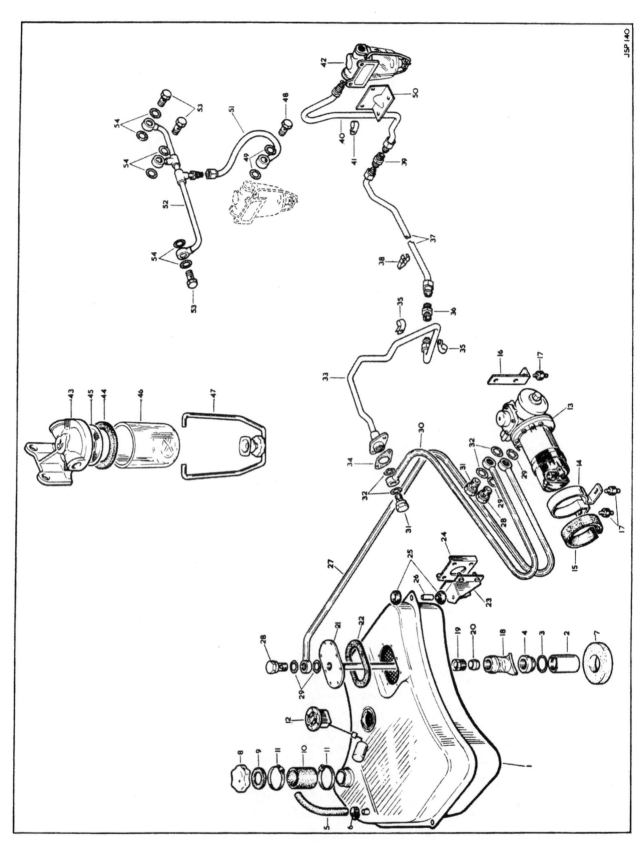

PLATE 44

JSP 140

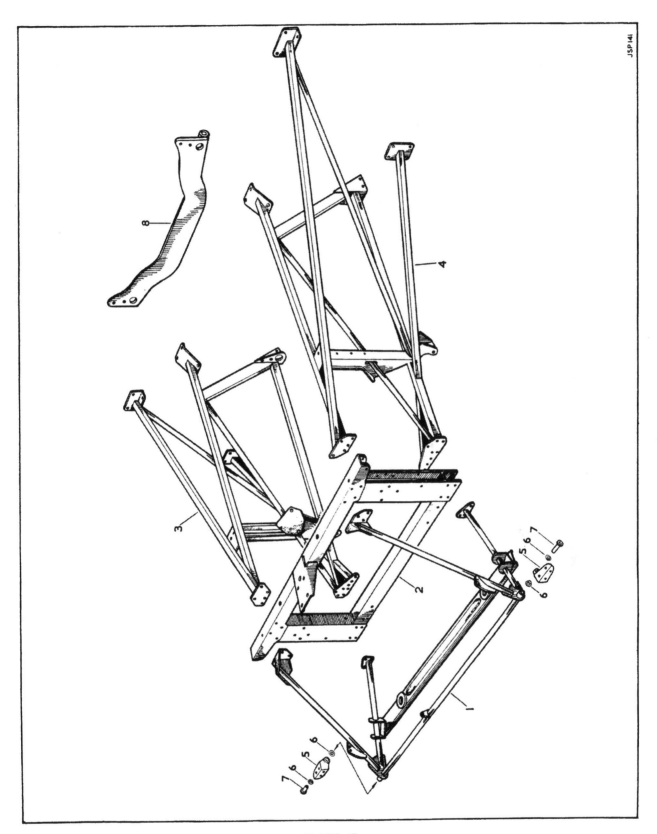

JSP 141

PLATE 45

279

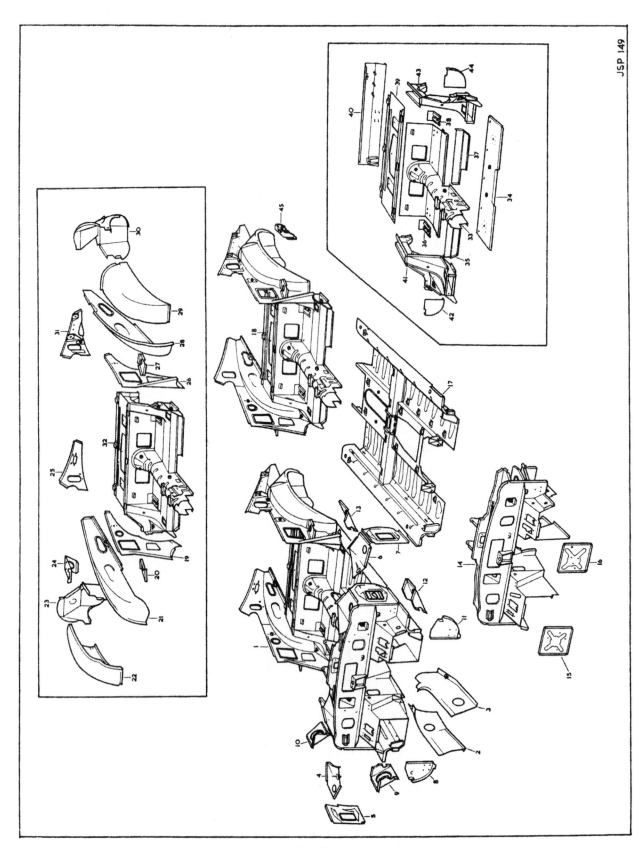

JSP 149

PLATE 46

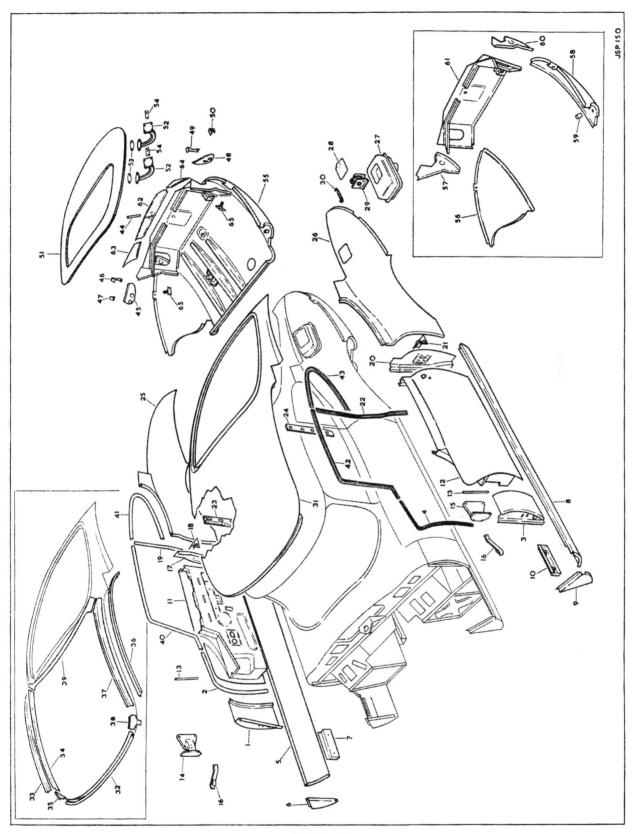

PLATE 47

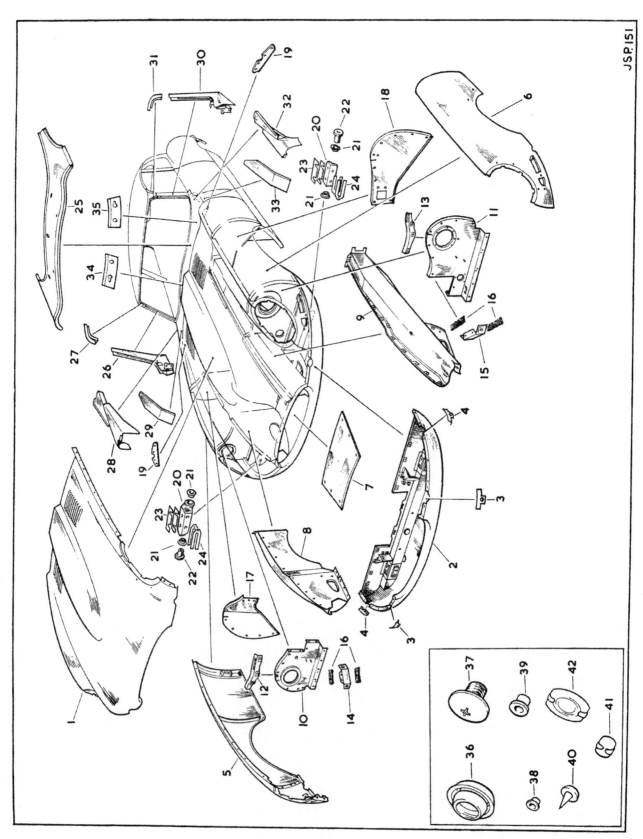

JSP.151

PLATE 48

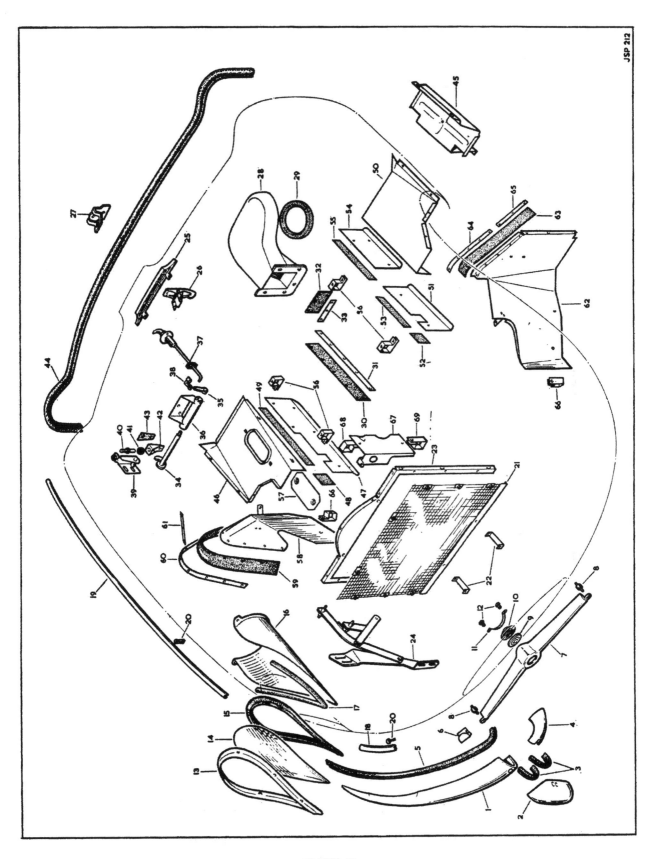

PLATE 49

283

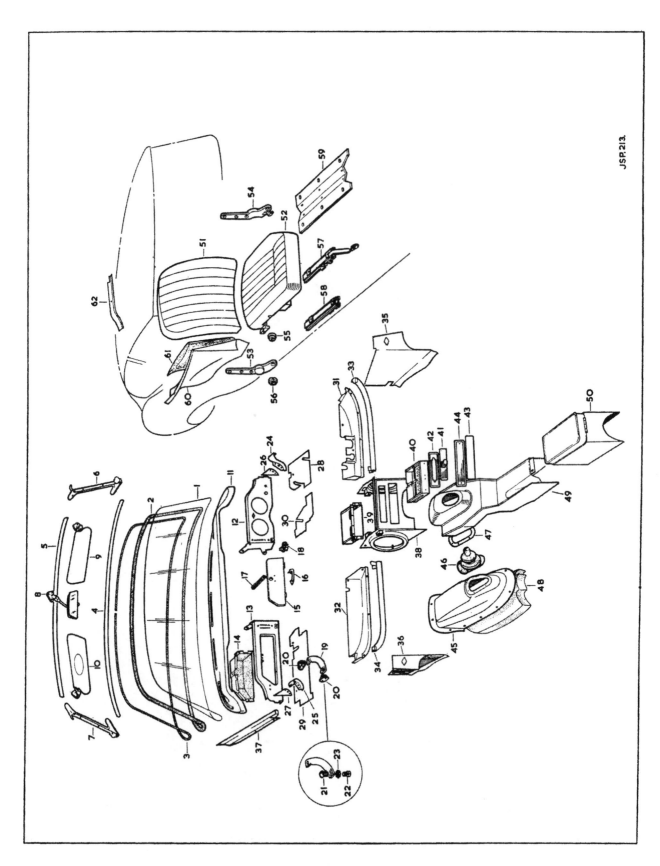

JSP.213.

PLATE 50

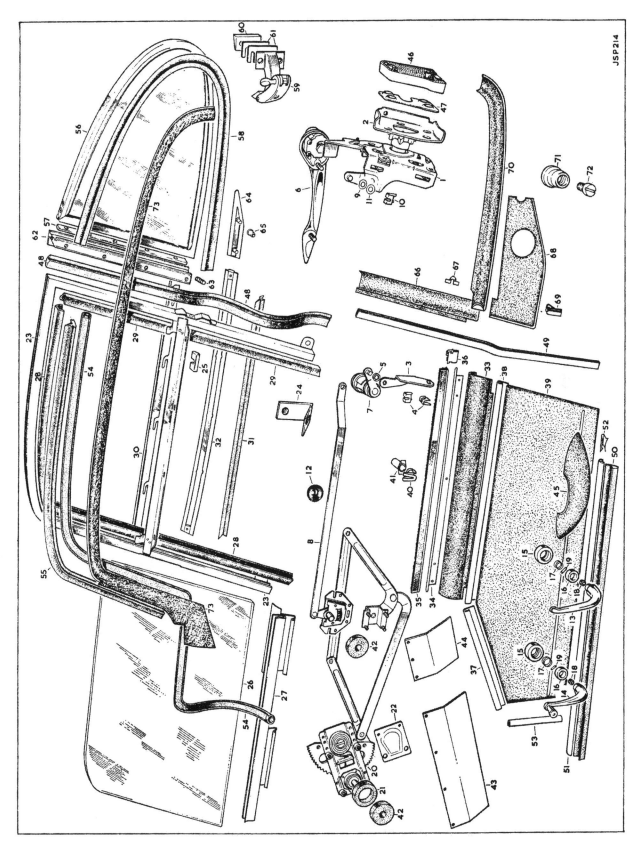

PLATE 51

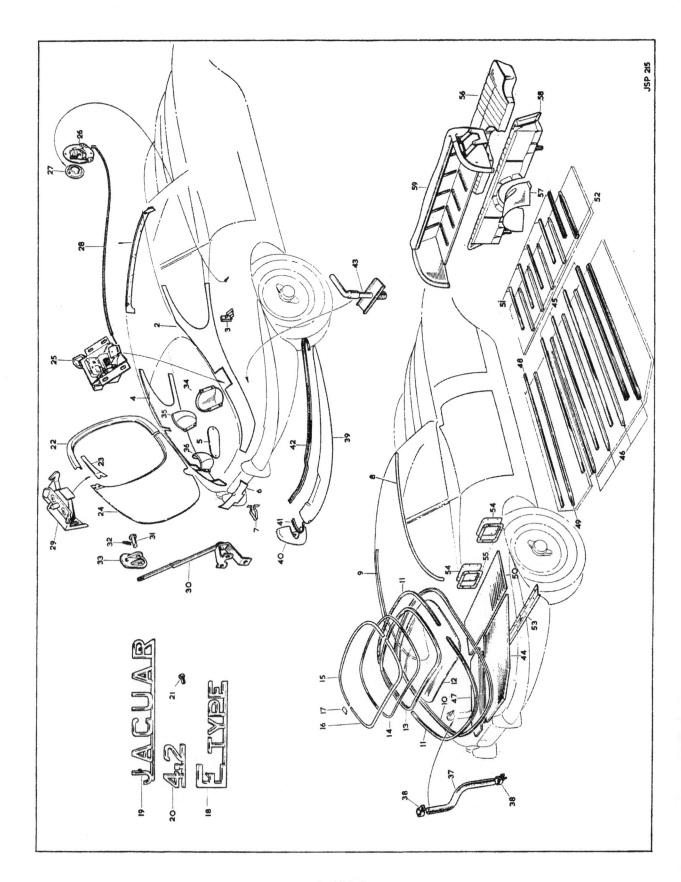

PLATE 52

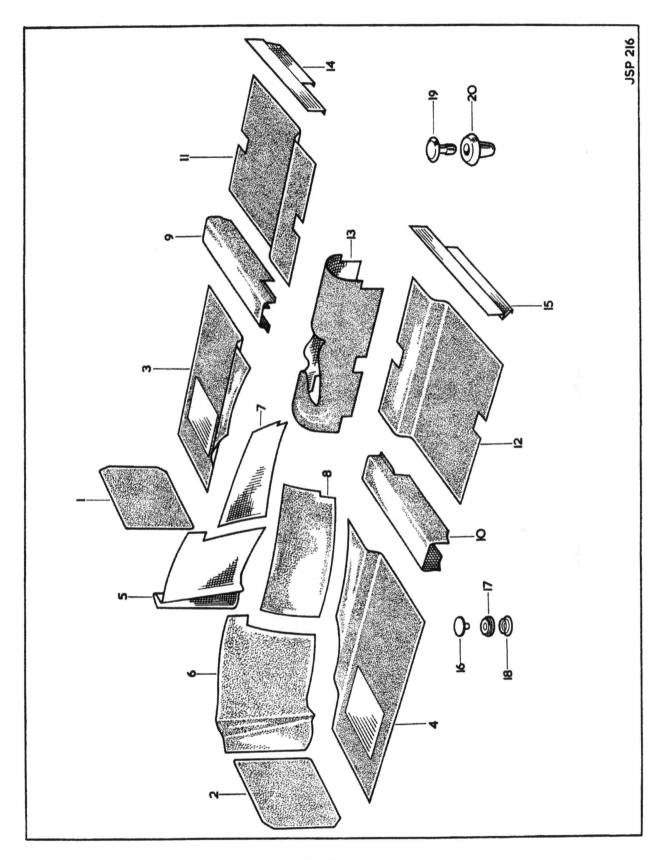

PLATE 53

287

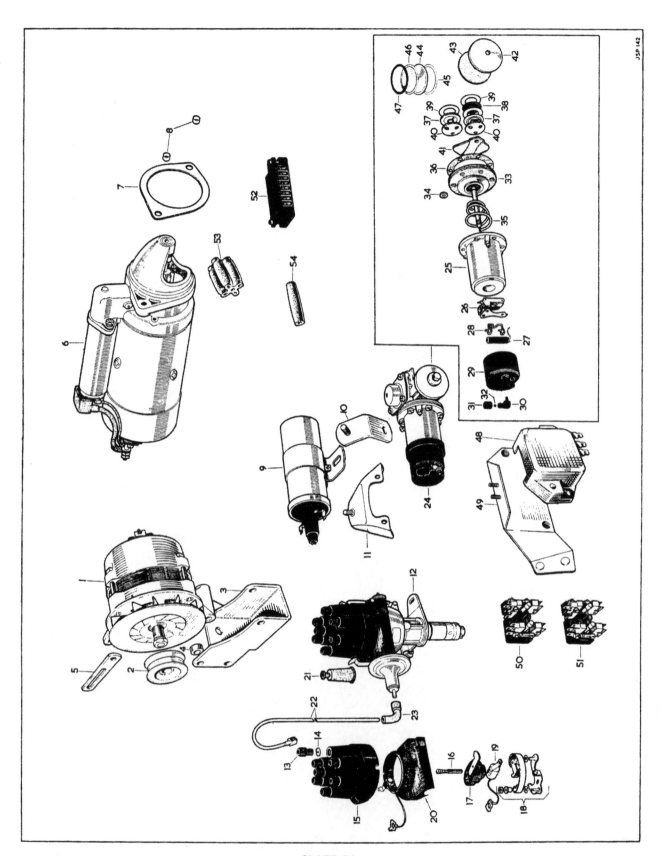

JSP 142

PLATE 54

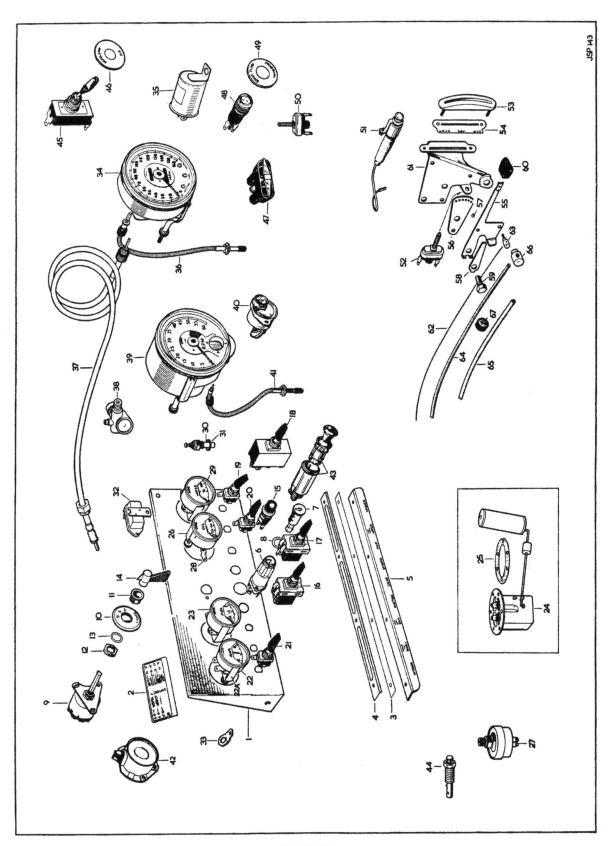

JSP 143

PLATE 55

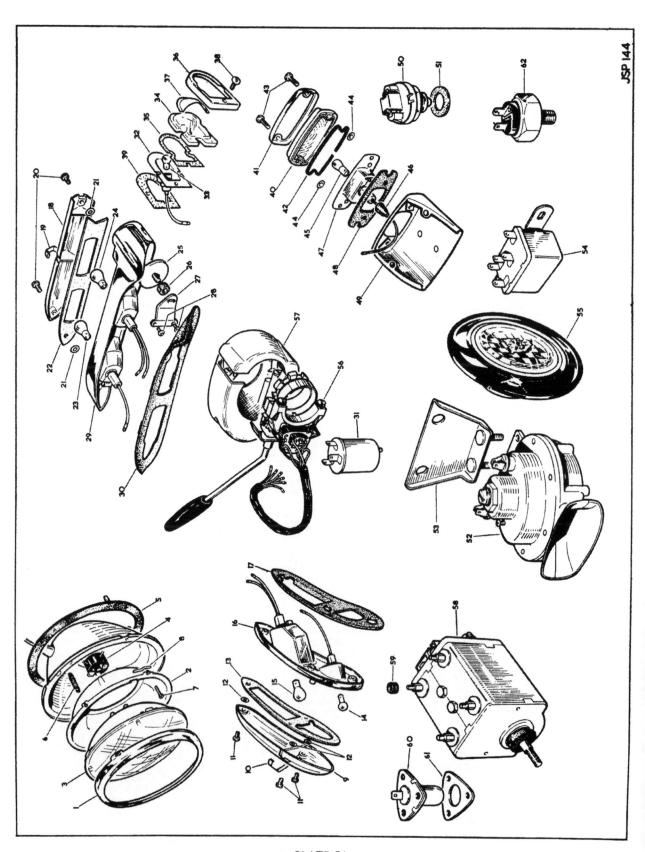

JSP 144

PLATE 56

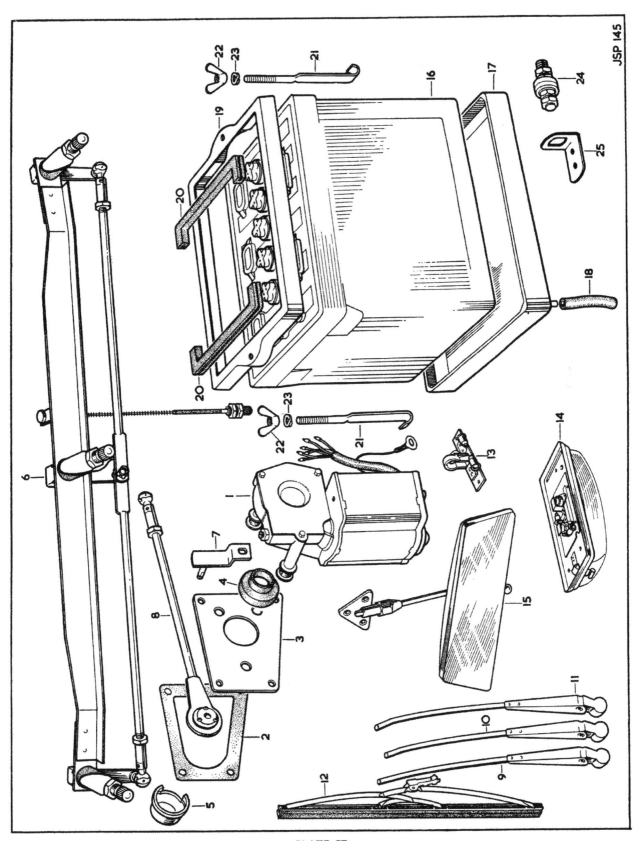

JSP 145

PLATE 57

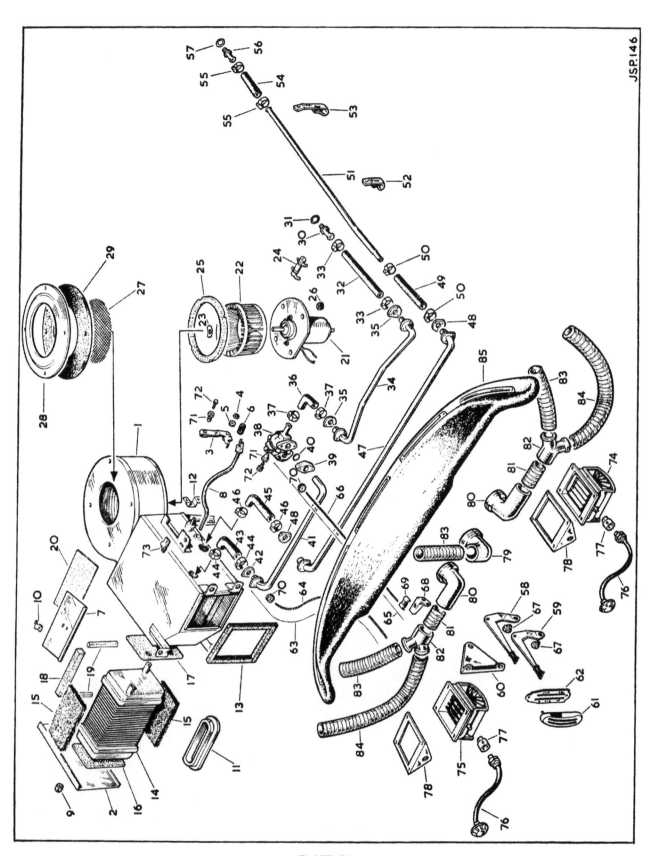

JSP.146

PLATE 58

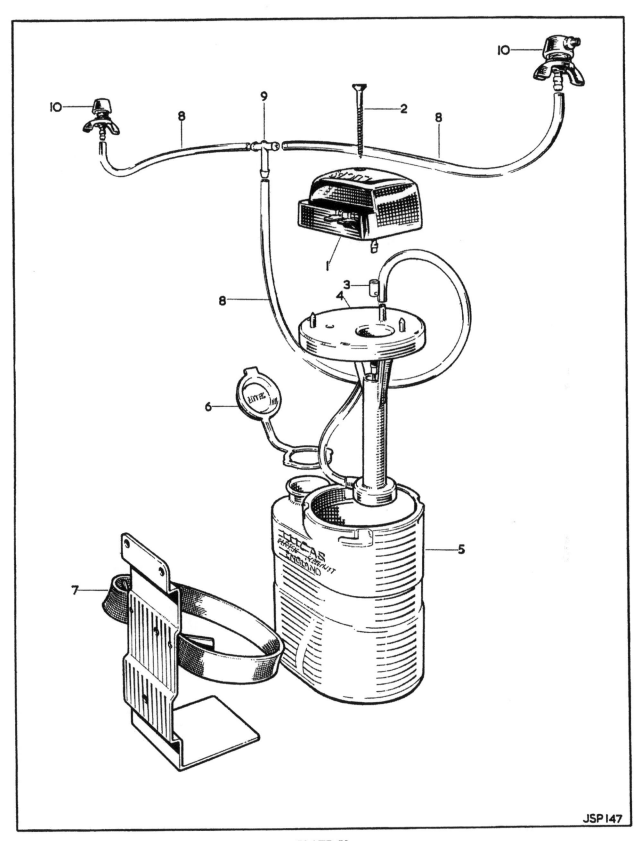

PLATE 59

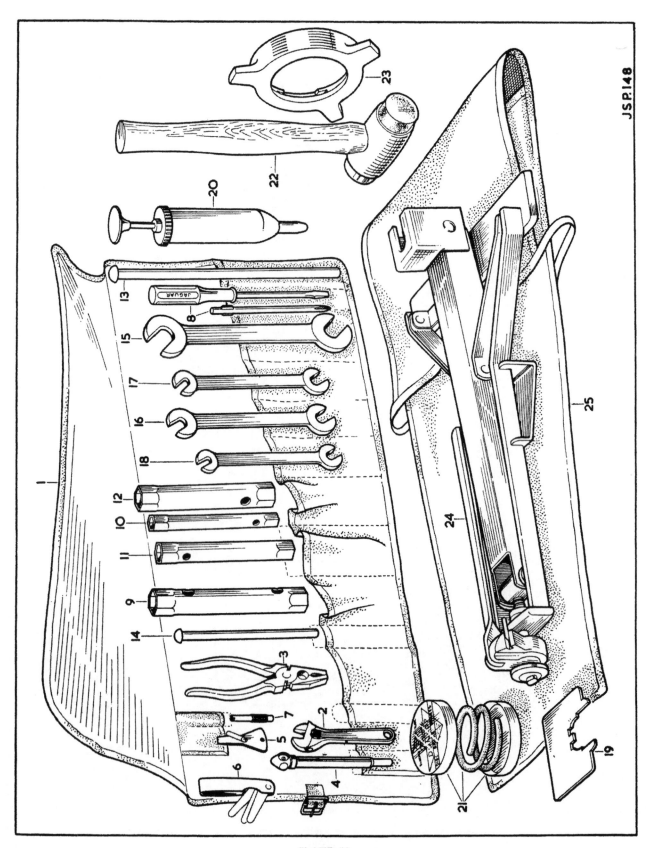

JSP.148

PLATE 60

294

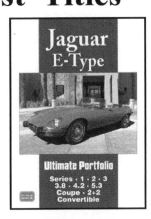

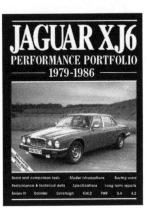

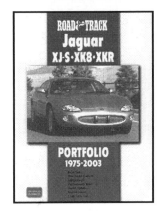
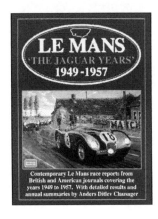
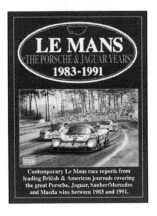

OFFICIAL TECHNICAL BOOKS

Brooklands Technical Books has been formed to supply owners,
restorers and professional
repairers with official factory literature.

Workshop Manuals

Jaguar Service Manual 1946-1948		9781855207844
Jaguar XK 120 140 150 150S & Mk 7, 8 & 9		9781870642279
Jaguar Mk 2 (2.4 3.4 3.8 240 340)	E121/7	9781870642958
Jaguar Mk 10 (3.8 & 4.2) & 420G	E136/2	9781855200814
Jaguar 'S' Type 3.4 & 3.8	E133/3	9781870642095
Jaguar E-Type 3.8 & 4.2 Series 1 & 2		
E123/8, E123 B/3 & E156/1		9781855200203
Jaguar E-Type V12 Series 3	E165/3	9781855200012
Jaguar 420	E143/2	9781855201712
Jaguar XJ6 2.8 & 4.2 Series 1		9781855200562
Jaguar XJ6 3.4 & 4.2 Series	E188/4	9781855200302
Jaguar XJ12 Series 1		9781783180417
Jaguar XJ12 Series 2 / DD6 Series 2	E190/4	9781855201408
Jaguar XJ6 & XJ12 Series 3	AKM9006	9781855204010
Jaguar XJ6 OWM (XJ40) 1986-94		9781855207851
Jaguar XJS V12 5.3 & 6.0 Litre	AKM3455	9781855202627
Jaguar XJS 6 Cylinder 3.6 & 4.0 Litre	AKM9063	9781855204638

Owners Workshop Manuals

Jaguar E-Type V12 1971-1974	9781783181162
Jaguar XJ, Sovereign 1968-1982	9781783181179
Jaguar XJ6 Workshop Manual 1986-1994	9781855207851
Jaguar XJ12, XJ5.3 Double Six 1972-1979	9781783181186

Parts Catalogues

Jaguar Mk 2 3.4	J20	9781855201569
Jaguar Mk 2 (3.4, 3.8 & 340)	J34	9781855209084
Jaguar Series 3 12 Cyl. Saloons		9781783180592
Jaguar E-Type 3.8	J30	9781869826314
Jaguar E-Type 4.2 Series 1	J37	9781870642118
Jaguar E-Type Series 2	J37 & J38	9781855201705
Jaguar E-Type V12 Ser. 3 Open 2 Seater	RTC9014	9781869826840
Jaguar XJ6 Series 1		9781855200043
Jaguar XJ6 & Daimler Sovereign Ser. 2	RTC9883CA	9781855200579
Jaguar XJ6 & Daimler Sovereign Ser. 3	RTC9885CF	9781855202771
Jaguar XJ12 Series 2 / DD6 Series 2		9781783180585
Jaguar 2.9 & 3.6 Litre Saloons 1986-89	RTC9893CB	9781855202993
Jaguar XJ-S 3.6 & 5.3 Jan 1987 on	RTC9900CA	9781855204003

Owners Handbooks

Jaguar XK120		9781855200432
Jaguar XK140	E101/2	9781855200401
Jaguar XK150	E111/2	9781855200395
Jaguar Mk 2 (3.4)	E116/10	9781855201682
Jaguar Mk 2 (3.8)	E115/10	9781869826765
Jaguar E-Type (Tuning & prep. for competition)		9781855207905
Jaguar E-Type 3.8 Series 1	E122/7	9781870642927
Jaguar E-Type 4.2 2+2 Series 1	E131/6	9781869826383
Jaguar E-Type 4.2 Series	E154/5	9781869826499
Jaguar E-Type V12 Series 3	E160/2	9781855200029
Jaguar E-Type V12 Series 3 (US)	A181/2	9781855200036
Jaguar XJ (3.4 & 4.2) Series 2	E200/8	9781855201200
Jaguar XJ6C Series 2	E184/1	9781855207875
Jaguar XJ12 Series 3	AKM4181	9781855207868

Carburetters

SU Carburetters Tuning Tips & Techniques	9781855202559
Solex Carburetters Tuning Tips & Techniques	9781855209770
Weber Carburettors Tuning Tips and Techniques	9781855207592

Jaguar - Road Test Books

Jaguar and SS Gold Portfolio 1931-1951	9781855200630
Jaguar XK120 XK140 XK150 Gold Port. 1948-60	9781870642415
Jaguar Mk 7, 8, 9, 10 & 420G	9781855208674
Jaguar Mk 1 & Mk 2 1955-1969	9781855208599
Jaguar E-Type	9781855208360
Jaguar XJ6 1968-79 (Series 1 & 2)	9781855202641
Jaguar XJ12 XJ5.3 V12 Gold Portfolio 1972-1990	9781855200838
Jaguar XJS Gold Portfolio 1975-1988	9781855202719
Jaguar XJ-S V12 1988-1996	9781855204249
Jaguar XK8 & XKR 1996-2005	9781855207578
Road & Track on Jaguar 1950-1960	9780946489695
Road & Track on Jaguar 1968-1974	9780946489374
Road & Track On Jaguar XJ-S-XK8-XK	9781855206298

Brooklands Books Ltd., PO Box 146, Cobham,
Surrey KT11 1LG, England Phone: (44) 1932 865051
E-mail: sales@brooklands-books.com   www.brooklandsbooks.com

ISBN: 9781855201705   Part No. IPL 5/2   Ref: J40PH   10T16/2014

Printed in Great Britain
by Amazon